Lincoln

& the Party Divided

The President in 1864, from a photograph by
Wenderoth and Taylor, at the White House

Lincoln
& the Party Divided

By William Frank Zornow

GREENWOOD PRESS, PUBLISHERS
WESTPORT, CONNECTICUT

The Library of Congress has catalogued this publication as follows:

Library of Congress Cataloging in Publication Data

Zornow, William Frank.
   Lincoln & the party divided.

   Bibliography: p.
   1. Lincoln, Abraham, Pres. U. S., 1809-1865.
2. Presidents--United States--Election--1864.
I. Title.
[E458.4.Z6 1972]   973.7'1   73-152619
ISBN 0-8371-6054-5

129351

Copyright 1954 by the University of Oklahoma Press

Originally published in 1954
by the University of Oklahoma Press, Norman

Reprinted with the permission
of the University of Oklahoma Press

First Greenwood Reprinting 1972

Library of Congress Catalogue Card Number 73-152619

ISBN 0-8371-6054-5

Printed in the United States of America

To My Parents

Preface

FOR THREE YEARS the fate of the North and, more important, the future of the United States reposed in the humble yet capable hands of Abraham Lincoln. The time was approaching when his policies had to be submitted to the people for review and endorsement, but early in 1864 there were many who doubted that an affirmative verdict could be obtained. He was losing popularity, and his party was openly divided over his program. Many of its leaders said it would be impolitic to accord him further support. They needed a man who could win battles and elections; Lincoln seemed unable to do either.

The story of how Lincoln used every resource of statesmanship, good fortune, and political acumen to reunite his party, to regain his prestige with the people, and to win their endorsement of his program reveals the most astonishing denouement of the war. Lincoln's victorious struggle to save his country, his program, and his party from defeat, rejection, and division is the story I have sought to tell.

A debt of appreciation is due to Professor Harvey Wish of Western Reserve University, who offered many helpful suggestions on the preparation of this manuscript. I am grateful also to his colleagues, Dean Carl Wittke and Professor Maurice Klain of the Political Science Department, as well as to my former colleague at Cleveland College, Professor Clarence T. Gilham, who corrected many factual errors in the text. I wish also to thank Professor

Arthur C. Cole of Brooklyn College, who first stimulated my interest in Lincoln and the Civil War.

I am indebted to the librarians and staffs of Western Reserve University, the Cleveland Public Library, the Western Reserve Historical Society, the Ohio State Museum, the Library of Congress, the Pennsylvania State Historical Society, Kansas State College, and the Kansas Historical Society for their kindness in assisting my research.

WILLIAM FRANK ZORNOW

Manhattan, Kansas
September 20, 1954

Contents

Illustrations

Lincoln

& the Party Divided

Lincoln
and the Unconditionals

THE GAUNT MAN *in the White House faced perhaps the most decisive and critical year of his life. Sure of no one and of nothing save his own integrity, Abraham Lincoln in 1864 was forced to fight his last and greatest battles to prevent the division of his own party and assure the future unification of his country. The significance of the titanic struggle which was about to take place in the political and military arena was not lost upon political observers, and early in the year speculation was rife concerning candidates and issues in the forthcoming presidential election.*

During the three years following the first shots at Fort Sumter a succession of military leaders had borne the banner of the Northern forces with indifferent success. But by 1864 momentous events were taking shape. The long, bloody years of attrition were being felt more keenly in Richmond than in Washington. Lincoln was preparing another iron thunderbolt to aim at the Confederacy, and he was assiduously seeking the man who could hurl it effectively.

Amid the preparations for the coming military campaign, however, Lincoln had to give thought to a campaign of more immediate personal concern. The many months of military stalemates, drafts, increasing taxes, arguments over war aims, and conflicts over patronage had shaken the foundation of the Republican party, so much that the party was in process of disintegration. An increasingly larger and more vocal element made it abundantly clear

Lincoln & the Party Divided

*that there was dissatisfaction in the ranks over the brand of leader-
ship and the policies being offered both the country and the party.
Thus Lincoln was forced into the position of having to fight,
almost singlehanded, a dual battle for unity. First and foremost
he had to push through his plans to secure the reunification of his
beloved land, at the same time engaging in an equally significant
struggle to assure the continued unity of his party. The complete
vindication of all that Lincoln stood for rested upon the endorsement of his program by the American people in 1864, and such an
endorsement was inextricably bound up with the necessity of keep-
ing the party intact. He had to secure the continued loyalty of the
diverse elements and to win back those who had already heeded
the siren call of other aspirants for the Presidency.*

*If the summer military campaigns failed, the blow would be
serious but not necessarily disastrous, while political defeat would
almost certainly prove catastrophic for both Lincoln and the United
States. If the President could not secure the endorsement of his
party—as represented by renomination—his whole moderate program would be lost, for the man chosen to replace him would
undoubtedly represent the opposite side of the political fence. Such
an outcome would, of course, be a defeat for Lincoln; and, should
the party divide completely, disaster might result for the whole
nation. With the disintegration of the Republican party, the
country could easily fall into the hands of men committed to the
principle of separation and peace at any price. The dismember-
ment of the United States would become, in that event, an accomplished fact.*

*Thus 1864 represented a decisive year—for Lincoln, for the
United States, and for history.*

"The canvass for the Presidential election is opening," wrote Secretary of State William H. Seward early in 1864. "That election
will probably be the first one held in forty years in which slavery
will have been held by all parties as unworthy of political defense.
Of course, the occurrence of the canvass at this conjuncture is a
subject of some anxiety." Seward, however, felt no trepidation,
for in his opinion "the nation has all the constancy and fidelity
necessary to secure its passage safely through this new political

4

Lincoln and the Unconditionals

trial."[1] The man who had been passed over in 1860 because he was marked with the stigma of "Black Republicanism" looked forward without fear to the first wartime presidential election in American history.

It was true that slavery was no longer considered worthy of defense by a large group in both parties, but there were many who did not accept as irrevocable the course which was charted on January 1, 1863. Slavery may have been dead in the opinion of many, but it was certainly not interred. There were still some who looked upon emancipation as a tragic error and the main cause for the prolongation of the war. Slavery, therefore, was still discussed in the election canvass, and it became an important issue.

For those who no longer regarded slavery as a signal issue there were new ones which had risen to fill the void. At the beginning of the election year the war was yet to be won; the Confederacy seemed still to possess unexpected capacities for survival. The incomparable Lee was fending off Yankee columns with his accustomed ease, and Lincoln was about to begin the third year of his yet fruitless quest for a man of sufficient courage, ruthlessness, and genius to pit against the champion. Before the year was out that man had come, but, in January, Grant was still only a comet on the distant horizon.

Though the war was still to be won, many were already thinking ahead to the peace. What new perplexities would the postwar period bring forth? First to be considered were the freedmen. If they were not returned to bondage, what was to be their future status in society, their civil and political rights, if any? Then there were the arrogant Southerners who had boasted they would defeat the Yankees in battle with cornstalks. Were they erring brothers to be welcomed back and invited to share the fatted calf, or were they unrepentant, unreconciled rebels whose birthright could be regained only after a long period of rededication and reconstruction? What of the triumphant capitalistic industrial society of the North which was being weaned through its infancy on fat war contracts and friendly tariffs into a promising adolescence? These and many other perplexing problems were already

[1] Frederick W. Seward, *Seward at Washington as Senator and Secretary of State*, III, 209.

present, demanding, if not a solution, at least consideration. By autumn the military balance shifted at long last irretrievably in favor of the North, and everyone knew that the end was in sight. The year 1865 would see the horror of civil war dissipated, and the problems of the Negro, reconstruction, and industrialization would be upon Congress and the people. It might conceivably be assumed that such salient questions would provide the major issues in the canvass, but although these ominous portents loomed menacingly, they played a minor role in the political canvass of 1864. Emotionalism was the order of the day.

The Democrats, whose defection had cost them the coveted office in 1860, were rebounding into the canvass of '64 with a renewed vigor which had been whetted by their astonishing triumph in '62. The future, they felt, belonged to them. They were destined to fill the atmosphere during the canvass with venomous assaults upon the President and his administration. The issues of the campaign from the Democrats' perspective were the inefficiency, corruption, and tyranny of the regime in power. Lincoln was a "dictator," a "coarse, vulgar joker," and a "third-rate lawyer who once split rails and now splits the Union." His administration was accused of dishonesty, of tyranny, of seeking to perpetuate itself in power, and of filling the pockets of shoddy contractors at the expense of the people. The war, they argued, should end at once, for its continuation was sapping the vitality of American institutions. Such arguments fitted well into the psychosis caused by three years of grueling war.

Nevertheless, the Democrats were often sincere in their accusations. There was no doubt in the minds of most of them that Lincoln was bent upon making himself a dictator. They feared that if he were allowed to continue unchecked in the course he was following, American liberties would perish along with slavery and the Confederacy. One can almost forgive their calling the Chief Executive an ape, a gorilla, a buffoon, and their constant allusions to his coarseness, for the fury of an election at such a moment could be expected to produce more heat than light. It must not be forgotten, too, that many in Lincoln's own party shared these views of the President's personal qualifications and appearance. Although such an attitude was undoubtedly emotion-

Lincoln and the Unconditionals

alism of the rankest sort, throughout all the persiflage, which more often degenerated into scurrility, the Democrats were pointing up one issue of major significance—the peril inherent in allowing a government to subvert the basic rights of its citizens in wartime on the pretext of necessity.

The Democrats feared that the foundations of freedom were being undermined by a war which was being prolonged unnecessarily by the insistence upon abolition. They deplored the "prevalence of doctrines subversive to the fundamental principles of civil liberty and tending directly to the overthrow of the Constitution of the United States."[2] The majority stood for peace as soon as practicable, a return to the full respect for civil liberties, and a constitutional recognition of slavery, if it were necessary, as a means of ending the war.

These Democrats represented a philosophy that had no chance to triumph in the chaos created by the war, but their appeals would still serve as a reminder to all Americans that the bitter hatreds and swift social changes generated by a civil conflict often lead to the deterioration of constitutional government and the erection of a dictatorship. Their dire predictions and warnings that the nation was headed toward tyranny were wrong largely because the resilience of American institutions and the character of the Chief Executive prevented a permanent subversion of the guaranteed liberties found in the Constitution. Nevertheless, they were discussing a significant issue in the election, although they may at times have coupled it with too much emotional emphasis.

To meet the Democratic issues which centered around war weariness, the violations of civil liberties, and the shortcomings of the "indecent joker," the Unionists relied primarily upon the device of unfettered emotionalism. There seemed to be no reply possible to the Democrats' charge that a despotism was imminent. It was a matter of record that many members of the Union party feared Lincoln's power, too, and they stood in favor of the "salutary one-term principle" as a means of hindering the rise of a dictatorship. This issue was conveniently ignored by the Unionists. The assaults on Lincoln's character were countered with equally dev-

[2] *The Constitution. Addresses by Prof. Morse, Mr. George T. Curtis, Mr. S. J. Tilden,* 4-9.

7

astating onslaughts against the hapless George B. McClellan, the Democratic nominee. In the exchange of insults the Unionists gave better than they received. The issue of war weariness was met by the utilization of an issue which provided an adrenalin shot for the fagging emotions of the public—the bogy of domestic treason.

The Unionists used the issue of domestic treason as their greatest weapon. Evidence of Democratic perfidy, Democratic treason, and Democratic conspiracies was unearthed, disclosed, and repeated into the ears and minds of audiences and readers until the public was nearly stupified. So effective were the speakers and editors in implanting the conviction in the mind of the public that the whole Democratic party was inherently a treasonable party that it was still identified as such two decades after the war.

The single issue of domestic treason, however extensively it was utilized, would probably not have turned back the challenge of the Democratic party had it not been for two other factors that were present during the canvass. In September the far-reaching military achievements of Sherman, Sheridan, and Farragut broke the back of the opposition, both southern and northern Democratic. The other element transcended both the treason issue and the military victories. It was to be found in the personality of the President—a man who had captured the imagination of the rank and file of American voters as no one else. There were many thousands who did not see in his little stories the evidence of an uncouth boor. Nor did they see in him a nineteenth-century Nero burning down the edifice of American democracy. Rather, they viewed him as a man especially created by an omniscient Providence for the task at hand. For any party seeking to win the election of 1864, the possession of a candidate like Abraham Lincoln would assure considerable advantage.

The myth of semidivinity which has grown up in recent decades around the martyred President often makes it difficult for people to realize that any man could seriously challenge or doubt his re-election, but early in 1864 the challenge was great, the doubts many. Two questions had to be answered: Would Lincoln wish to run again (this was by no means an inconsequential question, for no President had been re-elected since Jackson), and if he consented, would his party want him? The answer to the first

Lincoln and the Unconditionals

question was an emphatic affirmative, but there were many in the party who were willing to sacrifice a popular candidate for one of different views.

Whether Lincoln would choose to run again was a question which was not definitely settled before November, 1863. During the previous year there were often times when his resolution to stand for re-election seemed less definite. He must have frequently wondered during the unhappy days of '62 whether or not he was the man destined to steer the nation safely through the war. It is known, for example, that he once turned to Seward and suggested he should run in 1864. Perhaps as Lincoln contemplated the situation in 1862, he concluded that Seward should have the chance he was deprived of in 1860, and that he might prove to be the man to unite the discordant elements of the party and guide the country safely into the peaceful years ahead. Seward had increased in stature since the early days of the war when he was contemptuous of Lincoln's talents. He now wisely declined and assured the President his re-election was necessary to "reaffirm" the disputed results of 1860.[3]

In 1862, Lincoln also offered to step aside for New York Governor Horatio Seymour. This offer is even more amazing when one realizes that Seymour was a Democrat and hostile to the administration. What possible explanation can be offered for such an unprecedented move except that Lincoln was willing to rise above mere partisanship for the sake of the country? No wonder the Unconditionals in his party suspected his motives and opposed him so vehemently, for any man who was willing to endorse a candidate from the opposition party would appear to them as erratic, unpredictable, and certainly not endowed with the necessary attributes to carry out their program.

After his election to the governorship, Seymour seemed to Lincoln to be the man who might conceivably unite the conservative men of the North into a new bipartisan, moderate Union party. If the President was thinking ahead and planning the possible creation of a new alignment based on a combination of the moderate Republicans and Democrats, Seymour was a good choice to head such a party. When Thurlow Weed arrived in Albany

[3] Seward, *op. cit.*, III, 196.

9

carrying Lincoln's proposition, Seymour was reluctant to fill the proffered role.[4]

By November, 1863, Lincoln's decision to run again was well known.[5] As the months passed, he had come to agree with Seward's opinion that he must present himself as a candidate so that the people would have an opportunity to reaffirm his policies. The greatest blow which could be dealt the Confederacy and the strongest evidence which could be shown to the world of the unity of purpose pervading the North would be to have his administration sustained at the polls. It was primarily for this reason that Lincoln definitely decided late in 1863 to run again. He began to intimate to his friends his willingness to serve and hinted at the unwisdom of changing administrations at such a moment. In his opinion there was not sufficient time to groom a successor. For three years he had directed every critical stage of the operations as the Confederacy was placed in the crucible of war. Now that its resistance was beginning to melt slightly in the scorching flame, the time had come to strike the decisive blows, and Lincoln felt he was the man to do precisely that. Lincoln repeated on several occasions that he would gladly respond if the people wished him to stand for re-election. "I do not desire a renomination, except for the reason that such action on the part of the Republican party would be the most emphatic endorsement which could be given to the policy of my Administration," was the theme he repeated to everyone who inquired his intentions.[6]

Lincoln generally maintained that he wished to run again primarily for the purpose of putting the policies of his administration before the public for reaffirmation. But he did admit quite candidly to some of his intimates that he liked the job. Although the office was beset with difficulties on every hand, the hours long, the routine of interviewing office expectants, petty politicians, soldiers, party leaders, grieving parents, favor-seekers, and tourists was

---

[4] Thurlow Weed Barnes, *Memoir of Thurlow Weed,* 428.

[5] G. Brown to L. Trumbull, November 12, 1863, Trumbull Papers (MSS in Library of Congress).

[6] John Nicolay and John Hay, *Abraham Lincoln: A History,* IX, 58–59; Noah Brooks, *Abraham Lincoln and the Downfall of American Slavery,* 385; James M. Winchell, "Three Interviews with President Lincoln," *Galaxy,* Vol. XVI (July, 1873), 40.

depressing and exasperating, and the abuse from the press, pulpit, lectern, and floors of Congress often unbearable, there were few men who could resist the opportunity to occupy such a place; Lincoln was not the exception. His sympathetic understanding of Salmon Chase's aspirations to become president was undoubtedly due to the fact that he knew precisely how Chase felt. If Chase had an acute case of "White House fever," Lincoln did, too, although the thermometer would not have read so high in his case. "When the Presidential grub gets in a man it hides well," he once confided.[7]

In any event, by the new year it was universally known that Lincoln wished to run again. Senator Charles Sumner of Massachusetts once inquired of Gideon Welles whether the rumors he had heard from several friends concerning Lincoln's willingness to run again were true. Welles, the understander of the human heart, replied with a shrug, "I thought all Presidents had entertained dreams of that nature."[8] To Welles and hundreds of others, Lincoln's resolution to run again was accepted as the most natural thing in the world.

Late in October the *Philadelphia News* declared in favor of Lincoln's re-election, and soon other newspapers followed. In December the *Chicago Tribune* proclaimed its support. Simon Cameron, political boss in Pennsylvania, realized that the rank and file of the party wanted Lincoln and saw an opportunity to gain political advantage by taking the lead in an aggressive movement for the President's renomination; his powerful *Philadelphia Evening Bulletin* began singing Lincoln's praises early in January. He was speedily followed by John W. Forney, who threw the support of his three papers behind Lincoln's cause.[9] Once it was definitely established that Lincoln was willing to run again, Henry J. Raymond, editor of the *New York Times* and Lincoln's campaign manager, began working diligently to complete a biography of the President for distribution during the canvass. This time the subject of the sketch was better known than in 1860, and there

---

[7] William E. Dodd, *Lincoln or Lee*, 123.
[8] Gideon Welles, *The Diary of Gideon Welles*, I, 501.
[9] Forney owned the *Philadelphia Press, Washington Chronicle*, and *Harrisburg* (Pennsylvania) *Telegraph*.

was no need to inquire whether his name was "Abram" or "Abraham."

With Lincoln's hat in the ring, the next problem to be considered was the reaction of the public to his decision, and, even more important, the reaction of the party. There does not seem to be a shadow of doubt that in January, 1864, Lincoln was the choice of the voting public both in the army and on the home front. James Russell Lowell, prominent leader of the country's literary set, published an article in the *North American Review* entitled "The President's Policy," in which he hailed the Chief Executive and predicted he would have nothing to fear from the voters in the fall.[10] Local newspapers, as well as the big city dailies, and the private correspondence of prominent Washington politicians were filled with speculations about the approaching canvass, and most agreed with Charles A. Dana that Lincoln "would certainly be re-elected President."[11]

Harper's Weekly summarized the situation on January 2 when it said, "If the Presidential election took place next week, Mr. Lincoln would undoubtedly be returned by a greater majority than any President since Washington." In view of the evidence which was rapidly being assembled from many parts of the nation, this did not appear to be an overly optimistic estimate of the President's chances. The American public in January seemingly acquiesced in Lincoln's decision to stand for re-election. Unfortunately many of the most influential party leaders were reluctant to renominate Lincoln, and they were at that very moment seeking in the most febrile fashion for a satisfactory replacement. The same writer in *Harper's Weekly* pointed this situation out when

[10] *North American Review*, Vol. XCVIII (January, 1864), 238–65.

[11] Charles Dana to James Wilson, January 11, 1864, in James H. Wilson, *The Life of Charles A. Dana*, 303; Tappen Wentworth to Benjamin Butler, January 17, 1864, in Jessie A. Marshall (ed.), *Private and Official Correspondence of General Benjamin Franklin Butler*, III, 307; Albert G. Riddle, *Recollections of War Times, 1860–1865*, 267; Adam Gurowski, *Diary*, III, 60. Norman Judd to Trumbull, January 2, 1864; Richard Yates to Trumbull, February 16, 1864, Trumbull Papers. Elihu Washburne to Thomas Gregg, January 2, 1864. Gregg Papers (MSS in Western Reserve Historical Society). T. Brown to Salmon Chase, January 4, 1864; William Smith to Chase, October 31, 1863, Chase Papers (MSS in Library of Congress). Andrew Johnson to Horace Maynard, January 14, 1864, Edwin Stanton Papers (MSS in Library of Congress). John Purviance to Simon Cameron, December 3, 1863, Cameron Papers (MSS in Library of Congress).

Lincoln and the Unconditionals

he cautioned in his next sentence that Lincoln's roseate hopes might be ruined by a military disaster or if "some serious blunder is committed by the Union men in Congress."

There were many influential Unionists to whom the prospect of having Lincoln for four more years was entirely unpalatable. A strong conspiracy was brewing among these dissatisfied members of Congress, party leaders, abolitionists, and editors to shunt the highly popular Lincoln aside in favor of a candidate with what they considered to be more acceptable views. The men involved in this movement, explained the *Cleveland Leader,* were dissatisfied because the patronage spigot had been too tightly closed to them.[12] Such an oversimplified explanation presented an incomplete picture of the reasons for the mutiny on Lincoln's ship of state. It would be a mistake to underestimate the importance of the patronage question in appraising the anti-Lincoln movement, but the reasons for dissatisfaction went deeper than this. It was not merely the failure to obtain enough offices that drove men into a movement to shelve their party standard-bearer, whose popularity with the voters was admitted grudgingly even by his enemies. A fuller answer is to be found inherent in the very nature and composition of the party in power.

Republicanism was at its inception a sectional, almost entirely northern movement. No crusading army of old was ever composed of so many bands of vassals assembled under one banner to fight its common enemies as the Republican party in the 1850's. The common enemies of the Republicans were not the Southerners but the Democrats; the traditional rivalry of "ins" versus "outs" provided the nexus among the many groups composing the party. Lincoln's election in 1860 was due to the support given him by antislavery Whigs and Abolitionists, varying in shade from those who wanted to end slavery to those who wished merely to check its expansion, some Know-Nothings, disgruntled Democrats in opposition to their own party for reasons varying from personal to fanatical, protectionists, free-traders, machine politicians with their eyes on the main chance, plus many others who defy classification.

These heterogeneous elements presented an equally kaleidoscopic variety of issues. In 1860 the issue in the West was the rail-

12 March 4, 1864.

13

road and the overland mail. In Pennsylvania and New Jersey the tariff was the issue, and in New York and New England opposition to the extension of slavery, rum, Romanism, and an occasional Parthian shot at Stephen A. Douglas were the principal issues. In the old Northwest, homesteads, opposition to the extension of slavery, and "unionism" provided grist for the political mill. Yet the paramount issue, if one takes a bird's-eye view, was the opposition to slavery extension; not so much because it was ethically wrong, but because as an issue it was psychologically good. Even in the fifties every national issue became involved in the slavery question. The repeal of the Missouri Compromise, poor Kansas which "bled" like a hemophile over the editorial pages of the country, the Cuban question, and the Dred Scott decision all became suffused with the issue of slavery.

Although the desires of the "outs" to get "in" and the antislavery issue provided the principal ties which held the party together, another nexus was to be found in the fact that most of the elements of the party believed to some degree in the social ideology of free capitalism, which was seeking at that time to assert its supremacy.

Such a conglomerate party might have remained united during a peaceful period, but the war and its problems proved to be the catalyst necessary to drive the component elements assunder. The gradually widening fissures were recognizable as early as 1860, and the party began to split into a right and left wing.[13]

The President represented the moderate wing of the party, whose aim was to fight the war for the sole purpose of saving the Union. Regarding the institution of slavery, Lincoln and his friends preferred gradual, compensated emancipation followed by possible colonization. In their opinion slavery was morally wrong and would probably die as a result of the war, but they refused to tamper with it unless its abolition would directly influence the salvation of the Union. These moderates intended to deal fairly with the South and did not feel that the vanquished should be made to suffer unduly.

In opposition to the moderates stood a powerful faction which lost no time in applying the thumbscrews to the hapless President.

[13] T. Harry Williams, *Lincoln and the Radicals*, 3–18.

Lincoln and the Unconditionals

This was the group which John Hay, a dilettante student of the French Revolution, called "Jacobins," a name which was used interchangeably with "Radicals." Some historians have tended to feel that these titles are misnomers and that better sobriquets are to be found in the words "Reactionaries" and "Bourbons." James G. Randall called them "Vindictives."[14] In view of some of their policies, however, such a judgment seems too harsh. In many states they were often called "Unconditionals," and I have adopted this name for them in order to avoid the hostile implications which have been associated with the term "radical" when applied to these men. The four leaders of this group, Senators Charles Sumner, Zachariah Chandler, Benjamin Wade, and Representative Thaddeus Stevens, sought to carry out their program through the Committee on the Conduct of the War.[15]

A powerful ally of the Unconditionals were the extreme abolitionists led by Wendell Phillips and William L. Garrison. Phillips' hostility toward the President was so marked that he once avowed his willingness to "cut off both hands before doing anything to aid Abraham Lincoln."[16] In 1862, Garrison described Lincoln as a man as "near lunacy as any one not a pronounced Bedlamite."[17] The passage of time, however, mellowed Garrison, and in January, 1864, in a speech before the Massachusetts Anti-Slavery Society he took a stand in favor of Lincoln's re-election.[18]

The harassed President, encumbered with the multifarious problems of conducting the war, sought to restrain the Unconditionals and the abolitionists within the bounds of what seemed to him to be sound policy. His wisdom, statesmanship, and patriotism were instantly questioned, and the extremists organized a number of movements to prevent his nomination.

What policies did these Unconditionals represent which led them to feel such hostility toward Lincoln? In the first place, they

---

[14] James G. Randall, *Lincoln the Liberal Statesman*, 73.

[15] Williams, *op. cit.*, 64.

[16] Theodore Stanton and Harriet S. Blatch (eds.), *Elizabeth Cady Stanton as Revealed in Her Letters, Diary, and Reminiscences*, II, 100–101.

[17] Garrison to Oliver Johnson, September 9, 1862, in Randall, *Lincoln the Liberal Statesman*, 76.

[18] Wendell Garrison and Francis J. Garrison, *William Lloyd Garrison, 1805–1879*, IV, 104.

Lincoln & the Party Divided

distrusted Lincoln's tolerance and doubted that he was a good party man, especially after his offer in 1862 to step aside for the Democrat Horatio Seymour. Their second point of variance with the President was over the matter of the Negro. In their opinion slavery was at the root of the conflict, and its abolition was a vital necessity. Lincoln's Emancipation Proclamation in 1862 was regarded by them as a halfway measure at best, and their opposition increased as they sought to override what they felt was his inertia or stupidity. Nothing short of immediate emancipation would satisfy them. The Unconditionals also demanded the confiscation of so-called "rebel" property and the employment of Negro troops. As part of their long-range program some favored the enfranchisement and social equalization of the Negroes, in the hope that by this means Republican political and economic control could be saddled upon the South after the war. These were the men who in 1863 came to the conclusion that Lincoln must not stand for re-election.

Shortly after the elections of 1863 the differences between the moderates and the Unconditionals became more acute. The latter group hailed the Union party victory at the polls as a vindication of its program and a mandate for further action of the same sort. A determined effort was then made to acclimate public opinion to accept more extreme measures. On the supposition that the war was drawing to a close, many of them had worked out in some detail a scheme for readmitting the Southern states. It was a plan designed to insure Northern (it perhaps is better to say Republican) domination of the Southern economic and political system and the preponderance of the party in the national government. It was a plan so sweeping in its implications that the Unconditionals knew there was little likelihood that President Lincoln, with his warmheartedness and deep sense of moderation, would support it. For that reason they insisted that the problem of reconstruction lay exclusively within the jurisdiction of Congressional action.

The President, on the other hand, insisted that reconstruction lay within his sphere, and early in August, 1863, he had undertaken to carry out his own plan by authorizing General Nathaniel Banks to set up a civil government in Louisiana supported by the federal army. With the President's position so clearly stated, the Unconditionals were forced to agree with James Gordon Bennett of the *New York Herald,* who had been saying for several months that they would have to replace Lincoln if they hoped to control the reconstruction processes.[19]

The issue between the President and the Unconditionals was clearly drawn in December, 1863, when Congress reassembled. Some constituents urged Congressional leaders to take the initiative from him. "If the President hangs back and falters," wrote one Pennsylvanian to the old fire-eater Thad Stevens, "then should Congress show him that they are the representatives of the people."[20]

The Unconditional clique was present in full force to hear the Chief Executive's message on December 8. What they heard was a patient restatement of views which by that time must have become well known, but the President went a bit further. He promised executive recognition to any Southern state when 10 per cent of the number of voters in 1860 would take an oath of loyalty to the Washington government.

Toward the message the press reaction was as varied as one would expect. The *New York Herald* explained that it was submitted "more to conciliate the radicals than from any hope of its acceptance." Bennett went on to state further that it was done for political reasons. "The active work on all sides of the Presidential campaign begins," he wrote, and then he cautioned Lincoln, "There may soon appear much complications and combinations in his way to prove to Honest Old Abe himself that nothing is more uncertain or subject to accident than the next Presidency." The *New York Times,* representing the moderate point of view, said it was "perfectly adapted to the exigency." Greeley, still enjoying one of his periodic honeymoons with the administration, saw in the document the "wise and generous impulse of Abraham Lincoln." The Democratic press said it was "utterly abolitionist" and "simply absurd."[21]

[19] *New York Herald,* July 11, August 2, 8, 10, 25, 1863.

[20] Amos P. Granger to Thad Stevens, December 14, 1863, Stevens Papers (MSS in Library of Congress).

[21] *New York Herald,* December 10, 11, 1863; *New York Times,* December 11, 1863; *New York Tribune,* December 10, 1863; *New York Journal of Commerce,* December 10, 1863; *New York World,* December 10, 1863.

There was no immediate reaction among the Unconditional leaders in Washington. Three days after the message was delivered, Charles Sumner could write, "Everything is tranquil. Never before, since I have been in Congress, has the session begun so quietly." Even Zach Chandler, according to his biographer, was "delighted" with the message.[22]

The temporary lull before the storm was probably due to the fact that at the moment the Unconditionals were directing their fire at General Meade, whom they accused of cowardice. Many of them were clamoring that he be replaced at once by "Fighting Joe" Hooker, a general who neither deserved nor relished his nickname. Slowly the Unconditional leaders turned their attention toward Lincoln's message. "The reaction is beginning," wrote one of Benjamin Butler's friends; "Lincoln, I hear, is scared."[23]

The President's proclamation finally brought down upon his head all the wrath of the Unconditionals which had been pent up for several months. He had disregarded their wishes too often. He had repeatedly refused to remove the conservative influences of Seward, Edward Bates, Gideon Welles, and Montgomery Blair from his cabinet. He had declined to replace the conservative generals in his armies when requested to do so; and in December, 1863, he refused to acknowledge the supremacy of Congress and the Unconditional clique in dealing with the reconstruction problem. The Unconditionals were forced then to take steps to prevent his renomination. Such a move was to be taken with full cognizance of the President's popularity among the people. So bitter was their hatred of Lincoln that many of them were unwilling to admit that he really was the popular choice. In the summer of 1863, John Hay, Lincoln's private secretary, had written a letter drawing attention to this fact. "I know the people want him. There is no mistaking that fact," wrote Hay. "But politicians are strong yet, and he is not their 'kind of a cat.' "[24]

Many visitors to Washington and others who were intimately associated with the government service have left their impressions

[22] Sumner to Hamilton Fish, December 11, 1863, in George W. Smith, "Generative Forces of Union Propaganda: A Study in Civil War Pressure Groups" (Unpublished Ph.D. dissertation, Department of History, University of Wisconsin, 1940), 345; Wilmer C. Harris, *Public Life of Zachariah Chandler, 1851–1875*, 75.

of the strained relations which existed between Lincoln and the Unconditionals during this period.[25] Albert G. Riddle, who served in Congress during these years as a representative from Ohio, claimed that when the Thirty-seventh Congress adjourned, Lincoln's support came from only two men.[26] The nadir was reached in the next Congress; Carl Schurz glumly reported that "Mr. Lincoln had only one steadfast friend in the lower House of Congress, and few more in the Senate."[27] When a Pennsylvania editor came to the capital early in 1864, he visited Thad Stevens and requested that he be introduced to some congressmen who favored Lincoln's renomination. Without hesitation Stevens took the editor to Representative Isaac N. Arnold from Chicago and explained, "Here is a man who wants to find a Lincoln member of Congress. You are the only one I know and I have come over to introduce my friend to you."[28] Shelby Cullom canvassed the members of Congress and personally reported to Lincoln that there was scarcely a single member favorable to his re-election.[29]

There can be no doubt that early in 1864 Congressional opposition to the President was mounting because of the reconstruction problem and because of the perennial dissatisfaction over the distribution of patronage.[30] This great ground swell of disaffection was destined to spend itself harmlessly against the impregnable rock of the President's popularity among the voters. In the meantime, however, the quest for another candidate was going on feverishly. Trial balloons were aloft for General Benjamin

[23] J. W. Shaffer to Butler, December 17, 1863, in Marshall, *op. cit.*, III, 214; William Fessenden to his family, December 19, 1863, in Francis Fessenden, *Life and Public Services of William Pitt Fessenden*, I, 266–67.

[24] John Hay to John Nicolay, August 7, September 11, 1863, in John Hay, *Letters of John Hay and Extracts from His Diary*, I, 91, 102.

[25] Charles Dana to Charles Adams, March 9, 1863, in Don C. Seitz, *Lincoln the Politician*, 410; George Julian, *Political Recollections*, 1840–1872, 243. Julian claimed that only one in ten members supported Lincoln.

[26] Albert G. Riddle, *The Life of Benjamin F. Wade*, 255.

[27] Frederic Bancroft and William Dunning (eds.), *The Reminiscences of Carl Schurz*, III, 99.

[28] Carl Sandburg, *Abraham Lincoln: The War Years*, II, 561–62.

[29] Shelby Cullom, *Fifty Years of Public Service*, 98–99. See also Gurowski, *op. cit.*, III, 69–70; Theodore C. Smith, *The Life and Letters of James Abram Garfield*, I, 375; Edward Pierce, *Memoir and Letters of Charles Sumner*, IV, 194.

[30] Bancroft and Dunning, *op. cit.*, III, 99; Henry J. Raymond, *Lincoln, His Life and Times, Being the Life and Public Services of Abraham Lincoln*, II, 548.

Lincoln & the Party Divided

Butler, Secretary of the Treasury Salmon P. Chase, General John C. Frémont, Indiana Governor Oliver P. Morton, and a host of other satellites who revolved in the radical orbit. Ears were strained to the ground, eyes fastened upon the political seismograph to catch the slightest reverberation which might indicate an anti-Lincoln trend. Yet whichever way the die was thrown, Lincoln's number was always uppermost.

In contemplating a revolt against Lincoln and conspiring to prevent his renomination, the Unconditionals made the mistake of assuming that since they disapproved of him so heartily a similar view must prevail throughout the nation. Lyman Trumbull of Illinois sampled public opinion in the capital and wrote to his friend H. G. McPike that "the feeling for Mr. Lincoln's re-election *seems* to be general, but much of it I discover is only on the surface." The Senator had reached this conclusion after talking with some public men in Washington.[31] Trumbull made the error of assuming that the personal opinion of a few men in the capital reflected the feeling of the country as a whole. This entirely erroneous impression was shared by nearly all the Unconditional leaders.

The true well-wishers of the administration were not present in the capital; they were fighting at the front, tending their farms, running the nation's machines, and performing the myriad other tasks which would spell victory. They were the people, the voting public, who would have the final word on the candidate, but the Unconditionals did not at first take them into account when they planned their revolt against Lincoln. When they tried to put their plans into operation, they discovered that their desire to find another candidate was not shared by the people throughout the nation. "The people know what they want and will have it," John Hay had written prophetically in August, and the Unconditionals were compelled to admit that the President would have to be renominated.[32] The people would accept no one else.

Even though they secretly may have hoped to find another candidate, the Unconditionals were forced to play along with Lincoln because of the support being given him by the voters.

[31] Trumbull to H. G. McPike, February 6, 1864, Trumbull Papers.
[32] John Hay to John Nicolay, August 7, 1863, in Hay, *op. cit.*, I, 91.

Lincoln and the Unconditionals

Public opinion was too strong to be resisted. Shelby Cullom, who had interviewed several congressmen and reported to the President that he could find no sentiment among them in favor of his re-election, was amazed when he learned the true situation from the Chief Executive. Lincoln showed him a copy of the directory in which he had marked opposite each man's name a notation as to whether or not he could count on his support. Lincoln's backing was, Cullom admitted, actually much greater than his interviews had led him to believe.[33]

Lincoln understood that, although these men spoke against him in such insolent terms in their private conversations, they actually had no choice but to support him publicly in view of the attitude of the people. Lincoln had no illusions about their true feelings. He once told Attorney General Bates that he knew the Unconditionals would "strike him at once, if they durst." They held back only because they feared that the "blow would be ineffectual, and so, they would fall under his power, as *beaten enemies;* and, for that only reason the hypocrites try to occupy equivocal ground—so that, when they fail as *enemies,* they may still pretend to be friends."[34]

In view of the situation, the President's position was most perilous. One major group in his party eagerly wished for his overthrow and was awaiting only an opportunity or an excuse to oust him. Lincoln knew it was only his popularity with the people that assured him the support of these men, but the public was fickle. A military disaster, a new draft, or any of a dozen unforeseen events might dissipate this popularity, and the Unconditionals who were paying lip homage would seize the long-awaited opportunity. Lincoln's chief task was to retain his hold upon the affections of the voters.

Yet there was another danger, although not a great one. Some Unconditionals had already expressed their willingness to strike at him regardless of his popularity while others said that a defeat at the polls for the party was preferable to having him re-elected. "I believe it is better for us and for the country in the long run, to

---

[33] Cullom, *op. cit.,* 98–99. See also W. D. Lindsley to Chase, January 27, 1864; S. N. Wood to Chase, January 28, 1864, Chase Papers (Library of Congress).

[34] Howard Beale (ed.), *The Diary of Edward Bates, 1859–1866,* 333.

be defeated *if we must,* with Chase as our candidate, than to have the Blair-Seward, Lincoln administration upheld by our votes," wrote one man in this school of thought.[35] Lincoln's second task was to prevent the discontent from spilling over the dike of public restraint and from flowing into the waiting camp of his rival candidates.

There were two men who might have succeeded in rallying the Congressional opposition and the other extremists throughout the country into a force against him—Salmon Chase and John Frémont. It is highly doubtful that either of them could have carried the national convention against Lincoln at any time. The real danger lay in the fact that these men might become the candidates on a third-party ticket, and such a split would have ruined the Unionists as it had the Democrats four years earlier. The President cast anxious eyes on the insurgents. There were several lesser persons whose names were suggested as possible nominees, but only Frémont, with his strong following among the Germans, and Salmon Chase, with the great patronage of the Treasury Department at his disposal, had even a remote chance to supersede Lincoln.

[35] Joshua Leavitt to Sumner, November 18, 1864, George Smith, "Generative Forces of Union Propaganda," (Ph.D. dissertation), 350.

Chase,
the Unconditional Candidate

SALMON PORTLAND CHASE, who was born in 1808 in New Hampshire, was Lincoln's most formidable rival for the nomination. When still a child Chase was discovered one day reading a copy of Rawlins' *Ancient History*. Whereupon a friend remarked to his parents, "A boy with a head like that will certainly make his mark in the world." Throughout his life Chase was destined to make many marks: senator, governor, cabinet member, and chief justice, but the place which he felt it was his destiny to occupy was beyond his reach—a mirage which always beckoned him. He remained until death a man of unbounded ambitions, supremely confident in his transcendent ability to solve any problem and to handle any emergency. Chase was always the quintessence of cold dignity and reservation; the type of man who was admired and respected, but never loved as was his chief. He was vain, conceited, pompous; yet he displayed on several occasions a genuine fortitude, such as the time he defied a rum-soaked, howling mob bent on lynching James G. Birney and again as chief justice when in his superb dignity he faced Thad Stevens and the Unconditionals who were howling for Johnson's scalp.

Shortly after his graduation from Dartmouth he moved in 1830 to Cincinnati, where he imbibed deeply the antislavery spirit of the old Northwest. In 1841 he joined forces with Birney's new Liberty party, and in 1852 went to Washington as a senator. Three years later he began the first of two terms as governor of the Buckeye State, the first Republican to hold this seat of honor. As the election of 1860 drew near, it was generally felt that Seward or Chase were the most likely candidates whom the Republicans could nominate. Both men, however, were distrusted because of their radical antislavery sentiments. Chase entered the convention endorsed by the Ohio Republicans, but there was a growing feeling among the delegates at Chicago that he could not carry even his own state, so they turned to the lesser known Lincoln. With the Rail Splitter safely ensconced in the White House, Chase had to be content with the secretaryship of the treasury, but his dreams were always centered upon the fulfillment of his great ambition.

Chase had hardly taken up the duties of his department when he became thoroughly certain that Lincoln was unfit for the position in which fortune had apparently accidentally placed him. Almost at once there began to appear in his voluminous correspondence snide, supercilious remarks concerning the efficiency of the administration and the ability of the Chief Executive. The freshet of benevolent contempt which flowed steadily through his letters increased as the election year approached, and he continued to belabor the theme that the government was nothing more than a collection of unco-ordinated departments.[1] Moreover, he encouraged others to criticize the government.[2] It never at any time occurred to Chase that there was anything incompatible with perfect honor and good faith to indulge in and encourage such banter about his superior and the government he had taken an oath to uphold.

Since he was entirely convinced that the administration under Lincoln was merely a collection of unco-ordinated departments, he began looking about for someone who could provide the necessary leadership and cohesion. His quest did not carry him very far afield; modesty did not constrain him from naming himself as the man.[3] For anyone who might raise the otherwise embar-

---

[1] Chase to William Dickson, January 27, 1864, in Robert Warden, *An Account of the Private Life and Public Services of Salmon Portland Chase,* 564. Chase to E. D. Mansfield, October 18, 1863; to William Sprague, October 31, 1863; to Hiram Barney, July 21, 1863; to Thad Stevens, October 31, 1863; to Murat Halstead, September 21, 1863; to W. D. Bickman, October 18, 1863; to Theodore Tilton, October 31, 1863, Chase Papers (MSS in the Pennsylvania Historical Society).

[2] Warden, *op. cit.,* 505.

24

Chase, the Unconditional Candidate

rassing question as to how a member of Lincoln's cabinet could work against the President, Chase had a ready answer to rationalize his position. "If I were controlled by mere personal sentiments I should prefer the re-election of Mr. Lincoln to any other man," he once admitted magnanimously, and then went on to show that his opposition to Lincoln was prompted by the fact that he doubted "the expediency of re-electing anybody" and that "a man of different qualities from those the President has will be needed for the next four years."[4] Since January, 1862, Chase had been working to convince important leaders that he was that man.[5] Chase's clandestine machination did not escape the discerning eye of Gideon Welles, who noted in his diary that "Chase tries to have it thought that he is indifferent and scarcely cognizant of what is doing in his behalf, but no one of his partisans is so well posted as Chase himself." In fairness to Chase, it must be noted that his interests in the Presidency did not interfere with the working efficiency of his department, for as secretary of the treasury Chase did a splendid job and won the approbation of the American people.

Chase's position in the Treasury Department does not fall within the scope of this book, but for anyone seeking to win the Presidency the control of the financial agencies would naturally prove to be of considerable value. The department had in the last year of the war a patronage of nearly 15,000 places, and James G. Blaine later noted that this was the magnet which drew most of Lincoln's opponents to Chase.[6]

Chase, therefore, became the rallying point for the majority of the Unconditionals. It must not be concluded that his popularity was due solely to the fact that he could gratify their insatiable appetite for patronage. Salmon Chase's greatest asset was the fact that he agreed completely with the policies that the Unconditional clique was attempting to force Lincoln to adopt.[7]

[3] Chase to Joshua Leavitt, October 7, 1863; to Horace Greeley, October 9, 1863; to William Sprague, November 26, 1863, Chase Papers (Pennsylvania).

[4] Chase to William Sprague, November 26, 1863, in James W. Schuckers, *The Life and Public Services of Salmon Portland Chase*, 494.

[5] James Stone to Chase, January 15, 1862, Chase Papers (Library of Congress).

[6] Schuckers, *op. cit.*, 481; James G. Blaine, *Twenty Years of Congress*, I, 514.

[7] Chase's views are set forth in his correspondence. See Cyrus Grosvenor (quot-

Lincoln & the Party Divided

In Chase's views one finds the microcosm of the Unconditional program. The Unconditionals who refused to make any concessions to the South as a basis for peace and demanded that slavery be abolished unconditionally, that the Negro be accorded his full share of social and political rights, and that the terms for readmission into the Union be dictated by Congress, which would also take all reasonable precautions against future secession, found a perfect man in Salmon Chase. He agreed wholeheartedly with their program; he had extensive patronage; he had popular support, although somewhat limited; he held the friendship of many Unconditional leaders; and he needed no encouragement to induce him to run.

In reviewing Chase's quest for the Presidency the first question to be considered is whether or not he used his position in the Treasury Department to further his ambitions. It may be noted in passing that Chase's portrait on the reverse side of the greenbacks gave him a great deal of free publicity, but one cannot blame Chase for this situation. The main problem is whether he used his patronage to erect a machine for himself. On this important matter we have his own testimony that such was not the case. When someone implored him once for an appointment on the ground that it would help his campaign for the Presidency, Chase wrote with much repugnance, "I should despise myself if I felt capable of appointing or removing a man for the sake of the Presidency."[8] Yet on many occasions he betrayed much interest in the matter of making proper appointments for political reasons, and Edward Bates confided in his diary that "Mr. Chase's head is turned by his eagerness in pursuit of the presidency. For a long time back he has been filling all the offices in his own vast patronage with extreme partisans and contrives also to fill many vacancies properly belonging to other departments."[9]

Whether Chase made his appointments to foster his presi-

---

ing Chase) to Chase, July 28, 1862; Chase to James A. Stevens, July 23, 1863, Chase Papers (Library of Congress). Chase to Daniel S. Dickinson, November 18, 1863; to William Sprague, November 18, 1863; to E. D. Keyes, August 1, 1862, Chase Papers (Pennsylvania).

8 Clarence E. Macartney, *Lincoln and His Cabinet*, 254–55; Donnal V. Smith, *Chase and Civil War Politics*, 76–77.

9 Beale, *op. cit.*, 310.

Chase, the Unconditional Candidate

dential hopes can be considered a moot question, but one fact is irrefutable: it was the treasury appointees who did the most to keep his chances alive. Of Chase's most active managers the following were a few who held appointments from his departments: Thomas Heaton, Mark Howard, William Mellen, George Dennison, Richard Parsons, and James Briggs. Welles wrote in 1864 that Chase intended to press "his pretensions as a candidate, and much of the Treasury machinery and the special agencies have that end in view." George Dennison reported from New Orleans, "We are forming a Chase club here and meet for organization next Monday. . . . I believe we can control the election of delegates to the National Convention." Ben Wade heard from a friend in Ohio that "a great effort is now being made in this state in the interests of Mr. Chase for the next Presidency. Those holding positions under him are doing their very best."[10] Treasury agents in Indiana attempted to control the local Union party conventions and threatened to discharge William Bradshaw, revenue assessor in Indianapolis, if he did not support Chase. William Mellen ranged up and down the Mississippi River plugging for Chase, while Mark Howard attempted to control the Union League of America. Throughout the entire North, into the far West, down the Mississippi into conquered Louisiana, into the customhouses of the nation spread a host of his genuflecting agents surreptitiously working to advance Chase's ambitions for the Presidency.[11] Chase asked posterity to believe, in spite of all this, that he would have refused to appoint or remove a man for the sake of the Presidency.

Before proceeding further in tracing the course of Chase's unsuccessful bid for the Presidency, it is necessary to consider briefly his position among the people and the Unconditional lead-

[10] Welles, *op. cit.*, I, 525; George Dennison to Chase, February 19, March 5, 1864, Chase Papers (Library of Congress); S. S. Osborn to Benjamin Wade, February 8, 1864, Wade Papers (MSS in Library of Congress).

[11] For the work of treasury agents see J. H. Jordan to Chase, May 1, 1864; J. Fishback to Chase, April 11, 1864; William Mellen to Chase, June 27, August 6, September 10, 1863, Chase Papers (Library of Congress). H. J. Rudisill to Chase, February 2, 1864; Thomas Heaton to Chase, January 14, 1864; Chase to Heaton, January 28, February 8, 1864, Chase Papers (Pennsylvania). James Bingham to Andrew Johnson, November 15, 1863, Andrew Johnson Papers (MSS in Library of Congress); Nicolay and Hay, *Abraham Lincoln: A History*, VIII, 323.

ers. It has already been indicated that Chase was popular among the Unconditionals because he was one of them on the matter of policies and also possessed an extensive patronage with which to reward his followers. These two qualifications, however, were not enough to assure him support unless he could prove to them that his vote-getting appeal equaled Lincoln's. Chase's hope of receiving more than token support was futile until he could do so. His attraction to the Unconditional clique as a possible candidate was, mathematically speaking, directly proportional to the popular support given him. Since his following among the voters was never great, Chase's support among the Unconditionals was actually rather illusory.[12]

He received the proffered affections and hollow pledges of many minor bosses, editors, and Unconditional spokesmen, but the political dry flies Chase cast upon the waters failed to lure up from the depths the biggest prizes: Stevens, Wade, Greeley, et al. This game was too wary to commit itself without first ascertaining Chase's real position among the voters.

Chase personally overrated his support. To one well-wisher he wrote that he was gratified by the preference many showed for his candidature, "for those who express it are generally men of great weight, and high character and independent judgement."[13] Chase committed two basic errors in estimating his position: first, he assumed that these expressions of preference in his favor were shared by the American voters; and second, he erred in assuming that his support came from "men of great weight." Actually, as James K. Hosmer wrote, "He had no strength with the people, nor was there a single public man of prominence who actively favored his candidacy."[14] The prominent men who wrote him letters expressing their good wishes never were willing to go to the point of offering him public support. Their language remained equivocal; and well it should have, for they were intent upon learning the popular reaction to Chase's boom before openly committing themselves. As long as Lincoln remained the obviously

12 Williams, op. cit., 307.
13 Chase to Flamen Ball, February 2, 1864, Chase Papers (Pennsylvania).
14 James K. Hosmer, Outcome of the Civil War, 1863–1865, 147.

Chase, the Unconditional Candidate

popular choice, there was little likelihood that Chase's candidacy would receive the wholehearted support of the party leaders. The Secretary, however, remained a threat to Lincoln until March, 1864. The presidential boom, which he had planned so assiduously since 1862, assumed rather formidable proportions during and shortly after the state elections of 1863.

During the fall canvass of '63 Chase entered the hustings in Maryland, Ohio, and Indiana, while Welles expressed his opinion that the Secretary was firing the opening gun of his presidential campaign.[15] Ohio received Chase's fondest attention. He realized that if he could go into the national convention as Ohio's favorite son, he could seriously challenge Lincoln's claim for renomination. He threw his support to John Brough, the gubernatorial candidate, who apparently indicated he would reciprocate by helping the Secretary's presidential aspirations the following year.[16] In Indiana he appeared on the rostrum with Oliver Morton and at one time made a bid for the Governor's support by offering him the secretaryship of state.[17] The Governor was receiving some backing for the nomination himself at that moment, and he refused to help Chase.

Chase returned to the capital with a radiant confidence that he had served himself well by his junket into Ohio and the Hoosier State. When Brough carried the Ohio gubernatorial election against Vallandigham, many of his advisors and workers assured the Secretary that it was conclusive proof of his powers in that state. Others pointed to the heartfelt reception accorded him in Indiana as additional evidence.[18] Chase, who needed only a modicum of persuasion, fell in with their line of reasoning and admitted candidly that he was highly pleased with and impressed at the

---

[15] Welles, *op. cit.*, I, 469.

[16] Joseph Geiger to Chase, June 18, 1863, Chase Papers (Library of Congress); George H. Porter, *Ohio Politics During the Civil War Period,* 117–20. Chase spoke at Cincinnati, Xenia, Morrow, and Camp Dennison, Ohio; Indianapolis, Lawrenceberg, Greensburg, and Shelbyville, Indiana, as well as in Baltimore, Maryland.

[17] William D. Foulke, *The Life of Oliver P. Morton,* I, 251; Winifred A. Harbison, "Indiana Republicans and the Re-election of President Lincoln," *Indiana Magazine of History,* Vol. XXXIV (March, 1938), 50.

[18] R. S. Hart to Chase, October 16, 1863; Richard Parsons to Chase, October 17, 1863; James Briggs to Chase, October 17, 22, 1863; Flamen Ball to Chase, October 21, 1863, Chase Papers (Library of Congress).

spontaneity of the demonstrations which were accorded him wherever he went. It seemed a propitious omen for the future.[19]

While Chase was personally mending fences in Ohio and Indiana, he entrusted the carpentry work in Pennsylvania and New York to his friends. John Covode was instructed to help Governor Curtin in his struggle for re-election, probably with the hope that he would be appropriately friendly toward Chase's ambitions. In New York, Chase was served faithfully by his old Ohio wheel horse, Joseph Geiger, who went to the Empire State directly after arranging for a reception in Cincinnati honoring Chase. He was assisted by James Briggs, the deputy collector of the port of New York, and both gentlemen participated in the state canvass and never neglected an opportunity to speak a word in Chase's behalf.[20]

While Chase was busy fostering his political aspirations in September and October, the luckless President was wrestling with the Unconditionals over the Missouri question. The Missouri problem was one of long standing.[21] There was considerable tension between the radical (Charcoal) faction led by B. Gratz Brown and Henry Blow and the conservative (Claybank) faction led by St. Louis Representative Frank Blair and Governor Hamilton Gamble. The controversy had much to do with the question of emancipation and the control of patronage in Missouri. The Charcoals resented the influence which was exerted in the state by the Blair faction, and they especially despised General John Schofield, the military commander in that district, whom they regarded as a Blair tool. In September, 1863, the Charcoals sent a seventy-man delegation to Washington to beseech Lincoln to replace Schofield with Butler and to end the "intolerable oppression" of the Blairs. Lincoln said there was little hope that he could grant their requests.

[19] Chase to E. D. Mansfield, October 18, 1863; to John Conness, October 18, 1863, Chase Papers (Pennsylvania).

[20] Joseph Geiger to Chase, October 25, 1863, Chase Papers (Library of Congress).

[21] The literature on the Missouri question is plentiful. See Sceva Laughlin, "Missouri Politics During the Civil War," *Missouri Historical Review*, Vol. XXIII (April, 1929), 400–26, (July, 1929), 583–618; Vol. XXIV (October, 1929), 87–113. (January, 1930), 261–84. H. C. McDougal, "A Decade of Missouri Politics—1860–1870—from a Republican Viewpoint," *Missouri Historical Review*, Vol. III (January, 1909), 126–53.

Chase, the Unconditional Candidate

The whole matter was further complicated by the ill-timed attack on the Unconditionals which was launched by Frank Blair in St. Louis and by his brother, Postmaster General Montgomery Blair, in Rockville, Maryland. The selection of a conservative, John Henderson, as United States senator, and the removal of radical William W. Edwards, who was United States district attorney in the Eastern District of Missouri, provided the last insult. The Unconditionals were adamant and there were predictions of more violence in Missouri.[22]

Chase saw here an opportunity to make political hay and threw his support to the Unconditionals on the advice of his treasury agent in Missouri, William Mellen.[23] If he hoped to gain any permanent advantage from the situation, however, he was destined to be disappointed, for Lincoln at last awoke to the seriousness of the Missouri situation and removed Schofield. When he appointed Unconditional General Rosecrans, oil was poured upon the troubled waters. From the standpoint of the presidential question the most significant development growing out of the settlement of the affair was that the Unconditionals in Missouri now reciprocated Lincoln's kindness by stating that they did not plan to make Chase their candidate for the presidency unless they were compelled to do so by the retention of "Rockville" Blair and "Granny" Bates in the cabinet.[24] Thus, temporarily at least, Lincoln had resolved a delicate situation without sacrificing his friend Monty Blair or driving the Unconditionals into total opposition. Not all the Unconditionals were placated, however, for on the same night that Schofield was removed, Representative Henry Blow addressed the Union League in Washington and attacked Lincoln and the conservatives without mercy.

Not only did Chase's machinations for the Presidency involve him intimately in the politics of several states; he also sought to win the support of the Union League of America. The strength and activities of the league had greatly increased since its inception

[22] Horace White to William Fessenden, November 7, 1863, Fessenden Papers (MSS in Library of Congress); B. Smith to Elihu Washburne, January 15, 1864, Washburne Papers (MSS in Library of Congress).

[23] Mellen to Chase, June 27, August 6, September 10, 1863, Chase Papers (Pennsylvania); Chase to Henry Blow, September 23, 1863, Chase Papers (Pennsylvania).

[24] Donnal V. Smith, *op. cit.,* 84–85.

in 1862; according to the national executive committee the estimated membership of the society exceeded 700,000.

When the league met in Washington early in December, there was more than a little possibility that it would seek to dominate the coming presidential election. In New York, John Austin Stevens was working diligently to transform the powerful club there into a Chase society.[25] Thurlow Weed discovered, or at least suspected, that the "Loyal Leagues . . . are fixing to control delegate appointments for Mr. Chase."[26] The radical tendencies of the league had become well known, and it was generally felt that the meeting would be the signal for a general attack on Lincoln and his policies.[27]

The assembly gathered in Washington on the appointed day. The President's message had already been delivered and no effort had as yet been made to attack him. Perhaps the Unconditionals wished to consult together first at the league meeting before they opened their fusillade against Lincoln. The meeting was filled with Lincoln's enemies; in glancing down the list of delegates, one cannot help feeling that he is reading a roster of Chase supporters, many of whom were treasury agents. Though Unconditionals were present from every corner of the North, the attack on the President was milder than one would expect. After discussing fully the Missouri and reconstruction problems, the delegates adjourned to meet "at the same place and at about the same time as the Republican National Convention."[28]

Mark Howard was enthusiastic about the outcome of the league session at Washington. He felt confident the delegates preferred Chase for the Presidency, and he wrote to the Secretary that "the spirit of our Grand Council was fully in harmony with yours."[29] Another treasury agent at the meeting reported that a radical

[25] John Stevens to Chase, September 15, 1863, Chase Papers (Pennsylvania); George T. Brown to Trumbull, September 17, 1863, Trumbull Papers.

[26] Nicolay and Hay, *Abraham Lincoln: A History,* VIII, 315–16.

[27] The league refused to admit Montgomery Blair to honorary membership although this honor was extended to every other cabinet member. *New York Tribune,* December 8, 1863.

[28] George Smith, "Generative Forces of Union Propaganda" (Ph.D. dissertation), 369–73.

[29] Mark Howard to Chase, December 19, 1863, Chase Papers (Library of Congress).

spirit prevailed at the meeting and among the league in general. The league would *"make the* sentiment which would at least define the character of the nominee," he confided. Lincoln was "not up to their standard," and "they appreciated the *demand of the future* for a government and would not be satisfied with our [and he used a pet Chasism] administration of Departments."[30]

Chase must have tingled with anticipation when he read the glowing reports of his agents at the meeting that his views and those of the majority of the delegates coincided. It must have seemed to him that they would have to turn to him as the only possible man who could end the abominable "administration of departments" and bring the Unconditional program to fruition.

The question must be raised as to just how far the delegates at the convention were speaking for their more than 700,000 brothers? Could their opinions be taken as a fair barometer of public opinion? Apparently they could not. Within a few days Lincoln had adjusted the Missouri problem to the Unconditionals' satisfaction, and they were willing to pledge they would not make Chase their candidate. Even though the unrepentant Henry Blow assailed the administration before the Union League in Washington, the following evening when Lincoln's friend Isaac Arnold addressed a group in the same hall, his suggestion that Honest Abe be elected for another term was greeted by waves of cheering from the audience. The popularity of the President among the people, even in Washington, the stronghold of radicalism, could not be questioned by anyone who was honest enough to admit it.

Chase's position in the Treasury Department also gave him considerable opportunity to seek the support of the nation's powerful financial leaders. C. H. Ray, a prominent Chicago business executive and part-owner of the *Tribune,* was working for his nomination. In New York, John Austin Stevens was one of his staunchest supporters. William P. Smith of the Baltimore and Ohio Railroad attempted to secure a conference of Chase's supporters in Baltimore for the purpose of organizing for the presidential canvass. This proposed project fell through, but the Secretary's friends launched his campaign from Washington.

[30] John Hogeboom to Chase, December 28, 1863, Chase Papers (Library of Congress).

Chase's many business relations with the Cooke brothers, Henry and Jay, also won him considerable support from this quarter. An act of 1862 empowered Chase to select certain banks as depositories of public funds, and he chose these banks with a view to the possible favors they might be willing to reciprocate and the help they could give his presidential ambitions. It was to be wasted effort, however, for the bankers, like the politicians, supported Lincoln when he proved to be the popular candidate.[31]

One powerful element which Chase could not overlook in trying to erect his machine was the fourth estate, and he worked to win adherents among the most powerful editors of the nation. William Wales of the *Baltimore American* often printed flattering articles about him. Horace Greeley, whose love feasts with the administration were marred by periodic eruptions of dissatisfaction, confided that he would like a change of administration. He remained, however, an uncertain ally of Chase's, for his loyalties wandered to and fro from Rosecrans to Lincoln, and then to Chase and Frémont.[32]

Chase had much support from George Wilkes' *Spirit of the Times* and Theodore Tilton's *Independent,* as well as the *Indianapolis Gazette, Cincinnati Commercial,* and *Cleveland Herald.* On the other hand, James Gordon Bennet failed to throw the influence of his powerful *New York Herald* behind the Secretary, even though Chase used his most honeyed persuasions. Medill's *Chicago Tribune* was another paper which Chase could not win. Medill often opposed Lincoln, but the pressure from the President's friends in the Windy City was too great to permit the editor to line up with Chase. John Forney assured the Secre-

---

[31] C. H. Ray to Chase, November 14, 28, 1863; Chase to John Stevens, July 23, 1863; Stevens to Chase, June 11, 1863; William Smith to Chase, October 20, 1863; Clinton Rice to Chase, October 29, 1863, Chase Papers (Pennsylvania). Ellis Oberholtzer, *Jay Cooke: Financier of the Civil War,* I, 360. In making reports in the newspapers, Chase often included flattering references to his own superb financial ability to impress the readers.

[32] William Wales to Chase, September 19, 1863; Chase to Greeley, May 21, 1862, Chase Papers (Library of Congress). Greeley to Chase, September 29, 1863; Chase to Greeley, October 9, 1863, Chase Papers (Pennsylvania). James Gilmore, *Personal Recollections of Abraham Lincoln and the Civil War,* 86–101. Ralph Fahrney, *Horace Greeley and the Tribune in the Civil War,* 183–88.

Chase, the Unconditional Candidate

tary that he was "a Chase Democrat," but he backed Lincoln with his three influential journals.[33]

With all his corresponding and proselyting during 1863 to win the favor of prominent editors and business and political leaders, Chase made no effort to co-ordinate these activities into a well-planned and orderly system. Unless he succeeded in creating an organization, both state and national, there was little hope that his accession to the White House could be realized. Joseph Geiger, who served him faithfully during the fall canvass of 1863, understood the situation clearly and he characterized Chase's activities as "blind striking." He implored his chief to start building an organization or all would be lost.[34] Chase made no move in this direction, and it remained for his friends to set up an organization on December 9, 1863.[35]

On the basis of the evidence available it may be concluded that the Chase boom was officially launched by a central committee which consisted of three or four congressmen, two of them from Ohio, and four other gentlemen, of whom two were also from Chase's state. State committees were selected, but as Charles Wilson correctly observed, it was difficult to know how many of the men whose names appear on the list were actually supporters of Chase.

This first Chase national committee with its subordinate state organizations was a nebulous affair, but within a few weeks it assumed more definite shape and the membership became more permanent. It was also apparent that most of its strength came from Ohio. The national committee in its expanded form became known as the Republican National Executive Committee, with Senator Samuel Pomeroy of Kansas as chairman. Chase was fully aware of what was going on, for he wrote to a friend in Ohio on January 18 that a committee composed of "prominent Senators

---

[33] James Briggs to Chase, October 17, 22, 23, 1863, Chase Papers (Library of Congress); John Forney to Chase, August 26, 1863, Chase Papers (Pennsylvania); Don S. Seitz, *The James Gordon Bennetts: Father and Son*, 81.

[34] Geiger to Chase, November 10, 1863; Briggs to Chase, November 2, 1863; H. C. Bowen to Chase, November 16, 1863, Chase Papers (Library of Congress).

[35] Charles R. Wilson, "The Original Chase Organization Meeting and *The Next Presidential Election*," *The Mississippi Valley Historical Review*, Vol. XXIII (June, 1936), 61–79.

and Representatives and citizens" had been formed for the purpose of making him president. He also added, "This Committee, through a sub-committee, has conferred with me . . . and I have consented to their wishes."[36] As the election year dawned, Chase was afield in full panoply, and a committee had been organized to press his claims for the Presidency. "The fight will narrow between Lincoln and Chase," was the opinion of one observer, and it was shared by many.[37]

While the seeds of discontent which Chase sowed so furtively during 1863 were ripening for harvest early in the election year, what steps had the Chief Executive taken to combat his enemy? During this extremely critical period Lincoln seemed to be completely oblivious to Chase's threat; on the surface, at least, he seemed to hold the Secretary's sapping operations in complete disdain. Even John Hay, who saw Lincoln every day, was taken in by the President's outward calm and failed to recognize that his chief actually felt the deepest concern for the intrigues of Chase. Hay recorded in his diary that "he seems much amused at Chase's mad hunt after the Presidency."[38]

The President kept his feelings well hidden, and when his advisers and confidants came to him with reports of the grave situation which was developing in the Treasury Department, he frequently put them off with a facetious story. Lincoln's reticence to remove Chase from the cabinet provided subject for speculation and conversation throughout the capital. Was it ignorance of the true situation which deterred the axe from falling? It certainly was not; Lincoln knew of Chase's enterprises, but said, "I have determined to shut my eyes, so far as possible, to everything of the sort."[39]

[36] Chase to James Hall, January 18, 1864, in Schuckers, *op. cit.*, 497.

[37] George Stearns to his wife, January 23, 1864, in Frank Stearns, *The Life and Public Services of George Luther Stearns*, 326. Joshua Giddings to Chase, January 13, 1864; S. H. Boyd to Chase, January 10, 1864, Chase Papers (Library of Congress). A. Denny to Sherman, January 15, 1864, Sherman Papers (MSS in Library of Congress); Hay, *op. cit.*, I, 143.

[38] Tyler Dennett (ed.), *Lincoln and the Civil War in the Diary and Letters of John Hay*, 110.

[39] Nicolay and Hay, *Abraham Lincoln: A History*, VIII, 316; Cullom, *op. cit.*, 94; F. B. Carpenter, *Six Months at the White House with Abraham Lincoln*, 130; Hay, *op. cit.*, I, 113; Dennett, *Lincoln and the Civil War*, 110.

Chase, the Unconditional Candidate

Though Lincoln seemed unmindful of Chase's designs and deceived such constant companions as the youthful Hay, he did not for a moment gull the venerable Gideon Welles. The Naval Secretary correctly gauged Lincoln's true sentiments on Chase when he noted in his diary that "the President fears Chase, and he also respects him." On a second occasion he again observed, "Almost daily we have some indication of Presidential aspirations and incipient operations for the campaign. The President does not conceal the interest he takes."[40] The President was actually quite perturbed over the magnitude of the operations against him.

Even though Lincoln was aware of Chase's intent, he patiently played Damocles until the opportune moment arose to end the intolerable situation, and that favorable juncture did not present itself during the first months of 1864. General Butler once asked Simon Cameron, "Is Mr. Chase making any headway in his candidature?" Cameron admitted sadly that he was. Lincoln could solve the problem, said the impulsive Butler, by "tipping him out."[41] Such a drastic measure as Butler's "tipping out" treatment did not, in Lincoln's opinion, fall within the limits of sound policy. Chase was the darling of the Unconditional clique; it did not escape the President's discerning eye that many Unconditional leaders preferred the Secretary. He probably felt the removal of the treasury head would serve no purpose other than to add another black mark against the administration on the already lengthy list of the Unconditionals. The danger was present that the removal of Chase might have driven them into an open break with the administration, the repercussions of which might have irreparably shattered the Union party. It was to avoid this danger that he wisely decided to permit Chase to continue without molestation his surreptitious operations from the Treasury Department.

Many of Lincoln's associates were at a loss to explain his actions, and even a sapient political wizard like Thurlow Weed seemed to prefer the "tipping out" treatment. On one occasion he exploded with exasperation at Lincoln's tolerant attitude toward the Unconditionals. "Why," Weed bemoaned, "does he persist in giving them weapons with which they may defeat his renomi-

---

[40] Welles, *op. cit.*, I, 521, 525.
[41] Benjamin F. Butler, *Autobiography and Personal Reminiscences*, 635.

nation?"[42] Before the election year was three months old, he, too, saw the wisdom of retaining Chase in the cabinet and allowing him the privilege of being hoist with his own petard.

In his struggle to procure the renomination in the face of opposition from the Unconditionals in general and Chase in particular, the President drew many of the winning cards and the beneficent smiles of Dame Fortune. In the first place, as was indicated earlier, he had the unfailing support of the American voting public during the early months of 1864. Wherever the Unconditionals turned to gauge the public's reaction, they learned much to their discomfiture that the people wanted Lincoln again. The Unconditionals may have felt that Lincoln was an inept leader and that Chase or any one of a half-dozen other men would have made a more sagacious president; yet they heeded Lord Bryce's wise observation on American political life, "To a party it is more important that its nominee should be a good candidate than that he turn out a good President." As the supreme executive, Lincoln might have been, as Murat Halstead said, "an awful woeful ass," but there was no doubt that he was the candidate nonpareil. Political wisdom, therefore, required that he be supported.

Even if the Unconditionals were forced to support Lincoln against their own wishes, their position was by no means hopeless. There was always the possibility, as Gurowski once suggested, that they might succeed in forcing Lincoln to change his policies and his entourage. There were several instances when under their goading he had moved in the direction of radicalism. He may have been stubborn, the veritable "Kentucky mule" he was often denoted, but "with all his deficiencies" he proved repeatedly that he was "willing to grow."[43] The Unconditionals, therefore, hesitated to abandon Lincoln, the good candidate, for Chase, who would possibly be a better president. The men who felt that it was better to be defeated with Chase than to win with Lincoln were few in number, and there was little likelihood that the majority of the President's opponents would have adopted such a suicidal view.

[42] Barnes, *op. cit.*, 434.
[43] L. Marie Childs to George Julian, April 8, 1865, Giddings-Julian Papers (MSS in Library of Congress).

Chase, the Unconditional Candidate

Lincoln could abstain from direct action against Chase. He relied on the pressure of public opinion to keep the Unconditionals safely in the fold. His danger did not lie in Chase's grandiose, if somewhat impotent, preparations, but only in the fact that something might occur to divert public favor from himself and give the Unconditionals their much-sought-after justification for shunting him aside. It was Lincoln's good fortune that his popularity with the people came always at the correct moment. A temporary reaction against him came late in the summer because of the unpropitious military situation, but by then the nomination had already been made. The pendulum swung back shortly before the election and assured his triumph. Had the reaction occurred two months earlier, Lincoln might not have been nominated, and two months later his re-election would have been jeopardized.

The second trump card which Lincoln held was the extensive patronage of his office—the most influential men on the national executive committee of the party and the various state committees were federal officeholders, and consequently committed by their own welfare to support his campaign for re-election.[44]

The last advantage which Lincoln possessed was the inability of his Unconditional opposition to unite its strength on one candidate. It seems highly unlikely that, even had they united on one candidate, they could have prevailed against Lincoln's popularity, organization, and patronage; but the mere fact that they failed to do so greatly diminished the President's task.

The term "radical" often actually described the diverse opposition to Lincoln's administration within the Union party. One must not assume that there was perfect harmony among the leaders of this faction, nor would it be correct to believe that Chase was their only candidate. Thad Stevens, who was probably the most powerful leader within the group, had no greater affection for Chase than he had for Lincoln. Chase represented the western segment of the faction, and because of the East-West sectional animosity his friends were often at loggerheads with the eastern group. Even Benjamin Wade, an influential leader of the western group, was hostile to Chase. In Kansas, Unconditional leaders Samuel Pomeroy and James Lane could seldom agree. In Missouri,

[44] Harry Carman and Reinhard Luthin, *Lincoln and the Patronage*, 228–99.

Lincoln & the Party Divided

leaders B. Gratz Brown and Charles D. Drake were frequently moving in opposite directions. The same situation prevailed all over the nation, and illustrations can be found in many quarters.[45]

The bickerings and jealousies of various leaders hamstrung their efforts to unite on a common candidate. Joseph Geiger once reported to Chase that Lincoln's greatest weapon was the Unconditionals' inability to agree on one candidate.[46] Governor John Andrew of Massachusetts also said, "I am told that the Senators and Representatives are for the most part opposed to the renomination of President Lincoln; but, that there is no positive opinion among them, no union, or consent, or direction; so that nothing can easily come of their dissent to Lincoln."[47] One of Lyman Trumbull's correspondents echoed the same sentiments: "Some [of the Unconditionals] will vote only for Frémont, others only for Butler, allmost [sic] all would like a change, but they have no one to change for and they will vote indifferently."[48]

Taking advantage of his popularity, organization, patronage, and the internecine conflicts within the framework of his opposition, Lincoln worked to overcome Chase. As early as December, 1863, his friends began battering away at the foundation of Chase's hopes for the nomination. The galling situation which Lincoln had patiently endured for so many months was rapidly drawing to a close. Chase's movement was approaching its climax. "I presume it is true that Mr. Chase's friends are working for his nomination, but it is all lost labor; Old Abe has the inside track so completely that he will be nominated by acclamation when the convention meets," wrote Joseph Medill prophetically.[49]

45 Joseph Geiger to Chase, January 24, April 2, 1864; James Briggs to Chase, November 2, 1863, Chase Papers (Library of Congress). Edward McPherson to Stevens, September 21, 1863, Stevens Papers; *Chicago Tribune,* December 10, 1863; *Washington Chronicle,* December 14, 1863; William Zornow, "The Kansas Senators and the Re-election of Lincoln," *Kansas Historical Quarterly,* Vol. XIX (May, 1951), 133–44.

46 Geiger to Chase, April 2, 1864, Chase Papers (Library of Congress).

47 John Andrew to Gurowski, April 24, 1864, in George Smith, *"Generative Forces of Union Propaganda"* (Ph.D. dissertation), 397.

48 H. Baldwin to Trumbull, April 4, 1864, Trumbull Papers; Lafayette Holbert to Zachariah Chandler, March 11, 1864, Zachariah Chandler Papers (MSS in Library of Congress); Joshua Giddings to his daughter, March 7, 1864, Giddings-Julian Papers.

49 *Chicago Tribune,* December 17, 1863.

The Chase Pudding
Does Not Rise

J ANUARY was clearly the month when Chase's presidential aspirations reached their zenith, continued for a few brief weeks with no noticeable sign of diminishing, then abruptly fell away toward the end of February, and ended with the Secretary's withdrawal from the race in March. It was apparent that Lincoln's period of inactivity had ended, and he began to direct the operations which would deflate Chase's presidential balloon. As early as January 10, Francis P. Blair, Gideon Welles, and former Governor William Dennison of Ohio consulted with Lincoln on the coming campaign. What transpired in this conclave is unrecorded, but it undoubtedly had much to do with considering the tactics which could be suitably employed against Chase.

Another frequent visitor to the executive offices was Thurlow Weed, guiding instrument of the New York Republican machine. Weed was by no means an unqualified Lincoln man, for he often felt that the President had gone too far on the matter of emancipation and not far enough when dispensing patronage to the Weed faction. He was angry because Lincoln refused repeatedly to replace Hiram Barney as head of the New York Custom House, and he became even more so when the President appointed another Chase man, John Hogeboom, to the house.[1]

But though Weed growled about Lincoln's shortcomings, he was astute enough never to complain publicly. He realized that

[1] Glyndon G. Van Deusen, *Thurlow Weed, Wizard of the Lobby*, 306.

Lincoln & the Party Divided

Lincoln was too popular to be denied the renomination, and he had no intention of straying too far from the patronage fount. In the capital he spent countless hours closeted with the President, and they were joined by Simon Cameron of Pennsylvania, John Forney, and "other wire pulling politicians." Probably as a result of some promise concerning more patronage, Lincoln induced Weed "to [roll] up his sleeves and [to go] to work making his combinations."[2] It is interesting to note that shortly after this quadrumvirate began holding their meetings, Weed's *Albany Evening Journal*, Cameron's *Philadelphia Evening Bulletin,* and Forney's three papers declared for Lincoln. Chase was completely dumbfounded by these unexpected developments.[3]

The strategy of Lincoln and his advisers was simplicity itself. They worked to obtain endorsements in favor of Lincoln's renomination from the various state legislatures and from the Union party state conventions, the first of which was due to meet in January. Before the party's national convention assembled in June, Lincoln was endorsed in every northern state, and the delegates to the convention from all the states were instructed to vote for him. Only in the case of Missouri was there any opposition to his renomination, and from that state two delegations appeared, one pledged to Lincoln, the other to Grant. Had this former contingent of delegates been admitted to the convention, Lincoln would have been renominated by acclamation. The resolutions which were adopted in nearly every legislature commending his administration and urging his renomination were reputed to have been the work of the ever busy Weed. "It is positively asserted," wrote Adam Gurowski, who was probably transcribing some current talk in the capital, "that Weed . . . is the secret manager of the Lincoln pronunciamentos that are made by various state legislatures." The Count erred, however, in assuming that Weed's nefarious purpose was ultimately to swing the convention to Seward.[4]

Gurowski recognized that there were other factors at work

---

[2] *New York Herald,* May 24, 1864.

[3] Henry Cooke to Jay Cooke, January 14, 1864, in Donnal V. Smith, *op. cit.,* 100. Chase to Daniel Dickinson, January 16, 1864, Chase Papers (Pennsylvania).

[4] Gurowski, *op. cit.,* III, 90–91.

besides Weed which induced the legislatures to issue resolutions supporting Lincoln, and he listed them as the "contractors, the politicians, the officeholders, the office expectants, and finally the mass of honest country people." It is not known whether Gurowski intended to arrange these factors in what he considered to be their decreasing order of importance, but it is undeniable that each of the elements was present.

The frequent allusions already made to Lincoln's endorsement by the public are based upon evidence too irrefutable to be denied. Gurowski was, therefore, correct in listing "the honest country people" as one of the five elements which induced the various state legislatures to adopt resolutions in support of his renomination. If one were to rearrange the Count's list into order of importance, this factor would undoubtedly have to be placed first.

Yet the political situation which existed upon the state level often closely paralleled the one found at the capital. Each state legislature had its strong Unconditional element which was often pro-Chase, and in each state the Secretary's interests were well represented by active treasury agents. So strong was the Unconditional and treasury influence in some of the legislatures that the pressure of the "honest country people" would not have been sufficient to have prevailed upon them to adopt pro-Lincoln resolutions. It was here that the officeholders, expectants, and politicians were brought into play. The hard core of Unconditional, pro-Chase opposition in some of the legislatures was broken by the stubborn attacks of Lincoln's underlings. Often the ethics of the methods used by Lincoln's officeholders and the politicians were open to question, but there is no doubt that in the dog-eat-dog tactics of the campaign they had sharper teeth and took the telling bites.

The Unconditionals complained frequently and loudly that the unethical political dealings of Lincoln's friends during this all-important effort to gain endorsements in the states were deliberately circumventing the will of the majority. What truth is there in such an accusation? Here the answer depends upon the definition of "majority." If one is referring only to the majority of the members of the legislatures, then the accusation was often valid. In the Ohio Assembly, for example, Lincoln's friends re-sorted to parliamentary tricks to adopt a resolution in his favor when there were less than half of the members present at the meeting. The same was true in Indiana and Connecticut. These tactics are what the Unconditionals had in mind by their accusa-tion against Lincoln.

If the term "majority" referred to the voters, then the charge of the Unconditionals was probably false. At no time was the adoption of a pro-Lincoln resolution pushed through against the wishes of the people. On the contrary, such resolutions were in-variably hailed by the press as being in complete accord with pub-lic sentiment.

The major political and Unconditional Congressional leaders were forced to accept the President against their will and wish because of his great popularity with the people. The state legis-latures, which were not so responsive to public opinion on the presidential matter, were forced into line by the additional pres-sure of Lincoln's officeholders and politicians.

The influence of those who benefited through government contracts is an elusive factor to gauge and appraise. Undoubtedly they did exercise some influence in the assemblies, for there were many of them among the membership of each body, but their big role came in another connection. It was the contractors upon whom Lincoln's friends relied most heavily for campaign funds.

The New Hampshire Legislature was the first to convene. By a happy coincidence this state was Chase's birthplace, and the President's friends realized that a pro-Lincoln resolution would suggest that Chase was rejected by his own people. William E. Chandler carried out his mission successfully, and the legislature adopted a resolution calling for Lincoln's re-election. A second resolution warmly commended Chase's financial ability, but warned him to guard against fraud in his department. Shortly afterward fraud was discovered in the New York customhouse (which had been erupting frauds during the war with the well-regulated frequency of a geyser). Actually one of the Weed-Seward men was guilty, but he was passed off as a "ranting advocate of Chase" and held up as a horrible example of the type of conduct the Secretary permitted in his department.[5]

The Chase Pudding Does Not Rise

As the weeks passed, other legislatures and state party gatherings followed the lead of New Hampshire. There seemed to be no way to check Lincoln's rising star; in many states his personal friends and officeholders in Montgomery Blair's Postal Department broke the power of Unconditional cliques in legislatures and party conventions. "Providence has decreed your re-election and no combination of the wicked can prevent it," said Simon Cameron in reporting that a pro-Lincoln resolution had been signed by every Union party man in the Pennsylvania Legislature.[6] In New York, where the Chase forces were strong and active, Lincoln's friends also carried the day. "It is going to be difficult to restrain the boys, and there is not much use in trying to do so," wrote Edwin Morgan, while another of Lincoln's friends making a tour of the Empire State late in January wrote that on the political horizon "skies are bright, everything lovely." He was singularly impressed by the great unanimity of feeling favorable to the President's re-election.[7]

Lincoln's partisans organized a National Conference Committee of the Union Lincoln Association of New York under the presidency of Simeon Draper to work for his renomination. The activities of this organization of wealthy New Yorkers drew fire from both the Unconditionals and the Democrats. George Wilkes snarled that it was "a clique of rich conservatives . . . composed principally of the old Bourbons of the defunct Whig and Republican parties," and that it was formed to "be run in the Weed-Seward interest during the forthcoming presidential election."[8] August Belmont, one of New York's wealthiest and most active democratic leaders, addressed an audience at Cooper Union and cautioned his fellow millionaires against joining the society.[9]

This organization issued a circular on January 25 proposing that on February 22 all the people throughout the nation who desired Lincoln's re-election should meet in their respective towns

[5] *New York Tribune,* January 11, 1864.
[6] Dennett, *Lincoln and the Civil War,* 152–53.
[7] Nicolay and Hay, *Abraham Lincoln: A History,* IX, 55; William Pearne to Benjamin Field, February 5, 1864, Robert T. Lincoln Papers (MSS in Library of Congress).
[8] *Wilkes' Spirit of the Times,* February 13, 1864.
[9] August Belmont, *Letters, Speeches, and Addresses of August Belmont,* 116.

and "give public expression of their sentiments upon this most important question."[10] Proclamations for days of prayer and thanksgiving were not unknown, but a nationwide call for Lincoln men to attest their loyalty and faith was a new wrinkle in the political game, and neither the Unconditionals nor the Democrats knew how to deal with the situation. Manton Marble's *World* reported that bales of these circulars were sent out to every postmaster with orders for their distribution. "If Mr. Lincoln's military sagacity were equal to his political cunning," croaked Marble as he contemplated these astonishing developments, "we should have had peace long ago. That he will nominate himself and leave the Republican Convention, if there should be one, nothing to do but hold a ratification meeting, seems reasonably certain."[11]

On February 22, the Union National Committee, which had been chosen in 1860, met at the Washington home of New York Senator Edwin D. Morgan, who was the chairman. Only seventeen members were present, the others being absent from the capital at the moment except Representative Henry T. Blow of Missouri, who was denied admission.[12] Even though Blow was not present, an effort was made to introduce the Missouri question for consideration, but it was finally skillfully overruled by the efforts of the Lincoln men.

One of the most important initial decisions of the committee was the selection of Baltimore as the site of the coming convention, which it also scheduled for June 7. There was, at the moment, a strong movement in opposition to such an early date. Many preferred to postpone the convention until later in the year in order to see what the result of the summer military campaign would be. Others wanted to delay the convention in the hope that Lincoln's popularity would abate and another candidate could be more readily substituted. The selection of June 7, therefore, was a triumph for the Lincoln supporters, who wanted to convene early enough to capitalize on the President's popularity with the voters. Events in August were to justify the wisdom of preferring

10 Isaac Hazelhurst to Isaac Newton, February 5, 1864, Robert T. Lincoln Papers; *New York Herald*, February 7, 1864.
11 *New York World*, January 27, February 5, 1864.
12 *New York Times*, February 23, 1864.

an earlier date. The call sent our for the convention was sufficiently ambiguous to attract nearly everyone, for it was addressed to all those "who desire the unconditional maintenance of the Union, the supremacy of the Constitution, and the complete suppression of the existing rebellion with the cause there of by vigorous war, and all apt and efficient means."[13]

With the exception of the momentary attempt to introduce the troublesome Missouri question and the desire to delay the convention till later in the year, Gideon Welles was correct when he observed that "the proceedings were harmonious" and that four-fifths of the delegates favored Lincoln's renomination.[14] These men were all devoted to the Union; they all realized that Lincoln was the obvious choice of the public; but beyond that, as Carman and Luthin have noted, these men were personally interested in the continuation of the administration in power, for nearly all were either members of Congress or holders of positions by Lincoln's largess.[15]

By Washington's Birthday, the Union National Committee had selected the site for the convention and a date early enough to capitalize on the President's popularity with the voters. By that date the delegates to the national convention from New Hampshire, Connecticut, Maryland, and Iowa had been instructed to vote for Lincoln. He had also received overtures of support from the legislatures and other leading party organizations in Pennsylvania, Colorado, California, Wisconsin, Kansas, New York, and New Jersey. It is advisable now to see how Chase's forces were faring during this same period.

Much of the opposition to the President early in 1864 stemmed from a semisecret organization, the Strong Band Association. This society had been formed in 1863 by Joseph Medill and a Chicago attorney, John Wilson. From Illinois the order had spread throughout the country; and in February, 1864, Chase, who apparently counted very heavily on the society for aid, was informed that the membership was approximately seventy-five thousand and that its purpose was "solely to exert an influence in the coming presi-

---

13 *New York Times*, February 23, 1864.
14 Welles, *op. cit.*, I, 530.
15 Carman and Luthin, *op. cit.*, 239–42.

dential election."[16] About the same time one of Lincoln's friends estimated its membership at double that amount.[17]

The effectiveness of the association was greatly weakened by the inability of the Unconditional leaders to agree on a likely substitute candidate. Wilson wrote in February, 1864, that he wanted Butler in the White House, but admitted that the opposition to Lincoln could not yet agree on a single candidate and consequently no effective action could be taken. A few months later he had switched to Chase.[18]

The failure of the Unconditionals to agree on a candidate paralyzed their efforts and gave the President the opportunity to capitalize on his popularity. Clearly recognizing the weakness of their position, the Unconditionals sought to bargain with the President as Gurowski had suggested. Had their position been stronger, they would not have found it expedient to resort to such means but would have simply shunted Lincoln aside. Senator Chandler approached the President with their offer. The Senator claimed that he, personally, controlled one million votes, which he offered to throw to Lincoln if he would only remove Blair and Seward from the cabinet and Weed from the list of his close advisers. Lincoln did not have to accept the offer, for by February he felt sufficiently confident of his strength to make such tactics unnecessary. "I think the President will be renominated and re-elected and that is best; he should be," said Welles. "None would so cordially unite Union men. There would be contention over a new movement. Seward's friends would not be satisfied with Chase and Chase's friends would not be satisfied with Seward while both would oppose a new man. Besides a new contact would bring new issues and thus favor the rebels."[19] The complexity of the Union organization and the inability of the opposition to unite explained

[16] Daniel Butterfield to Chase, February 27, 1864; Delano Smith to Chase, November 23, 1863, Chase Papers (Library of Congress). *Missouri Democrat,* March 26, 1863; *Milwaukee Sentinel,* January 25, 1864.

[17] David Kilgore to Lincoln, February 1, 1864, Robert T. Lincoln Papers.

[18] John Wilson to Butler, February 16, 1864, in Marshall, *op. cit.,* III, 421–23; Horace White to Fessenden, August 24, 1864, Fessenden Papers; George Smith, "A Strong Band Circular," *The Mississippi Valley Historical Review,* Vol. XXIX (March, 1943), 557–64.

[19] Welles to E. T. W. Brockett, January 16, 1864, Welles Papers (MSS in Library of Congress).

The Chase Pudding Does Not Rise

to a great extent Lincoln's ability to maintain his supremacy over the many fragments.

Senator Pomeroy's Republican National Executive Committee, in the meantime, continued its work in behalf of Chase. In February a document entitled *The Next Presidential Election* was given wide circulation throughout the old Northwest under the frank of Senator Sherman, Representative Ashley, Blow, and others. Ward Lamon described it as a "most scurrilous and abusive" document.[20] The pamphlet maintained that Lincoln's reelection was doubtful and even undesirable, and called instead for a man who was "an advanced thinker; a statesman profoundly versed in political and economic science, one who fully comprehends the spirit of the age in which we live."

The President and his friends did not have to take any action on the matter, for the power of public opinion rose to sustain them against the attack. Sherman was bombarded with letters from constituents throughout Ohio. A few acquiesced meekly in the views set forth in the document, but most were indignant at this shabby attempt to defame the President.[21]

Miscalculating the effect of their first pamphlet on the American public, Chase's managers prepared a second circular, dated February 8, for distribution. Since this document bore the signature of Senator Samuel Pomeroy, it has gone down in history as the "Pomeroy Circular," although that gentleman was not its author. As in the case of the first document it was franked out by several prominent Unconditional congressmen. This second pamphlet was allegedly distributed in response to the circular sent out in January by Simeon Draper's committee. The Pomeroy Circular was marked "strictly private," but as is frequently the case with such things, it soon appeared in the public journals, and on February 22 it was given to the people generally over the wires of the Associated Press.[22]

The Next Presidential Election and the Pomeroy Circular in-

[20] Charles Wilson, "The Original Chase Organization Meeting and *The Next Presidential Election*," *The Mississippi Valley Historical Review*, Vol. XXIII (June, 1936), 61–79. Lamon to Lincoln, February 6, 1864, Robert T. Lincoln Papers.

[21] The John Sherman Papers contain many of these letters.

[22] The document appeared first in the *Washington Constitutional Union* on February 20.

tensified public opinion against Chase and his managers. "The Pomeroy Circular has helped Lincoln more than all other things together," was the opinion of one of Sherman's constituents. The circular has made enemies for Chase, wrote the *Pittsburgh Gazette,* the document was "not manly—not truthful—mean." Pomeroy's "yeast don't [*sic*] make the Chase pudding rise," was the triumphant observation of one of Lincoln's partisans.[23] The storm was rising to such alarming proportions that the Unconditionals soon had to seek means of denying their connection with the episode.

John Sherman, one of the chief offenders in the affair, found the political ground slipping from beneath his feet. "If you were to resign tomorrow," wrote a pessimistic friend, "you could not get ten votes in the legislature provided it could be shown that you have been circulating such stuff as this."[24] This may not have been an exaggeration, for Sherman was forced soon to quell the storm against him by publishing an open letter in the *Cincinnati Daily Gazette* explaining that he had been the victim of an unfortunate mistake or a deliberate deception.[25] Others insisted that the first document had been written by Anna Ella Carroll and distributed with the Pomeroy Circular by mistake.

The Unconditionals' explanations do not seem to hold up. Charles Wilson has analyzed both documents and concluded that the similarity of content indicates that possibly they were written by the same person. He also concluded that there is "good reason to doubt that the two manifestoes had become mixed by mistake and were distributed concomitantly."[26] The two pamphlets are precisely alike in all principal points except their conclusions: *The Next Presidential Election* merely hinted broadly that a man of different talents was needed in the White House during the next term, while the circular stated openly that Chase had "more of

[23] Lewis Gunckel to Sherman, February 29, 1864, Sherman Papers; *Pittsburgh Gazette,* February 24, 1864; George Lincoln to William P. Doyle, February 26, 1864, Robert T. Lincoln Papers.

[24] G. W. Gordon to Sherman, February 26, 1864, Sherman Papers.

[25] *Cincinnati Daily Gazette,* March 3, 1864; James White to Sherman, February 7, 1864, Sherman Papers. This letter would seem to indicate that Sherman knew of the existence of the document in question.

[26] Charles Wilson, "The Original Chase Organization Meeting and *The Next Presidential Election," The Mississippi Valley Historical Review,* Vol. XXIII (June, 1936), 66.

the qualities needed in a President during the next four years than are to be found in any other candidate."

In the final analysis it does not matter who the author or authors of these pronunciamentoes were; what is important is that the documents were sired by Chase's friends for the purpose of helping his election cause and that, instead, they did much to ruin his chances. The very intemperance of the attack on Lincoln embodied in the pamphlets aroused public opinion first against Sherman, who had disseminated one of them, then against the committee, and finally against Chase himself. The indignation caused by the pamphlet and circular led directly to the Ohio State Legislature's declaring in favor of Lincoln, and this declaration was to be the final blow to Chase's hopes.

At the very moment the Pomeroy Circular was receiving its just due in the Northern states, the Union National Committee was in session, the Union party state conventions were assembled in Maryland and Iowa, and Lincoln's friends in Indiana were preparing to drive another nail into the coffin of Chase's ambitions. Chase had always felt that he commanded considerable strength in the Hoosier State, especially after his reception there in 1863. His treasury agents continued their intense activity, and efforts were made to line up Governor Morton, as well as Indiana's two most prominent congressmen, George Julian and Schuyler Colfax.[27] At the same time, however, many of Lincoln's officeholders "serving their country at prices ranging from $3,500 to $6,000 *per annum*" were equally as active in the President's behalf.[28] At the state convention on February 23, Lincoln's men, former Governor Cyrus Allen, Provost Marshall Richard Thompson, and John Defrees, superintendent of the Government Printing Office, surprised Chase's supporters by forcing through a resolution endorsing the President's re-election even before the temporary organization had been completed. It was a stunning blow to the Chase men, who were taken completely by surprise.[29]

[27] Julian, *Political Recollections, 1840–1872*, 237–38; Grace Clarke, *George Julian*, 250–51; Nicolay and Hay, *Abraham Lincoln: A History*, VIII, 315.

[28] *Indianapolis Sentinel*, February 18, 1864.

[29] B. F. Tuttle to Chase, February 27, 1864; H. B. Carrington to Chase, February 27, 1864, Chase Papers (Library of Congress). Harbison, "Indiana Republicans and the Re-election of President Lincoln," *Indiana Magazine of History*, Vol. XXXIV (March, 1938), 52.

129351

Lincoln & the Party Divided

While Allen's resolutions were being rushed through the Indiana convention, the President was faced with another problem requiring his most careful consideration. The Secretary, after having read the text of the Pomeroy Circular in the *Union,* hastened to dispatch a letter to the Chief Executive offering to resign. As he held this letter in his hand, Lincoln may have toyed with the idea of applying Butler's "tipping out" treatment at last; but if the thought entered his mind, he disregarded it and embarked upon a wiser course. He could not at that moment accept the Secretary's offer of resignation, for that would have been an open admission that he feared Chase as an opponent for the nomination. But, more important, such a move might have convinced the Unconditional leaders that Lincoln was wholeheartedly committed to the conservative cause. Keenly aware of the repercussions created throughout the country by the publication of the pamphlet and circular, the President sat back to sound public opinion further before giving Chase a final reply.

On February 24 came the news of the affair in Indianapolis, and within a few days word from Ohio that a pro-Lincoln resolution had passed the legislature. Chase's own state had disowned him—a blow which his pride could not endure. Many attempts had been made to force a pro-Lincoln resolution through the legislature, but to no avail. At length the two forces struck a bargain: the Lincoln men would introduce no more resolutions if the Chase men would help them get Columbus Delano chosen to the state supreme court.[30]

The bombshell which wrecked these well-laid plans was the Pomeroy Circular. "You have no idea of the effects produced by that Circular," Richard Parsons hastily wrote to Chase: "It . . . produced a perfect convulsion in the party."[31] Lincoln's friends quickly summoned a caucus of Union party members and adopted a pro-Lincoln resolution, although Chase's friends insisted that there were not enough members present to constitute a quorum.[32]

[30] Porter, *op. cit.,* 123. The Chase Papers contain many letters from his agents in Ohio detailing the whole course of developments in that key state.

[31] Richard Parsons to Chase, March 2, 1864, Chase Papers (Library of Congress); L. Devin to Sherman, February 26, 1864, Sherman Papers.

[32] James Hall to Chase, March 2, 1864, Chase Papers (Library of Congress); Isaac Gass to Sherman, February 29, 1864, Sherman Papers; Elizabeth Yager, "The

Lincoln in profile, February 9, 1864,
from a photograph by Mathew B. Brady

The Chase Pudding Does Not Rise

There was great consternation among Chase's friends after this incident, but it was too late to undo the fateful stroke. One of Sherman's correspondents told him that the only way adoption of the resolution could have been prevented would have been for Chase to have stated publicly that he had nothing to do with the circular. Chase had already denied connection with the circular to Lincoln, but he did not do so publicly because "he could not publicly disavow the action of his own friends, however ill-advised and inopportune that action was."[33] Lincoln may have deliberately refrained from answering Chase's letter because he wanted to keep the whole affair out of the press until after the Ohio Legislature had spoken. Then a public disavowal by Chase would not benefit him in any way.

The unfortunate Secretary's troubles were not yet ended, for while he was impatiently awaiting Lincoln's final reply, he had to bear the ignominy of another attack from Lincoln's henchmen, the Blair brothers. Frank Blair introduced a resolution in Congress calling for an investigation of illegal practices in the Treasury Department, which was pigeonholed only after a great deal of parliamentary manipulation by Thad Stevens and James Garfield. The matter was not closed so easily, however, for shortly afterward the Postmaster General began sending copies of his brother's speech to various newspapers throughout the country for publication. Dipping his own pen into literary arsenic, Montgomery Blair produced a statement of his own in which he accused Chase of having written the Pomeroy Circular himself.[34] The Blairs disturbed the already ruffled feathers of peacock Chase so badly that he wrote Greeley he would resign if they did not stop their belittling.[35]

While Frank Blair was salting Chase's wounds on February 27 and 29, Lincoln presented the Secretary with his final reply to the offer of resignation. The President assured him he saw no reason for making a change in the treasury headship, but the reply

Presidential Campaign of 1864 in Ohio," *Ohio State Archaeological and Historical Quarterly*, Vol. XXXIV (October, 1925), 553.

[33] Schuckers, *op. cit.*, 476–77.

[34] *Congressional Globe*, 38 Cong., 1 sess., 779–82, 876–78, appendix 46–51. Parsons to Chase, March 7, 1864, Chase Papers (Library of Congress).

[35] Chase to Greeley, February 29, 1864, Chase Papers (Pennsylvania).

did little to soothe Chase's distressed spirit. He disliked Lincoln's patronizing attitude and his failure to reciprocate the hollow platitudes of affection which Chase had incorporated into his own letter. He revenged himself, however, by publishing all the letters despite Lincoln's instructions not to do so.[36]

By the first week in march, Chase's candidacy was a dying cause. The evidence of Lincoln's popularity was too great to be denied. There was nothing for Chase to do but withdraw from the race. Early in January he had written to his ally James Hall that "if . . . it should be the pleasure of a majority of our friends in Ohio to indicate a preference for another, I should accept their action with that cheerful acquiescence which is due from me to the friends who have trusted and honored me."[37] The Ohio Legislature's action convinced him that he was not wanted, and on March 7 he wrote to Representative Albert Riddle, "Our Ohio folks don't want me enough, if they want me at all, to make it proper for me to allow my name to be used."[38] Forty-eight hours before, after much consideration, Chase had written to James Hall asking that no further consideration be given him. The Chase boom was deflated, although Chase did not realize it fully at the moment.

[36] Alonzo Rothschild, *Lincoln Master of Men: A Study in Character,* 207. After this there was little cordiality between Lincoln and Chase until the latter left the cabinet. Lincoln was also down on Pomeroy. Dennett, *Lincoln and the Civil War,* 181. Donnal V. Smith, *op. cit.,* 123–24.

[37] Chase to Hall, January 18, 1864, in *Daily Ohio State Journal,* March 11, 1864; Chase to W. D. Lindsley, February 1, 1864, in Warden, *op. cit.,* 568.

[38] Chase to Riddle, March 7, 1864, in Warden, *op. cit.* 576.

) IV (

To Meet
or Not to Meet

"IT SEEMS CLEAR to me," counseled James A. Garfield on February 25, "that the people desire the re-election of Mr. Lincoln and I believe any movement in any other direction will not only be a failure but will tend to disturb and embarrass the unity of the friends of the Union." This was an interesting admission from a man who a few weeks earlier deplored the possibility of having to "push" Lincoln for another term. He advised Chase to withdraw and reduce the danger of splitting the party, for "it would be a national calamity to alienate the radical element from Mr. Lincoln and leave him to the support of the Blair and Thurlow Weed school of politicians."[1] Chase continued to receive such sensible advice from many of his most enthusiastic workers, who realized the absurdity of opposing Lincoln further and hesitated to endanger party solidarity by continuing Chase's candidacy.[2]

It remained, however, for William Orton of the New York Chase committee to make a suggestion which finally galvanized the hesitant Secretary into action. Orton advised him to withdraw from the race to prove his patriotism and silence his calumniators, but to permit his friends to continue their clandestine efforts so that they could bring his name forward unexpectedly at the national

[1] Garfield to Chase, February 25, 1864, in Theodore C. Smith, *op. cit.*, I, 375–76.

[2] Greeley to Chase, March 2, 1864, Chase Papers (Pennsylvania). L. Holbert to Chase, February 28, 1864; William Mellen to Chase, March 2, 1864; Richard Parsons to Chase, March 2, 1864; W. P. Gaddis to Chase, March 5, 1864, Chase Papers (Library of Congress). *Cleveland Herald,* March 4, 1864.

convention.[3] After sampling this fruit and finding it good, Chase replied that he would use the recent declaration of the Ohio Legislature as a pretext for a letter of withdrawal.

On March 5, Chase dispatched a letter to James Hall in which he said that "the recent action of the Union members of our Legislature indicates" that they wanted Lincoln. He was dutifully bound to "ask that no further consideration be given [his] name."[4] Hall published this letter in the Ohio press on March 11.

Some of his friends understood that the letter did not mean that his name was no longer to be considered, and the undercover work was pushed with a vengeance on all sides. Many wrote confidently predicting that there would soon be a change in popular sentiment which would revive the Secretary's star.[5]

The undercover work that Chase's friends wished to carry on in his behalf did not remain secret for long. The consensus of opinion at the capital was that the race was not ended but merely entering a new phase. "Mr. Chase will subside as a presidential candidate after the nomination is made,—not before," wrote one skeptic. Judge David Davis told Weed that Chase's "declination is a mere sham, and very ungraceful at that." Edward Bates was from Missouri both literally and figuratively, for he wrote, "This forced declination of Mr. Chase is really not worth much. It proves only that the *present* prospects of Mr. Lincoln are too good to be openly resisted, at least, by men within the party; the extreme men who urge Mr. Chase, afraid to array themselves in *open* opposition to Mr. Lincoln, will only act more guardedly—get up as many candidates as they can, privily, with the hope of bringing in Mr. C. at last, as a compromise candidate. And, in the meantime, strain every nerve to commit Mr. L. to as many as possible of their extreme measures."[6]

[3] Orton to Chase, March 3, 1864; Chase to Orton, March 4, 1864, Chase Papers (Library of Congress). Donnal V. Smith, op. cit., 124–30.

[4] Chase to Hall, March 5, 1864, in Schuckers, *op. cit.,* 502; Chase to Hall, March 6, 1864, Chase Papers (Pennsylvania). Hall unwisely published Chase's letter of withdrawal together with his earlier letter of January 18, thus creating the impression that Chase was withdrawing in acknowledgment of defeat rather than because of intense patriotism, as the Secretary wished.

[5] Parsons to Chase, March 11, 1864, Chase Papers (Library of Congress). R. W. Taylor to Sherman, March 18, 1864; J. Guthrie to Sherman, March 20, 1864, Sherman Papers.

To Meet or Not to Meet

These were the opinions of Lincoln's partisans; Chase's friends offered even more convincing proof that the movement was still alive. Pomeroy announced in Congress that his committee intended to continue work even after it had become known in Washington that Chase had written a letter of withdrawal.[7] We know that James Winchell, secretary of Pomeroy's committee, did not regard Chase's letter of withdrawal as bona fide. Winchell also insisted that Lincoln personally offered him a choice of two highly lucrative positions in the government. This action shows conclusively that Lincoln considered his cabinet member very much in the running, for it is hardly likely that he would have made such an offer had he considered the Pomeroy committee defunct. Lincoln was not in the habit of doing this kind of work himself; he generally left it to a subordinate unless the matter was of such importance that it could not be entrusted to one of his many go-betweens.[8]

In spite of Chase's fond adieu to the presidential race in March his friends were still working and his name was before the voters. His men continued their subterranean efforts. Their mole-like work in behalf of Chase was, perhaps, in the final analysis no worse than what Lincoln's friends were doing in Ohio, Connecticut, and Indiana, where the power of patronage hung like a weight over all the conventions and legislatures. Such activity is undoubtedly an integral part of every presidential race; if it is unethical or wrong, then one can say that in 1864 the blame was equally shared by Lincoln's and Chase's friends.

After having failed to best the President in numerous encounters from December to March, the Unconditionals abandoned their direct approach temporarily and sought to find other means of removing him from the race. Chase's boom was, for the moment, in need of revival, and as his friends worked to repair their battered machine, there was a growing fear among them that time was running out. Lincoln's officeholders were steam-rolling more

---

[6] Edwin Morgan to Weed, May 29, 1864; David Davis to Weed, May 21, 1864, in Barnes, *op. cit.*, 444–45. Howard Beale, *op. cit.*, 345.

[7] Harold Dudley, "The Election of 1864, *The Mississippi Valley Historical Review*, Vol. XVIII (March, 1932), 502–503; Donnal V. Smith, *op. cit.*, 130–33.

[8] Winchell, *loc. cit.*, 38–39.

endorsements through state legislatures and getting state conventions to instruct their delegates to support him. The Unconditionals' fruitless quest continued for a candidate upon whom all factions could agree.

The declarations in Lincoln's favor coming from various legislatures and Union party state conventions were conveniently dismissed by the Unconditionals as the work of placemen and political chicanery; other politicians, however, who were in closer contact with the people, wrote that there could be no doubt of the people's love for Lincoln. Several of the President's friends noted that the opposition to his renomination came from a few politicians rather than the public at large.[9]

Not only did these letters reporting the status of public opinion come to the White House from Lincoln's partisans, but similar ones flowed increasingly into the mail boxes of leading Unconditionals, who were anxiously trying to discern some evidence of anti-Lincolnism, however minute it might be.[10]

With the evidence continuing to roll into Washington nearly every day that the President would certainly be renominated if the people had anything to say, the Unconditionals were at a loss to know precisely what to do to prevent it. No other man of sufficient stature appeared on the political horizon after Chase's ignominious defeat to merit any further attempts, for a while at least, to run another candidate. Ben Butler's friends were busy,

[9] A. B. Cooley to Lincoln, February 10, 1864; J. W. Stokes to Isaac Newton, February 10, 1864; Arthur Rich to Lincoln, February 27, 1864; Samuel Galloway to Lincoln, February 25, 1864; Roscoe Conkling to Lincoln, February 27, 1864, Robert T. Lincoln Papers. I. B. Gara to Cameron, February 26, 1864; John Purviance to Cameron, February 25, 1864, Cameron Papers.

[10] W. D. Bickman to Sherman, March 1, 1864; R. W. Clarke to Sherman, February 20, 1864, Sherman Papers. J. F. Jordan to Chase, March 12, 1864; Geiger to Chase, April 2, 1864; Thomas Heaton to Chase, May 31, 1864, Chase Papers (Library of Congress). Susan Anthony to Anna Dickinson, April 14, 1864, Dickinson Papers (MSS in Library of Congress). A. Belcher to Washburne, February 8, 1864; S. G. Speer to Washburne, February 11, 1864; Jason Hobart to Washburne, April 25, 1864, Washburne Papers. A. Hamilton to Schuyler Colfax, April 10, 1864, Colfax Papers (MSS in Library of Congress). W. Hanna to Trumbull, February 5, 1864, Trumbull Papers. J. Bolles to Welles, April 27, 1864, Welles Papers. Gurowski, op. cit., III, 154, 159; C. E. Norton to C. Sumner, April 29, 1864, in Edith Ware, Political Opinion in Massachusetts During the Civil War and Reconstruction, 140.

but his was a hopeless cause from the start. John Frémont, the old Pathfinder, was seeking to blaze a new trail to the White House, but his movement did not assume significant proportions until late May. From the date of the publication of the Hall-Chase letters until the nomination of Frémont at Cleveland on May 31, Unconditional leaders were vainly seeking another candidate. The more they talked, however, the greater Lincoln's popularity seemed to become; and as his hold upon the people increased, the greater became their inability to agree on a suitable replacement.

Until such time as the recriminatory opposition to Lincoln could unite their forces, some device had to be found to give them more time to organize. This device assumed the form of a large-scale movement to postpone the Baltimore convention from June 7 to a later date, on the pretext that it was folly to select a party standard-bearer before the outcome of the military campaigns was learned.

The sire of this artful political dodge was undoubtedly the New York editor Horace Greeley, who had argued in favor of an autumn date for the convention since September of the preceding year.[11] During the early months of the election year he continually insisted that winning the war should take precedence over winning the election, and he became one of the prime movers in the attempt to postpone the convention. His all too brief honeymoon with the administration terminated early in '64, and his editorial column alternated affectionate platitudes for Chase, Butler, and Frémont, those paragons of statesmanship who preserved the "salutary one-term principle."[12] In February he explained that it was his intention to keep up a "quiet and steady opposition" to the President and work for a postponement of the convention.[13] Greeley realized from the very beginning that such an attempt would be feeble and nugatory; his only reason for supporting such a movement was to force the President further to the left. "I am not at all confident of making any change," he wrote to Mrs. R. H. Whipple, "but I do believe I shall make things better by trying. There are

[11] Fahrney, *op. cit.*, 184.

[12] *New York Tribune*, February 23, 1864.

[13] Greeley to Beman Brockway, February 28, 1864, Greeley Papers (MSS in Library of Congress).

those who go as far as they are pushed, and Mr. Lincoln is one of these. He will be a better President . . . for the opposition he is now encountering."[14]

In New York, which was the center of this movement to delay the convention, Greeley sought the assistance of Theodore Tilton's *Independent* and William C. Bryant's *Evening Post*. Although Tilton was known to be pro-Chase and his editorial pages frequently delivered scathing indictments against the administration, privately he admitted that Lincoln would be renominated.[15] He gave Greeley's project only lukewarm support. Bryant, on the other hand, fell in behind the banner of hectoring Horace and joined the movement.[16]

During March an appeal was prepared in New York and sent to the Union National Committee calling for the postponement of the convention until September 1.[17] Greeley and Bryant were active in directing the work of this committee which prepared the appeal; and their efforts were most thorough if one judges by the impressive list of names appended to the document. "This list," crowed Greeley, "contains the names of two thirds of the Unionists chosen to our present state Senate, the absence of others prevented their signing. We understand that but two Senators declined to affix their names."[18] Henry Raymond's *Times* denounced the appeal as nothing more than a cheap electioneering trick of the Unconditionals to defeat the President's nomination.[19] John Forney also took the defensive in favor of the June 7 date for the convention in editorials in his papers, but in private conversations he often agreed that a postponement would be better.[20] The whole

[14] Greeley to Mrs. R. H. Whipple, March 8, 1864, Greeley Papers.

[15] George B. Lincoln to William P. Dole, February 26, 1864, Robert T. Lincoln Papers; DeAlva Alexander, *A Political History of the State of New York*, III, 89.

[16] *New York Evening Post*, February 23, 1864.

[17] *Appleton's Annual Cyclopedia for 1864*, 785. For additional information on the postponement see W. Hutchins to Cameron, March 28, 1864, Cameron Papers; J. Goodrich to Welles, March 24, 1864, Welles Papers; J. Goodrich to Washburne, March 24, 1864, Washburne Papers.

[18] *New York Tribune*, April 1, 25, 1864.

[19] *New York Times*, April 8, 1864.

[20] *Detroit Advertiser and Tribune*, April 11, 1864. W. Blair to Cameron, April 12, 1864, Cameron Papers. The writer said he was glad Cameron had defeated the Forney-Curtin scheme to postpone the convention.

affair in New York, however, collapsed in its own insignificance when the Union National Committee refused to take cognizance of the appeal, which had been made on March 25.[21] By early April, Greeley was writing that he still preferred someone other than Lincoln, but that from present appearances his wishes were to be disregarded. He still hoped to see the convention postponed, "but if Lincoln's friends will not agree to this, we had better quietly acquiesce and await the progress of events."[22] The disconsolate editor then faded out of the movement. About the same time Simon Cameron reported that the effort to postpone the convention had been thwarted; "the people were too strong for the politicians," he noted.[23]

Lincoln's friends had by no means heard the end of the clamor for postponement; it continued without interruption until early in May. Even though Greeley reluctantly confessed his inability to stem the Lincoln tide, other prominent Unconditionals continued the unequal struggle to the last. Governor John Andrew of Massachusetts, Whitelaw Reid, war correspondent of the *Cincinnati Gazette* and prominent member of the Chase for President committee, B. F. Prescott, political luminary from New Hampshire, Richard Henry Dana, John Murray Forbes, and Peleg Chandler had all taken a stand in favor of delaying the meeting.[24] Governor Curtin of Pennsylvania was also active in the movement.[25] In April, Welles recorded in his diary that the pressure for postponement was growing stronger, while simultaneously Trumbull heard the rumor that there was danger the dissatisfied might "start out on Butler or Frémont." In this case, his correspondent assured him, the Union party would be whipped.[26] The editors of a pro-Frémont journal, *The New Nation*, early in April urged all the friends of the various Unconditional candidates to form a national

[21]Nicolay and Hay, *Abraham Lincoln: A History*, IX, 57–58.

[22] Greeley to B. Brockway, April 9, 1864, Greeley Papers.

[23] Cameron to Montgomery Blair, April 7, 1864, Blair Papers (MSS in Library of Congress).

[24] Horatio Woodman to Sumner, March 23, 1864, in George Smith, "Generative Forces of Union Propaganda" (Ph.D. dissertation), 395–96; Whitelaw Reid to Anna Dickinson, April 10, 1864, Dickinson Papers.

[25] W. Blair to Cameron, April 12, 1864, Cameron Papers.

[26] Welles, *op. cit.*, II, 4–5; W. A. Baldwin to Trumbull, April 4, 1864, Trumbull Papers.

committee to secure an acceptable platform and to nominate a reliable man for the Presidency.[27]

The futile effort to delay the opening of the convention was overshadowed late in April by a revival of the Blair-Chase tiff. The Blair brothers had been silent for a short time after their attack on the Secretary late in February, but the controversy was resumed during the following month. At that time it was one of Chase's friends who opened the attack by accusing Frank Blair of profiting from the illegal trade on the Mississippi. Blair met this challenge with his accustomed vigor and demanded a Congressional investigation of his activities.

The committee's report exonerated Blair on April 23. This vindication was insufficient, however, and Blair proceeded to exact his pound of flesh. In one of the most acrimonious tirades of his career, the congressman tore into the Unconditionals and their darling Chase with the fervor of a Demosthenes. He sneered at Chase's alleged withdrawal from the race and said that only after the Pomeroy Circular had "unearthed his underground and underhand intrigue against the President" was the letter written. "He wanted to get down under the ground and work there in the dark as he is now doing," screamed Blair. The torrent rolled on until he felt he had completely exposed to public view the activities of Chase and the Unconditionals against Lincoln's renomination. With his task completed, Blair hurried down Pennsylvania Avenue to see Lincoln.[28]

For several months the President had been holding in his office Blair's commission as major general in the United States Army, which Blair had relinquished to assume his political duties. Lincoln had assured him at the time that the commission would be restored whenever Blair wished it. He now asked for the commission, and the President, saw no reason why he should break his word. Chase went into a rage when the news reached him. Although Lincoln personally assured him that he was ignorant of Blair's attack on Chase at the time the commission was returned,

[27] George Smith, "Generative Forces of Union Propaganda" (Ph.D. dissertation), 396.

[28] *Congressional Globe*, 38 Cong., 1 sess., 1013–17, 1251–53, 1827–32.

the Secretary continued to feel that the attack had been made with the President's heartiest approval.[29]

After Frank's speech in Congress, the attack on the Blair family continued during April. Joseph Medill wrote that he did not care if the convention was delayed till August. In the *Tribune* he took a stand against delay, but in his correspondence he admitted that if Lincoln preferred to lose the renomination instead of the Blairs, he did not care. Lincoln has "Blair on the Brain" he wrote to Elihu Washburne. "If he prefers the Blairs to the Presidency, why should he be deprived of his choice? I am free to say that if it shall be known to be his intention to continue his present cabinet, I don't believe we could elect him if nominated. The country is heartsick and horribly disgusted with the Blairs—to say nothing of his sticking to Frank B. Halleck, Schofield, etc, and giving the cold shoulder to the Mo. radicals. Lincoln has some very weak and foolish traits of character."[30]

The Blair episode proved to be a safety valve to take the pressure from the demands for postponement. There was a general shift from the agitation favoring delaying the convention toward an attack on the administration for countenancing the Blairs. "The country at this time can better afford to lose both Mr. Lincoln and the Blairs than Mr. Chase," said one of the Secretary's journals.[31]

Realizing the futility of trying to postpone the convention, the Unconditional press may have been secretly thankful for the Blair episode since it afforded a convenient pretext for abandoning the demands for delay. Henry Raymond was still fearful on the last day of April that they might succeed in their schemes, but his fears proved groundless.

The agitation for postponing the convention died rather ignobly during May, with Greeley, who had begun the whole affair, strangely missing from the death scene. He had wisely pulled out in March, and those who remained behind learned once again the

[29] Riddle, *Recollections of War Times*, 266–76. W. S. Hickox to Sherman, April 30, 1864, Sherman Papers; Chase to Parsons, May 6, 1864, Chase Papers (Library of Congress).

[30] Medill to Washburne, April 7, 12, 29, 1864; J. Miller to Washburne, April 16, 1864; J. F. Polter to Washburne, April 16, 1864, Washburne Papers.

[31] *Indianapolis Gazette*, April 29, 1864.

oft proved truth of politics: you cannot defeat somebody with nobody. All the talk about the desirability of forestalling the convention until September was doomed to failure as long as no candidate appeared who could unite the diverse elements in opposition to Lincoln and who could command the popular support that Lincoln did. The President summed up the situation nicely when he remarked, "Perhaps some other man might do this business better than I. That is possible. I do not deny it. But I am here, and that better man is not here." He then put his finger on the whole kernel of the Unconditionals' problem. "If I should step aside," he continued, ". . . It is much more likely that the factions opposed to me would fall to fighting among themselves, and that those who want me to make room for a better man would get a man whom most of them would not want in at all."[32]

The Unconditionals worked on; even late in May they were still trying feverishly to find an alternate candidate in spite of the fact that every state except Missouri had declared in favor of Lincoln's re-election. Chase no longer carried much weight with them, but there were still three other possible men who might be used. General Benjamin Franklin Butler had a moderately strong following. His boom developed during March and April, but it never reached very formidable proportions. A second possible nominee was still the radical Germans' choice, John C. Frémont, whose boom developed sufficiently in May that he was nominated by a rump convention at Cleveland, Ohio. For those who could not accept either of these two military leaders, a third possible candidate was suggested—Ulysses S. Grant. It is necessary now to trace the course of the movements which were launched for these three men.

[32] Bancroft and Dunning, *op. cit.*, III, 103–104.

) v (

Lincoln
and the Beast

THE COVERT and open intrigues to push Chase into the Presidency came to a temporary halt with the Secretary's letter of withdrawal in March. It was at this point that the name of Ben Butler was brought forward with increasing frequency by his partisans, who attempted to sell him to the Unconditional clique as the man who could succeed where Chase had failed.

Butler was originally a War-Democrat, but his activities since the very opening of the war had endeared him to a large number of extreme Republicans. Even the irrepressible Gurowski brimmed over with unrestrained platitudes when he contemplated the General's abilities. "Ben Butler would make an excellent president," was the Pole's unqualified opinion. "He has all the capacities of a statesman. . . . Many of the best men think of Butler as I do; Butler would have good chances for the White House if leading and influential men would speak out their convictions."[1]

The name of one of the most controversial and colorful men of the period was suggested as a possible Unconditional nominee. Few generals in the Union Army were fawned upon by the public as much as Butler, a fact doubly amazing when one realizes that there was no basis in his military accomplishments for such lionization. Grant and Sherman earned their praises by hard campaigning and sweeping victories, but Butler won his by shrewd, bold moves which captured imagination rather than citadels. It

[1] Gurowski, *op. cit.,* III, 86, 87.

was his innate theatrical sense and mastery of press-agentry which made Butler's exploits such worthwhile copy. Whatever he did was news, and public opinion was divided sharply on the question of his greatness. Was he really a genius, military or otherwise, as most of his friends readily admitted, or was he, as Hay's friend Judge Cartter said, merely the "smartest damned rascal that ever lived"?[2] Whether he was a genius or the prince of rascals made no difference, for either title would assure him at least a passing reference in history.

The secret of Butler's success seems to be that he gave the public what it wanted. In Louisiana he treated the rebels as everyone felt rebels ought to be treated, and he was acclaimed for it. If the administration was stewing over the troublesome problem of emancipation, Butler had a simple solution: cut through the red tape, ignore the legal, moral implications in the situation, and free the Negroes as contrabands. It was as simple as that, and the uninformed public applauded him as a man of action, a man with insight, who could dispense with the folderol and get to the heart of the matter. The administration unfortunately did not seem to appreciate Butler's self-admitted genius, and he was pushed into relatively unimportant positions but never into obscurity. The public immortalized its hero with more distinctive appellatives than any man in public life except Lincoln. In the South he earned such sobriquets as "Beast" Butler, who insulted and defamed southern womanhood; and "Spoons" Butler, brigand and plunderer of plantations. In his own section he was known affectionately as "Old Cockeye" Butler, sufferer from strabismus, and admiringly as "Bold Ben" Butler, because of his overrated military achievements and his dazzling, if somewhat farfetched, legal flight of fancy, in freeing slaves as "contraband of war."

Whatever Bold Ben's shortcomings or favorable attributes, his role in the election of 1864 was unique. Prominent enough to be mentioned occasionally as a possible dark-horse nominee, he was also offered the vice-presidency by both Lincoln and Chase. It was one of those historical ironies that he refused Lincoln's offer because the job would have been a political blind alley, only to see later that Booth's pistol would have opened the greatest door for himself rather than the Tennessee tailor.

Lincoln and the Beast

The mere fact that Lincoln sought to make Butler his running mate shows how important the General must have been. It was not through personal preference that Lincoln turned to Butler, for he once characterized him as a man "as full of poison gas as a dead dog."[3] Only Lincoln's fear of the Unconditionals would have induced him to turn to Butler. He also sought to make the Union party live up to its name; he wanted to rise above mere partisanship by uniting his fortunes with a War-Democrat as his running mate. His decision to invite Butler to share the honor with him was a double stroke of wisdom, for not only would he bring in an outstanding War-Democrat, but he would also ally himself with a man who was an idol of the Unconditionals. It was for these reasons that Lincoln decided to have "Old Cockeye" on the ballot with himself.[4]

In November, 1863, Butler had been reassigned to active duty at Fortress Monroe as commander of the Department of Virginia and North Carolina, a position which seemed to provide an abundance of paper work but little opportunity for glory, as in Louisiana. Shortly after arriving at Fortress Monroe, Butler received a confidential letter from the unpredictable Gurowski that he should do "something bold, dazzling and decisive" to capture the public imagination and the White House. Gurowski modestly proposed that he might capture Richmond.[5] This attack on Richmond was carried out (not as secretly as Gurowski had suggested, but with the full cognizance of the War Department), and it was a complete fiasco because the plans had been betrayed to the Confederates.

The failure of what Gurowski hoped would be the winning *"coup d'éclat"* did nothing to reduce Butler's military reputation or political prospects.[6] After all, the failure was not his, but it

[2] Dennett, *Lincoln and the Civil War*, 115.

[3] George F. Milton, *The Age of Hate: Andrew Johnson and the Radicals*, 25.

[4] *Ibid.*, 30; Alexander McClure, *Old Time Notes on Pennsylvania*, II, 140. There were some who doubted that Lincoln ever made this offer to Butler. Henry Dawes to Charles Hamlin, April 19, 1896, in Charles Hamlin, *The Life and Times of Hannibal Hamlin*, 484.

[5] Gurowski to Butler, January 30, 1864; Butler to Henry Lockwood, January 31, 1864; Butler to Lincoln, February 8, 1864, in Marshall, *op. cit.*, III, 348–49, 351, 400. Louis Merrill, "General Benjamin F. Butler in the Presidential Campaign of 1864," *The Mississippi Valley Historical Review*, Vol. XXXIII (March, 1947), 537–70.

[6] Gurowski, *op. cit.*, III, 86.

could be laid at Lincoln's door and upon General Isaac Wistar, who had commanded the strike. In anticipation of the coming canvass, James Parton, one of Butler's supporters, had written a volume entitled *General Butler in New Orleans*. This highly eulogistic paean to the military prowess of Butler was hailed by Parton as "decidedly the most successful book of the season."[7]

Chase's backers looked to Butler as a likely teammate for their candidate. Such a move would undoubtedly have strengthened Chase's ticket, and it would also have removed one of the Secretary's rivals for the nomination. An emissary was sent from the Treasury Department to sound out Butler at Fortress Monroe. After listening to his offer, Butler replied that at the age of forty-five he had no desire to become interred in the vice-presidency, nor did he intend to seek elective office before the end of the war.[8]

Shortly after this offer was made, Chase's candidacy began to falter and was soon completely discredited. Butler was wise in not yoking himself with a loser, for as the Secretary's star began to wane, the General's grew correspondingly brighter. It is highly doubtful that Butler ever really had a chance to procure the nomination, but his friends were loath to give up hope. Lincoln could not afford to disregard him. In fact, at the time of the Missouri controversy over Schofield there were some who said that the President feared that the whole matter was essentially a conspiracy to make Butler his successor.[9]

When Chase's fire had burned down to a few sickly embers, Butler's friends reminded him that the sentiment against Lincoln had not abated as yet, and "if this sentiment . . . should continue to increase, why may we not hope that the public attention will be turned towards you?"[10] Still another observed that "Lincoln's safety depends on the events of the next sixty days. Any Bull Run achievements would floor him absolutely. If he is down, the tug comes then whether *place,* or *brains* shall win. I have not given up hope that Providence may yet give us a *President.*"[11] The Ger-

[7] Parton to Butler, February 22, 1864, in Marshall, *op. cit.,* III, 448.

[8] Benjamin F. Butler, "Vice-Presidential Politics in '64," *North American Review,* Vol. CXLI (October, 1885), 331–32.

[9] Horace White to Fessenden, November 7, 1863, Fessenden Papers; B. Smith to Washburne, January 15, 1864, Washburne Papers.

[10] Tappan Wentworth to Butler, March 13, 1864, in Marshall, *op. cit.,* III, 513–15.

man voters, Butler learned from still another well-wisher, desired "some live man at the helm" and they looked for such a man in "Butler, Frémont, or Chase."[12]

In Butler's own state, Massachusetts, Abolitionist leader Wendell Phillips excoriated Lincoln and praised Butler in a speech entitled "Pilots don't drift, they Steer," but the refluent tide which drew the Unconditionals back toward Lincoln proved too strong for any pilot to resist. The President's prior claims seemed too well based, and Butler's partisans were forced to admit that he could not be dislodged. Congressman George Boutwell of Massachusetts believed sincerely that if Butler entered the White House the "rebels would at once give up." Gurowski, to whom Boutwell addressed these comments, agreed wholeheartedly, but added hopelessly, "It would be useless for the patriots now to oppose the current."[13] Butler's closest friend, Colonel John W. Shaffer, reluctantly admitted that Butler's hope for the nomination was slight. "Mr. Lincoln will be the man," he wrote. "I don't believe that you or I can do much to change things. We must let them drift, hoping that something may turn up to change the current, and if the current should once be checked Mr. Lincoln is gone up."[14]

The current flowed on, however, and the spring freshet became an irresistible flood; the tidelands were overflowed, Chase's dikes were breached, Butler's hopes smothered in the turbid waters, and the Unconditionals struggled in vain for a pilot or a rudder to keep them from being swept under by the Lincoln tide, but it was of no avail. The current was too strong, and late in March Butler hurried to Washington to see Lincoln. What the purpose of this flying visit was can only be guessed. It is known only that Butler saw Lincoln and Seward, both of whom were very gracious to him. Whether they discussed the coming election or merely the military situation is unrecorded, but the conversation must have been important, for Butler would not tell even his wife what had transpired in the executive offices.[15]

[11] N. G. Upham to Butler, March 3, 1864, in *ibid.*, III, 481–82.
[12] S. Wolf to Reverend McMurdy, March 7, 1864, in *ibid.*, III, 496–98.
[13] Gurowski, *op. cit.*, III, 154.
[14] John Shaffer to Butler, March 12, 1864, in Marshall, *op. cit.*, III, 518.
[15] Butler to his wife, 1864, in *ibid.*, III, 515.

Lincoln & the Party Divided

Lincoln's interest in "Old Cockeye" remained unabated. He may have made an attempt to take a sounding during Butler's visit to Washington, but the waters were running too deep. Lincoln sought to gain some information by sending an emissary to one of the General's friends. The problem bothering Lincoln was ascertaining the degree of truth in a persistent rumor at the capital that "Butler, Frémont, Chase, and Banks were going to make common cause for his defeat in the nominating convention." Lincoln had Seward's secretary fetch Ohio politician Tom Ford to the White House, where he detailed the situation to him. "Lincoln said that he did not believe the story as to Chase but was credulous as to the balance of it," Ford said later, and he wanted the Ohioan to "find out just what Butler was doing in the matter." Ford probably got his information from the Reverend McMurdy, one of Butler's closest friends, who assured Lincoln through Ford that Butler "was no aspirant for the Presidency." Ford reported his findings to Lincoln, who was "greatly delighted" to learn that Butler had no design on the Presidency.[16]

It was in March that Lincoln formulated his plan for appeasing the Unconditionals by selecting a running mate who subscribed to their policies. Butler seemed to be precisely such a man. According to the Pennsylvania politician Alexander McClure, Lincoln chose him during the month "without specially consulting any of his friends."[17]

To perform the delicate task of bearing this offer to Butler, Lincoln carefully selected Simon Cameron, a staunch worker for the President's renomination and also a personal friend of Butler's. According to Butler's recollection, Cameron arrived at Fortress Monroe about three weeks after the visit from Chase's emissary. Once again the General saw fit to refuse the offer because it was a political blind alley.

The interview concluded with Cameron and Butler discussing the merits of Chase's bid for the Presidency. Butler recommended that Lincoln should "tip" the Secretary out of office. It was not until June that Lincoln finally followed Butler's suggestion in

16 McMurdy to Mrs. Butler, March 25, 1864; J. K. Herbert to Butler, April 12, 1864, in *ibid.*, III, 575–76; IV, 66.

17 Alexander McClure, *Abraham Lincoln and Men of War-Times*, 119, 441–42; Merrill, *loc. cit.*, 549–51.

regard to Chase, but in the meantime the Massachusetts general had tipped himself out of the golden opportunity of his lifetime.[18]

Butler's unwillingness to inter himself in the mortuary of the vice-presidency is perfectly understandable. We need not look for hidden motives in his arbitrary refusal; this one would be sufficient. With the immediate prospects of a glorious campaign against Richmond and Lee in the offing and the possibility of winning eternal fame on the battlefield and possibly winning higher political recognition at some subsequent date, who can blame Butler for his incontrovertible refusal?

Cameron reported back to Lincoln the news of the General's refusal. "He seemed to regret General Butler's decision," commented Cameron later.[19] The President may still have hoped to sway Butler by a personal interview; plans were made for Lincoln and his wife to visit Fortress Monroe.[20]

Whatever Lincoln had in mind in connection with this proposed visit is impossible to tell. Whether it was merely to be an exchange of social amenities or whether Lincoln hoped to succeed where Cameron had failed cannot be ascertained because the visit was never made. It was canceled on the excuse that Mrs. Lincoln was ill. Had Lincoln really wanted to discuss politics with Butler, he could have made the trip alone. In view of the fact that no additional attempts were made to induce Butler to join the Union ticket, it might be concluded the President was not really too sorry he had refused. The Chief Executive still had another card to play; Butler was not the only War-Democrat and Unconditional hero. The vituperative Andrew Johnson was stamped from the same die. His career in Tennessee had aroused as much public attention as Butler's had in New Orleans. Lincoln was never a man to be caught without an alternative plan. At the very moment that Cameron was sounding out Butler in Virginia, another of Lincoln's agents was observing Johnson in Nashville as a possible vice-presidential nominee. With the reluctant Lowell leader out of the running by his own refusal, Lincoln now directed his attention toward the tailor whose political rise had been equally as meteoric.

[18] Butler, "Vice-Presidential Politics in '64," *North American Review*, Vol. CXLI (October, 1885), 333–34. Butler, *Autobiography*, 632–35.

[19] Butler, *Autobiography*, 634–35 n.

[20] Lincoln to Butler, April 7, 1864, in Marshall, *op. cit.*, IV, 29.

) VI (

The Radicals
at Adullam

SIMULTANEOUSLY with the growth of the opposition to the President which centered about Chase, there developed a less completely organized effort to present the name of General John C. Frémont.[1] He had been in Paris when the war broke out, but he returned promptly, was given a major-generalcy, and placed in command of the Western Department with headquarters in Missouri. In the controversy between the Charcoal and Claybank factions the General soon aligned himself with the former group and immediately earned the hatred of the Blairs. His position in Missouri was further complicated in August, 1861, when he issued his famous order emancipating the slaves of Confederate sympathizers. Although this move was hailed by the abolitionist element as a death blow aimed at the fundamental cause of the war, Lincoln refused to go along with his General and rescinded the order after Frémont had consistently refused to modify it.[2]

During the summer months of 1861, Frémont became the stormy petrel of Lincoln's administration. His slavery proclamation, his ruinous strife with the Blairs, and the disheartening military campaign in his state left Lincoln no alternative but to remove him. The following year he was reassigned to duty in the

[1] Ruhl J. Bartlett, *John C. Frémont and the Republican Party*, 89 ff. William Zornow, "The Cleveland Convention, 1864, and Radical Democrats," *Mid-America*, Vol. XXXVI (January, 1954), 39–53.

[2] Allan Nevins, *Frémont the West's Greatest Adventurer*, II, 561–623.

The Radicals at Adullam

Mountain Department. Here again he was beset with difficulties and was removed at his own request.

Frémont's military career was over, but he did not know it at the time, nor did his friends. The General went to New York, where he rusticated on the inactive list until 1864 when he finally resigned from the army. During the interval he became interested in railroad construction in the Far West, but at length decided to seek vindication of his wrongs in the political arena. Many of his friends and especially his ambitious wife encouraged him. As early as May, 1863, it became know among a few select friends that the General was going to seek the Presidency.[3]

As Frémont's support developed, it came from the German population and the abolitionists. A meeting of the former had been held in Cleveland on October 20, 1863, and a platform was adopted which foreshadowed the one adopted at the same city the following year.[4]

As far as the abolitionists were concerned, their chief spokesman, Wendell Phillips, was loud in his denunciation of Lincoln and Chase. His speeches radiated cordiality for Frémont, especially after the issuance of the 1861 proclamation. Phillips probably had more to do than any other man in shaping the deliberations of the Cleveland convention, although he was not present.[5]

Not all the abolitionists, however, were willing to lend their support to an anti-Lincoln crusade. At the meeting of the Massachusetts Anti-Slavery Society in January, 1864, when Phillips had spoken against Lincoln's premature reconstruction program based on the nonenfranchisement of the Negroes, William Garrison supported Lincoln. "What about Frémont?" cried Garrison.

[3] George Brown to Chase, May 25, 1863, Chase Papers (Library of Congress). Bartlett, *op. cit.,* 70–83, 89.

[4] The platform of the 1863 meeting denounced states' rights and demanded the suppression of the rebellion, the abolition of slavery, and a revision of the Constitution in accordance with the spirit of the Declaration of Independence. The South was to be regarded as "territories for the purpose of reconstruction," estates were to be given to the slaves, a national militia modeled after the Swiss was to be established, and they also demanded that support be given to all European revolutionary movements. Carl Wittke, *Against the Current: The Life of Karl Heinzen, 1809–80,* 192.

[5] Effie May McKinney, "The Cleveland Convention" (unpublished Master's thesis, Department of History, Western Reserve University, 1928), 3 ff.

"Events have occurred within a year greatly to diminish my faith in Frémont."[6] In February, Owen Lovejoy, another important abolitionist leader wrote, "I am satisfied . . . that if he [Lincoln] is not the best conceivable President, he is the best possible."[7] Francis Lieber, the German antislavery leader, declined an offer in March to become the leader of the New York Frémont Club. "I am convinced," he wrote, "that every personal election movement at this time can only tend to weaken us. . . . I believe the nomination of my friend General Frémont can have no other effect than the division of our forces, but not his election."[8] Although not all the important abolitionists were willing to join the Frémont movement, a sufficient number did so to make it formidable. After Chase's withdrawal in March, many Unconditional leaders reluctantly confessed that they had no choice but to support Lincoln. Nevertheless, "opposition to Mr. Lincoln continued and was secretly cherished by many of the ablest and most patriotic men in the party." The opposition was further aggravated during the spring by military failures; however, "it lacked both courage and leadership and culminated in the nomination of General Frémont."[9]

The movement in support of Frémont probably started in Missouri. As has been indicated, the removal of Schofield did not placate all the dissatisfied persons in that state. Many Germans were keenly aware of their strength and suspected that they could play an important role in the coming presidential election. "The Germans," boasted their journal, *Neue Zeit,* "will hold the balance of power in the radical party." The editor, who claimed that Lincoln should be rejected, said, "The present time is the time to elevate a new standard."[10] This German opposition to Lincoln was manifested shortly after the removal of Schofield. The Blairs were working among their friends in Missouri to procure a declaration in favor of Lincoln's re-election, but word arrived that when a

---

[6] Garrison and Garrison, *William Lloyd Garrison,* IV, 94.

[7] Owen Lovejoy to William Garrison, February 22, 1864, in *ibid.,* IV, 97.

[8] Francis Lieber to Sinclair Tousey, March 17, 1864, in Frank Friedel, "The Life of Francis Lieber" Ph.D. dissertation, Department of History, University of Wisconsin, 1941), 628–29.

[9] Julian, *Political Recollections,* 238.

[10] St. Louis *Neue Zeit* in *National Intelligencer,* July 25, 1863.

meeting was held "considerable opposition was manifested by some of our truest and best men."[11] An attempt to get an endorsement through the state legislature was also voted down despite the herculean efforts of Blair's men from the Post Office Department.[12]

In February, B. Gratz Brown and some members of the Missouri Legislature helped arrange a meeting at Louisville, Kentucky. Efforts were made at this meeting to arrange for a national convention in May at St. Louis for the purpose of nominating Frémont, but it was not given sufficient support.[13] When they returned home, the Missouri delegates continued their work for Frémont, and the *Neue Zeit* and *Westliche Post* urged all Unconditionals to join this movement openly. Pro-Frémont movements began to develop in New York, New England, and the old Northwest.

By February the prospects of having Frémont in the race as a third-party candidate were obvious to many persons. Gurowski noted on February 14 that he had recently heard that "Frémont's chances increase in proportion as Lincoln's chances decrease."[14] Medill of the *Chicago Tribune* was alarmed at the German opposition to Lincoln. He wrote that most Germans were bitter toward Lincoln because of his treatment of Frémont, and he proposed that the General should be returned to command in West Virginia.[15] It is difficult to gauge accurately the full strength of the German movement for Frémont. Caspar Butz, militant leader from Illinois and editor of the *Deutsche Amerikanische Monatshefte,* remarked in February that the Germans controlled 400,000 votes, but whether all these would support Frémont was a moot question.[16] Several observers who were close to the movement reported conflicting estimates of its strength.

Frémont had no real support from influential men throughout the country. His strength was actually even more illusory than

[11] R. J. Howard to Montgomery Blair, December 28, 1863, Blair Papers.

[12] *St. Louis Democrat* in *National Intelligencer,* February 25, 1864.

[13] E. Merton Coulter, *The Civil War and Readjustment in Kentucky,* 179–80; Bartlett, *op. cit.,* 95–96.

[14] Gurowski, *op. cit.,* III, 101.

[15] J. Medill to Washburne, February 12, 1864, Washburne Papers; J. A. Briggs to Chase, February 15, 1864, Chase Papers (Library of Congress); S. W. Masters to Washburne, January 25, 1864, Washburne Papers.

[16] *Cincinnati Enquirer,* February 23, 1864.

Chase's had been earlier in the year. He had no patronage with which to construct a machine, and he had no organization in existence, nor did he create one. Even Gurowski had to confess that "Frémont's movement . . . has in it too much of the foreign element, and it does not seem that men of real weight care to enter into it."[17]

One factor which undoubtedly accounts for the often over-estimated strength of the Frémont movement was the attitude of the Democratic press. Since many editors representing that party gave the movement considerable space, a number of observers believed that the Democratic party would swallow up the radical German faction by making Frémont its candidate. Actually, however, there seems to be little evidence to indicate that the Democrats were interested in Frémont. They probably overemphasized his importance in order to encourage the Germans to continue their disruptive work, to frighten the administration, and to rouse the lagging spirits of their own partisans by showing them that the Unionists were torn by strife.

The Frémont leaders continued to plan for a national convention to put the Pathfinder forward as the nominee of a third party. Plans were first formulated for a meeting at Cleveland on May 10, but the date was finally set for three weeks later. A group of malcontents in St. Louis, who had persistently refused to accept the renomination of Lincoln, were responsible for issuing a call for this convention. Joining forces with a small but vocal organization in New York, the Central Frémont Club, they denounced the "imbecile and vacillating policy of the present Administration" and demanded "the immediate extinction of slavery throughout the whole United States, by congressional action, the absolute equality of all men before the law," and the confiscation of all rebel property.

A second call to the convention was addressed simply to "the People of the United States." Forty-seven signatures were affixed to this document, representing Illinois, Pennsylvania, New Jersey, Iowa, Wisconsin, Mississippi, Ohio, Maine, New York, Massa-

17 Gurowski, *op. cit.*, III, 161; E. Reinach to Washburne, March 12, 1864, Washburne Papers.

chusetts, and Missouri. The call stated that after having "labored ineffectually to defer . . . the critical moment when the attention of the people must inevitably be fixed upon the selection of a candidate," the time had come for "independent men" to confer together and unite to resist the "swelling invasion of an open, shameless, and unrestrained patronage which threatens to engulf under its destructive wave the rights of the people, the liberty and dignity of the nation." The signers declared that they were "deeply impressed" with the fact that in revolutionary times the patronage and the administration which sought to control "the remotest part of the country in favor of its supreme chief" was a danger which threatened all Republican institutions. Therefore, they believed that the one-term principle should be adhered to in 1864. The document went on to explain that they did not recognize the Baltimore convention as a truly national convention since its propinquity to Washington would make free deliberations impossible. Cleveland was, therefore, selected as a better site for a national meeting. The call named no candidate.

A third call, like the second, also came from New York and was issued by State Comptroller Lucius Robinson. It was addressed to all who believed that the rebellion could be suppressed without infringing upon individual rights, and to those who favored economy and an amendment abolishing slavery. Although there was a wide difference of principles evident in the three calls, they were in agreement on their common antipathy to the President.[18]

As the organization for the Cleveland meeting began to take shape, the names of several men who actively supported it came before the public. Amazingly enough, few really prominent men were involved, even though so many were known to be opposed to Lincoln's renomination. Among the most distinguished names associated with the proposed convention were those of Wendell Phillips, Elizabeth Cady Stanton, Lucius Robinson, Emil Pretorius, B. Gratz Brown, Karl Heinzen, and Caspar Butz. There was some suspicion that Pomeroy was also working for Frémont; he was known to be trying to get the Cleveland meeting postponed

[18] Edward McPherson, *A Political History of the United States of America During the Great Rebellion,* 410–11.

until June and then transferred to Baltimore, and this attempt probably gave rise to the rumor that he was working for Frémont's selection.[19]

Of the convention itself, one gets widely variant notions, depending largely upon whether a Republican or Democratic paper supplies the information. The Democratic papers for days before the assembly enthusiastically told of the vast crowds that were to attend the meeting, asserting that several thousand delegates would be present to voice their displeasure with the administration—two thousand delegates were allegedly coming from St. Louis alone. A local Democratic journal crowed, "The Cleveland convention will efface Old Abe's last chance for the Presidency and will completely extinquish the proposed convention at Baltimore."[20] An exaggerated account of the excitement prevailing in Cleveland during the days preceding the convention appeared in the *Plain Dealer,* which predicted that there would not be sufficient hotels in Cleveland to accommodate the throngs.[21]

Among the more prominent men who arrived before the opening of the convention must be included General John Cochrane; Edward Gilbert, president of the Frémont Club of New York; Colonel Charles Moss of Missouri; former Senators Colvin and Carroll of New York; and some members of Frémont's military staff. Many who had been prominent in arranging the meeting were conspicuously absent: Wendell Phillips, Horace Greeley, and Frederick Douglass among them.

Before the convocation of the regular meeting a group of twenty-seven Germans, representing ten states and the District of Columbia, assembled and drafted resolutions favoring the creation of a new party to be known as the "Liberty party." The rest of the resolutions adopted were similar to those drafted the preceding year and foreshadowed those to be adopted at the regular meeting.[22]

The first session of the regular convention opened in Chapin Hall on May 31. The president of the New York Frémont Club

[19] Mellen to Chase, May 16, 1864, Chase Papers (Library of Congress); E. Reinach to Washburne, March 12, 1864, Washburne Papers.

[20] *Cleveland Plain Dealer,* May 17, 1864.

[21] The convention is not well reported in the Cleveland papers, but there is excellent coverage in the papers of most of the principal cities.

[22] Wittke, *op. cit.,* 193.

called the meeting to order and asked for the nomination of a temporary chairman. Former Governor William Johnston of Pennsylvania was selected. The formal organization resulted in John Cochrane's being chosen presiding officer, with vice-presidents selected from several states.

During the preliminary work of organizing the meeting, a lively debate arose on the matter of credentials. Since many delegates had been sent from political bodies that had given them no credentials, it was decided to withdraw this requirement; however, Ganz of Missouri forced the reopening of the discussion, for "the time would come," he said, "when it would be considered an honor to have been a member of such a convention, therefore, there should be a record to show the world and all lovers of liberty and law that we are here for a great and good purpose in spite of Lincoln and the Devil."[23] After a lengthy discussion it was decided to register the names of all present with the statement that each delegate had come in response to the calls issued. Only 158 signed the register, but these may have been actually only a small fraction of the delegates present, for the total was estimated as high as 400. In any event, the turnout was a disappointment, for many had predicted that the convention would be a giant mass rally in protest against the injustices of Lincoln's administration. The *Detroit Tribune* asked derisively, "Were the immortal 158 the masses? Truly answers Echo—Them Asses!"[24]

The afternoon session opened with a report of the Committee on Credentials that delegates were present from fifteen states and the District of Columbia. While awaiting the Resolutions Committee's report, the assembly was addressed by various speakers who belabored the theme of Lincoln's usurpations and called for absolute and unconditional emancipation. After these speeches were concluded, the chairman of the Resolutions Committee returned the following report:

1. That the Federal Union shall be preserved.

[23] *New York Times*, June 1, 1864; *Detroit Tribune*, June 1, 1864; *Cleveland Plain Dealer*, May 31, 1864.

[24] *Detroit Tribune*, June 6, 11, 1864.

2. That the Constitution and laws of the United States must be observed and obeyed.

3. That the Rebellion must be suppressed by force of arms and without compromise.

4. That the rights of free speech, free press, and the *habeas corpus* be held inviolate, save in districts where martial law has been proclaimed.

5. That the Rebellion has destroyed slavery, and the Federal Constitution should be amended to prohibit its re-establishment, and to secure to all men absolute equality before the law.

6. That integrity and economy are demanded at all times in the administration of the Government; and that in time of war the want of them is criminal.

7. That the right of asylum, except for crime and subject to law, is a recognized principle of American liberty; that any violation of it cannot be overlooked, and must not go unrebuked.

8. That the national policy known as the "Monroe Doctrine" has become a recognized principle, and that the establishment of an anti-republican government on this continent by any foreign power cannot be tolerated.

9. That the gratitude and support of the nation are due to the faithful soldiers and the earnest leaders of the Union army and navy for their heroic achievements and deathless valor in defence of our imperiled country and of civil liberty.

10. That the one-term policy for the Presidency, adopted by the people, is strengthened by the force of the existing crisis, and should be maintained by constitutional amendments.

11. That the Constitution should be so amended that the President and Vice-President shall be elected by a direct vote of the people.

12. That the question of the Reconstruction of the rebellious states belongs to the people, through their representatives in Congress and *not* to the Executive.

13. That the confiscation of the lands of the rebels, and their distribution among the soldiers and actual settlers, is a measure of justice.[25]

The Radicals at Adullam

After the formal presentation of the resolutions, a letter was read from Wendell Phillips, who had disappointed the delegates by his failure to come to the meeting.

Phillips' letter was written from Boston under date of May 27. It began with formal charges against Lincoln for conciliating the rebels instead of subduing them when he had at his disposal the necessary weapons to end the struggle. By way of constructive criticism Phillips suggested what he believed was an expedient plan for reconstructing the rebel states, which was the admission of the Negro to citizenship and the ballot, for "the Negro together with the white man must be used as the basis of states," he wrote, "thus making every man and race equal before the law." He regarded Lincoln's administration as "a civil and military failure," and predicted that if Lincoln were re-elected, he did "not expect to see the Union reconstructed in [his] day unless on terms more disastrous to liberty than even disunion would be." The letter closed with a call for a constitutional amendment abolishing slavery and ending all distinctions between races. Phillips also made it clear that he hoped to see Frémont nominated.

The entire letter was received enthusiastically by the convention, and that it was influential in determining the course of the debates that followed is evident from the frequency with which it was quoted. Wild, unreserved cheering disturbed the hall at the announcement that Phillips favored Frémont. It became apparent at once that a majority of the delegates at the meeting were there for the purpose of pressing the presidential aspirations of the Pathfinder.

The Phillips letter served to point up the division which existed among the delegates at Cleveland. There was a large group from the West, primarily Missouri, which wanted to nominate Frémont. A second and somewhat smaller group of War-Democrats came from New York; they were thinking in terms of securing the nomination of Grant, with Frémont as his running mate. There were also a great many Democrats present who had supported General George B. McClellan. They were interested in fusing with the Grant men from New York and other Eastern states and presenting Grant as a compromise candidate who could unite the

[25] McPherson, *op. cit.*, 413.

War and McClellan Democrats against Lincoln. When it became apparent that Frémont might be nominated, the McClellanites lost interest in the meeting. To them, Frémont's radicalism was "too much of a neck stretcher for conservative Democrats to swallow."[26]

The Grant supporters, who were led by Cochrane and Andrew Colvin, came to the defense of their man after Phillips' letter was read. Colvin offered Grant as a candidate who could carry New York State by 100,000 over Lincoln, and a letter from Lucius Robinson was read exalting Grant as an able man dedicated to the cause of freedom. Although the military successes of Grant were stressed and his popularity as a national hero emphasized, it was clear from the lack of applause that it was Frémont and not Grant who was the choice of the majority of the delegates.

At this point a call was made for consideration of the resolutions. Only the fifth and eighth provoked any discussion, and only the latter was slightly modified at the insistence of the delegates. These resolutions were adopted with a rapidity and lack of deliberation that was amazing. A few raucous speakers from Missouri took charge of the meeting and bludgeoned their program through in a harsh, domineering manner that seemed inconsistent with the principles in the call of the convention.

Now that the question of a platform was settled, a motion was made by Moss of Missouri that the convention should proceed to the nomination of a candidate for President. An immediate objection was raised by the delegates from New York and New Jersey on the ground that the people of their respective states should have an opportunity to study the platform, and they further contended that the nominee could not be elected without the support of the populous Eastern states, and that it would be impossible to get this support if summary action were taken at the convention. The Westerners had hoped to name a slate of candidates, and they now insisted upon immediate action. To accomplish the selection of Frémont, they had sent large delegations, while the Eastern states with smaller representation were clamoring for time to return to their homes to stir up interest for their favorite—Grant.

Further controversy arose over the manner in which the can-

[26] *Cleveland Herald*, May 27, 30, 31, June 1, 1864.

The Radicals at Adullam

didates were to be named. Since the Westerners had sent much
larger delegations, they favored the plan of having each registered
delegate vote; the Easterners claimed that it was unjust for such
populous states as their own to be outvoted by the thinly settled
states of the West. They argued in favor of apportioning votes
among the states on the basis of the number of electors to which
each was entitled. This plan was suggested originally by the Committee on Organization, which was packed with Easterners. Caspar
Butz was on his feet at once denouncing such a move. It would
be unfair, he argued, to permit a large state represented by only
three or four men to cast more votes than a small state represented
by a much greater number. He proposed that each delegate cast
one vote. His recommendation was received with considerable
applause and was sustained by Moss. "If you vote by men," shouted
an Easterner, "nothing will stop them from bringing in people
from the street." His objection was speedily overruled; the committee's recommendation was voted down. A counterproposal
from the Eastern group that the convention should adjourn so
that the nomination could be made at a later date was also shelved.
Frémont was then nominated without further opposition, and as
a sop to the Easterners, Cochrane was chosen as his running mate.

The press made much of the fact that the convention had committed a ludicrous *faux pas* by nominating two men from New
York, thereby making it impossible for the electors of that state
to vote for both of them without violating the Constitution.[27]
Actually this situation had been discussed at the convention, and
the delegates had concluded that Frémont was still a resident of
California, since his residence was still so listed in the army
register.[28]

In a lengthy letter of acceptance Frémont took occasion to
criticize the administration's conduct of the war and to hold
Lincoln responsibe for division and disloyalty within the ranks of
his party. The resolutions adopted by the convention all met with
his approval except the one concerning confiscation. He objected
to this plank on the grounds that it savored of revenge, that peace

[27] Alexander, *op. cit.*, III, 92; Nicolay and Hay, *Abraham Lincoln: A History*,
IX, 41.
[28] *Cleveland Herald*, June 1, 1864.

and abiding happiness could not be attained in such fashion, and that an amendment to the Constitution forever prohibiting slavery was the only way to settle the matter. He concluded by offering a bribe to the Baltimore convention. He asserted his willingness to withdraw from the nomination if the regular conclave selected anyone except Lincoln; otherwise, there was no course for him but to accept the candidacy so as to prevent bankruptcy for the country and a continuance of the destructive policy of the preceding three years. At first Cochrane declined the proffered nomination "with a virgin coyness, so novel and refreshing in a politician of his antecedents," but he later reconsidered and accepted.[29]

The die had been cast; Frémont was afield as the candidate for the new party, which called itself the "Radical Democracy." The whole affair had aroused little enthusiasm among the Unconditional clique; George Julian expressed his opinion that the incident had been a sad mistake, and Zachariah Chandler said that its only usefulness might be to serve as a rallying point in the event sufficient anti-Lincoln sentiment developed. Senator Trumbull heard from a Western friend that Frémont's support was actually very slight. Garrison said that in his recollection there never had been a more abortive or a more ludicrous gathering. Welles characterized the assembly as a "meeting of strange odds and ends of parties, and factions, and disappointed and aspiring individuals . . . a heterogeneous mixture of weak and wicked men."[30]

The press reaction was quite similar. The *Philadelphia Evening Bulletin* described the personnel as "broken down politicians" disgruntled because Lincoln had not given them "a fine fat office or a high military position." *Harper's Weekly* insisted that the only reason they made the journey to Cleveland was to gain revenge against Lincoln; Raymond's paper said the meeting was a "form of mental hallucination." The *Baltimore Clipper* and *De-*

[29] *Detroit Tribune*, June 2, 1864; *Cleveland Leader*, June 1, 2, 1864; Horace Greeley, *The American Conflict*, 1861–1865, II, 658.

[30] Grace Clark, *op. cit.*, 251; Harris, *op. cit.*, 79–80; Lindsay Swift, *William Lloyd Garrison*, 337; Welles, *op. cit.*, II, 41–43; John Palmer to Trumbull, June 8, 1864; J. Conkling to Trumbull, June 29, 1864, Trumbull Papers; Simeon Nash to Chase, June 10, 1864, Chase Papers (Library of Congress).

troit Tribune insisted that the platform adopted at Baltimore was actually far more radical in tone than the resolutions adopted by the self-styled radical party. A similar sentiment was expressed by the Democratic *Chicago Times,* which jubilantly added, "The Cleveland convention has insured the defeat of Lincoln, and the election of a better man than Frémont."[31]

The President also tended to minimize the action taken at Cleveland. When his friends told him that the number of delegates present was estimated at about four hundred, he was reminded of how a like number of the distressed and discontented Israelites had rallied behind David at the cave of Adullam, and he read them a quotation from the Bible, much to their amusement.

The Radical Democracy began its short career. Its platform, drawn largely from the suggestions of the abolitionists and German radicals, was not as extreme as the proposals made by the German convention of 1863, which had supported the creation of a national militia and American assistance to European revolutionary crusades. Nor did it go as far as Wendell Phillips, who proposed the enfranchisement of the Negro. To avoid the appearance of foreign domination the principal officers of the convention were Americans, but there were six Germans on the fourteen-man Committee on Resolutions, and one can feel their influence at work. The proposed constitutional amendments for direct election of the president and vice-president for one term were their work, but little was done to bring these matters clearly before the general public.

The delegates were soon chagrined to find their nominee repudiating the most radical of their planks—confiscation. Within a few days the regular party convention at Baltimore was to adopt a platform which robbed them of their second most important plank—a constitutional amendment prohibiting slavery. Frémont's party ran its course late in September and was liquidated. There was a growing conviction among Union party members that they could not win with any candidate other than Lincoln. Before the

---

[31] *Philadelphia Evening Bulletin,* May 31, June 1, 1864; *Harper's Weekly,* June 18, 1864; *New York Times,* June 2, 1864; *Baltimore Clipper,* June 2, 1864; *Detroit Tribune,* June 10, 1864; *Chicago Times,* May 26, June 2, 1864.

election there was a general tendency for the malcontents to close ranks for the sake of the party. Frémont's group was soon left without an issue.

The German and abolitionist movement failed because of its inability to align with the Democrats. The Democrats were interested in the Cleveland movement, and they hoped to see Grant chosen. They lost interest, however, immediately after the selection of the too extreme Frémont. General McClellan, who was the choice of conservative Democrats, was too proslavery for the radicals at Cleveland. Had the two groups been able to agree on a compromise candidate, they could have ruined Lincoln's hope of re-election. The selection of Frémont prevented this coalition, and at the same time Frémont was destroyed because the issues his group represented, confiscation and a constitutional amendment prohibiting slavery, were repudiated or taken over by the Union party.

Although many ridiculed the Cleveland convention as a misfortune and a sad affair, it is possible that live issues at a later time may have had their origin, or at least been stimulated, by the Cleveland movement. Wendell Phillips later maintained that it was here that the idea of a constitutional amendment prohibiting slavery had its origin, affirming that the action in favor of an amendment would not have been consummated without the pressure the convention exerted in bringing the idea before the public.[32]

The claim of the abolitionists that they conceived the Thirteenth Amendment is open to doubt, but it is quite possible that their determined stand on the question brought sufficient pressure upon the Baltimore convention to make it expedient to include in its platform an article favoring an antislavery amendment. At any rate, it seems that the Cleveland meeting gave added impetus to the growing sentiment for such a measure.

[32] *New York Independent,* July 7, 1864.

The Baltimore Convention

WITH the Chase and Butler booms succumbing through lack of support, there remained only Grant as a possible threat to the President's position. Lincoln had never disguised the fact he was interested in Grant as a potential rival. Shortly after the Battle of Vicksburg he had occasion to seek reassurances from friends of the General that he was not ambitious for the Presidency.[1]

Late in 1863 the *New York Herald* took occasion to label Grant "the peoples' candidate."[2] Other papers joined the parade, and as the chorus grew, Sam Medary of the Columbus, Ohio, *Crisis* predicted Grant would become such a threat to Lincoln that "it might blow the political calculations of the president makers at Washington 'higher than a kite.' "[3] Early in 1864 when the rumors continued, Grant took occasion to announce that he intended to refrain from running, but the skeptics failed to be impressed.[4]

Not only was Grant's name continually before the public in connection with the Union party nomination, but he was con-

[1] James H. Wilson, *op. cit.*, 311–12.

[2] *New York Herald*, November 5, December 15, 23, 1863; Sandburg, *op. cit.*, II, 539.

[3] *The Crisis*, December 23, 1863.

[4] Anna Green, "Civil War Opinion of General Grant," *Journal of the Illinois State Historical Society*, Vol. XXII (April, 1929), 58–59; A. Rawlins to Washburne, January 20, 1864, Washburne Papers; J. Palmer to Trumbull, January 24, 1864, Trumbull Papers; Peter Fay to F. P. Blair, January 31, 1864, Robert T. Lincoln Papers.

sistently advocated as the ideal Democratic candidate, too. His appointment as lieutenant general in March was regarded by many Democrats as a calculated attempt on Lincoln's part to deprive them of their best candidate.[5] The group of War-Democrats which went to Cleveland in May with the intention of still trying to press Grant's name for the nomination encountered too much opposition from Frémont's supporters. Thereafter they gave no further attention to Grant.

Many Unconditionals in the Union party did not give up hope of making him their candidate even after the confirmation of his new appointment. The *Herald* and the *Tribune* continued to print flattering articles about him, and the Democratic *World* sang his praises, too.[6] The possibility that the Unconditionals would make Grant their candidate persisted until the very eve of the Baltimore convention.

The Unconditionals' last attempt to make Grant the nominee came just three days before the national convention assembled. A meeting was scheduled in New York for the purpose of thanking him for his services. There was much suspicion that it was being engineered actually to present him as a candidate. If such a plan existed, it was thwarted by the cleverness of Lincoln and by Grant's refusal to have his name brought forward. The President was invited to attend but declined to do so. He wrote a letter to the assembly worded in such a way that it robbed the delegates of their opportunity to present Grant as a candidate. When the meeting was held, it fell into the hands of Lincoln's friends.[7]

There seemed to be no obstacle now in the way of securing Lincoln's renomination. In turn both Chase and Butler had entered the list against him only to suffer the ignominy of defeat. The boom for Grant had expired with a mild sputter after Lincoln had dampened its fuse and the General himself had expressed little interest in any movements other than Lee's. Frémont was gathering his little brood at Adullam, seeking to find a devious path

[5] William Zornow, "Lincoln's Influence in the Election of 1864," *Lincoln Herald*, Vol. LI (June, 1949), 28.

[6] *New York Herald*, April 25, 1864; *New York Tribune*, May 10, 1864; *New York World*, May 2, 1864; *New York Times*, May 9, 1864.

[7] Nicolay and Hay, *Abraham Lincoln: A History*, IX, 50–51; Blaine, *op. cit.*, I, 516.

which might lead to the White House. His adherents were not strong enough to prevent Lincoln's renomination; nevertheless, they were important enough to bear close watching, for they might drain off enough votes in some areas to influence the outcome of the election. "The Frémont movement is a weak thing," wrote one man, "but just about as strong as the Birney movement which defeated Henry Clay in 1844."[8] Lincoln would have to deal with Frémont before November, but for the time being, no obstacle seemed to stand in the President's path. Although a majority of the delegates were instructed to vote for him, Lincoln was still cautious and told several friends that he was worried about the outcome of the convention.[9]

The disheartening news of the butchery at Cold Harbor did not diminish the enthusiasm of the delegates bound for Baltimore. Washington was alive with activity as politicians from the hinterlands stopped off to pay their respects to the Chief Executive. "Washington is overrun with politicians, with contractors, and with busy-bodies of all kinds and sizes," quipped Gurowski. "The Baltimore Convention is at the door, and the ravens make due obeisance to the White House."[10] After a brief consultation with the White House sage, they were off again for the convention.

In Baltimore the delegates from New York and the Eastern states took up their residence at the Eutaw House, while those from Pennsylvania and the West took up their abode at Barnum's City Hotel. The city was rife with intrigue and speculation. There was considerable discussion about who the vice-presidential nominee would be, which of the two delegations from Missouri would be admitted, and what action would be taken on the matter of reconstruction. There did not seem to be much speculation as to whether Lincoln would be selected; this apparently was a foregone conclusion.[11] Many expressed the opinion, however, that the

[8] George Lincoln to Andrew Johnson, June 11, 1864, Andrew Johnson Papers.
[9] Alexander McClure, *Lincoln and Men*, 124; Alexander McClure, *Our Presidents and How We Make Them*, 184; Abram J. Dittenhoefer, *How We Elected Lincoln*, 77, 80–81.
[10] Gurowski, *op. cit.*, III, 246–47.
[11] William Zornow, "The Union Party Convention at Baltimore in 1864," *Maryland Historical Magazine*, Vol. XLV (September, 1950), 176–200; Dittenhoefer, *op. cit.*, 82; Andrew White, *Autobiography*, I, 120.

Lincoln & the Party Divided

Unconditionals would not accept the results of the convention but would bolt. Campaign biographies of Chase were in evidence, which served to remind many delegates that his friends still had hope of the impossible happening. On June 6, the Unconditionals printed and distributed a circular among the delegates. This document asked a series of questions concerning the efficiency of Lincoln's administration. "Is it not a fact that large numbers of the Baltimore Convention regret that they have been instructed to nominate a man for President whom they feel is the most vulnerable to attack of any who might be named by the Party?" asked the Unconditionals as they sought to sow seeds of doubt in the delegates' minds. The circular hinted that Lincoln had stolen his whole program from Frémont and Chase.[12]

The full scope of this dissatisfaction with Lincoln among the delegates was difficult to estimate accurately; therefore, to gain a better clue to its extent, the meeting of the National Grand Council of the Union League of America—scheduled on June 6—in Baltimore—was awaited with special interest. This session would be a most revealing preliminary to the main event, for it was here that the Unconditionals would probably make their last bid against Lincoln's power.[13]

At the meeting Lincoln's friends, most notably Senator James Lane of Kansas, defended him against the threadbare accusations of malfeasance, tyranny, corruption, favoritism, and frivolity leveled against him by his enemies. At length the Unconditional opposition to Lincoln subsided before Lane's eloquent appeal and a resolution was adopted recommending his renomination. Other resolutions were approved which anticipated to a large extent those which would comprise the party's platform. Having blown off one last head of steam against Lincoln's renomination, the National Grand Council of the Union League of America adjourned its session.[14]

12 *Baltimore Gazette,* June 9, 1864.
13 William Stoddard, *Inside the White House in War Time,* 238–39. Stoddard insisted that the membership of the Union League Grand Council represented a majority of the total membership of the regular convention. This hardly seems to be possible since only 156 attended the council meeting, and many of these were not members of the convention, but had to request tickets to gain admission.
14 Anna Hardie, "The Influence of the Union League of America on the

The Baltimore Convention

By some connivance the malcontents reputedly under the direction of the wily Henry Winter Davis managed to rent the regular Baltimore convention hall for June 7. Thus the delegates suddenly found themselves without a hall in which to assemble. Various counterproposals were made; some wanted to have a special meeting hall constructed, others wanted to move to Philadelphia, but at last it was decided to hold the meeting in the Front Street Theatre, and it was here the delegates took their seats at the appointed hour. "What a crowd of sharp faced, keen, greedy politicians. These men would literally devour every one in their way . . . everywhere shoddy contractors, schemers, pap journalist, expectants, etc. The atmosphere, the spaces are filled with greedy and devouring eyes. The moral insight of the convention would disgust one with the people, but I know the various combinations and events which brought this scum to the surface, and I know that it is not the genuine people," said Gurowski as he surveyed the assemblage.[15] The conditions in the cramped theater were by no means ideal. Andrew White described the meeting later in his memoirs in the following passage:

> Although I have attended several similar assemblages since, no other has ever seemed to me so interesting. It met in an old theater, on one of the noisiest corners in the city, and, as it was June, and the weather already very warm, it was necessary, in order to have as much air as possible, to remove curtains and scenery from the stage and throw the back of the theater open to the street. The result was, indeed, a circulation of air, but, with this, a noise from without which confused everything within.[16]

It is no wonder the delegates were impatient with the speakers and refused to permit any of the longer-winded politicians to occupy the floor for more than a few moments. The deliberations of this

Second Election of Lincoln" (unpublished Master's thesis, Department of History, Louisiana State University, 1937), 43–45; John Speer, *Life of General James H. Lane*, 279.

    [15] Welles, *op. cit.*, II, 30; Milton, *The Age of Hate*, 42–43; Gurowski, *op. cit.*, III, 249. *Baltimore Gazette*, June 8, 1864.

    [16] Andrew White, *op. cit.*, I, 117.

body were characterized by the same speed which had been the hallmark of the Cleveland meeting. Anyone who attempted to make an unnecessary address was speedily silenced by jeers and catcalls from the delegates and spectators.

New York Senator Edwin D. Morgan, chairman of the National Executive Committee, called the convention to order on June 7. The most significant remark in his opening address was an appeal for a constitutional amendment prohibiting slavery.[17] A torrent of applause and cheering followed this assertion. Though Wendell Phillips later insisted that it was his abolitionists and the Cleveland convention which had given birth to the idea of a Thirteenth Amendment, it was the President himself who had suggested to Morgan several days before that this reference should be included in his opening message.[18] Lincoln showed again his remarkable aptitude for accomplishing two objectives with one stroke; he placated the abolitionists and robbed the Frémont movement of its important remaining plank. These opening remarks were followed by the selection of Dr. Robert J. Breckinridge of Kentucky as president pro tem.[19]

In the evening session former Governor William Dennison of Ohio was chosen as the permanent presiding officer.[20] His brief address emphasized that the old party lines were now obliterated by the formation of the Union party; he called for a vigorous prosecution of the war and for the assembly to make certain that slavery would never be restored in the country. All of the speakers made little reference to the presidential question; they seemed to take it for granted that Lincoln would be renominated.

The important keynote speeches having been concluded and

[17] Noah Brooks, "Two War-Time Conventions," *The Century Magazine,* Vol. XLIX (March, 1895), 723–24.

[18] Carpenter, *op. cit.,* 168.

[19] Nicolay and Hay, *Abraham Lincoln: A History,* IX, 65; Brooks, "Two War-Time Conventions," *The Century Magazine,* Vol. XLIX (March, 1895), 724. There was a story current at the time that Lincoln had offered the vice-presidential nomination to Breckinridge. As part of his election strategy to compliment Breckinridge and also to show the truly national character of the Union party, Lincoln proposed the Kentuckian be given the temporary chairmanship. Milton, *The Age of Hate,* 50.

[20] Albert Riddle suggested to Lincoln that it was a good idea to have Chase's man, Dennison, named to the presidency of the meeting, and it was so arranged. Riddle, *Recollections of War Times,* 277.

the permanent organization having been erected, the convention busied itself with three remaining tasks: the settlement of the status of some contested delegations, the adoption of a platform, and the nomination of the candidates.

The report of the Committee on Credentials, which was presented by Preston King of New York, provoked some discussion. No question was raised in regard to the admission of those delegations from the northern states or the border states of West Virginia, Delaware, and Maryland. There were some delegations present from the freshly reconstructed states of Tennessee, Virginia, South Carolina, Florida, Louisiana, and Arkansas. Most of these men were known to be conservative so that opposition from the Unconditional clique was inevitable, but there was much opposition too from some New England delegates who were backing Hannibal Hamlin for renomination and knew that he would get little support from these southern states.[21] The assembly voted to admit the delegates from Tennessee, Louisiana, and Arkansas with all the privileges of the floor. Many in the crowded theater nodded approvingly when the Tennesseans were admitted by a vote of 310 to 151; it was regarded by them as a marked indication of the preference for Andrew Johnson for the vice-presidency.[22] The delegates from Nebraska, Colorado, and Nevada were also admitted with voting privileges. Those from Virginia, Florida, and the remaining territories were admitted without the right to vote, and the delegation from South Carolina was barred from the convention entirely.[23]

Some discussion was engendered by the fact that Missouri had sent two delegations, one conservative and the other Unconditional. The Committee on Credentials recommended that "those styling themselves the Radical Union Delegation be awarded the seats." They were pledged to vote for Grant. Amid tumultuous applause the assembly voted in favor of seating them 440 to 4; this move was regarded as a notice served upon Lincoln that his party would no

21 Milton, *The Age of Hate*, 46, 53.

22 Brooks, "Two War-Time Conventions," *The Century Magazine,* Vol. XLIX (March, 1895), 724; James W. Patton, *Unionism and Reconstruction in Tennessee, 1860–1869*, 45–46.

23 McPherson, *op. cit.,* 405–406.

longer tolerate the Blair influence and the border state policy.[24]

Though many Unconditionals gloated over the belief that the seating of the radical delegates from Missouri was a word of warning spoken by the convention against the President's policies, it was Lincoln himself who had actually recommended their admission. Acting through his secretary, Nicolay, Lincoln sent instructions to the Illinois delegation to support the admission of the radicals. The rest of the convention followed the lead of Lincoln's own state. The President realized that they would vote for Grant, and thus deprive him of the honor of being nominated by acclamation, but there was much more at stake. He saw the necessity of uniting all the elements of the party. Lincoln wished to give the Unconditional clique no further excuse for later claiming that the convention had been closed to them and that the party was merely his tool. By admitting them to the deliberations he bound them to accept the action which the convention took and deprived them of any reason for casting their lot with Frémont's Radical Democracy.[25]

Henry Raymond, as chairman of the Platform Committee, presented the following eleven planks to the assembly for its consideration:

> RESOLVED, That it is the highest duty of every American citizen to maintain against all their enemies the integrity of the Union, and the permanent authority of the Constitution and laws of the United States; and that, laying aside all differences of political opinion, we pledge ourselves as Union men, animated by a common sentiment and aiming at a common object, to do everything in our power to aid the government in quelling by force of arms the rebellion now raging against its authority,

---

[24] Laughlin, *loc. cit.*, 265–66; Walter Stevens, "Lincoln and Missouri," *Missouri Historical Review*, Vol. X (January, 1916), 109–10; McDougal, *loc. cit.*, 141–42. "The Radicals were not mistaken in the notion that the admission or exclusion of these delegates would define the position of the convention with reference to radical policies," *Missouri Republican*, June 9, 1864.

[25] Clark Carr, "Why Lincoln Was Not Renominated by Acclamation," *The Century Magazine*, Vol. LXXII (February, 1907), 504–506. Nicolay to Hay, June 5, 1864, Robert T. Lincoln Papers.

The Baltimore Convention

and in bringing to the punishment due to their crimes the rebels and traitors arrayed against it.

RESOLVED, That we approve the determination of the government of the United States not to compromise with rebels, or to offer them any terms of peace except such as may be based upon an unconditional surrender of their hostility and a return to their just allegiance to the Constitution and laws of the United States; and that we call upon the government to maintain this position, and to prosecute the war with the utmost possible vigor to the complete suppression of the rebellion, in full reliance upon the self-sacrificing patriotism, the heroic valor, and the undying devotion of the American people and its free institutions.

RESOLVED, That, as slavery was the cause and now constitutes the strength of this rebellion, and as it must be, always and everywhere, hostile to the principles of republican government, justice and the national safety demand its utter and complete extirpation from the soil of the republic; and that, while we uphold and maintain the acts and proclamations by which the government, in its own defence, had aimed a death-blow at this gigantic evil, we are in favor, furthermore, of such amendment to the Constitution, to be made by the people in conformity with its provisions, as shall terminate and forever prohibit the existence of slavery within the limits or the jurisdiction of the United States.

RESOLVED, That the thanks of the American people are due to the soldiers and sailors of the army and navy who have perilled their lives in defence of their country and in vindication of the honor of its flag; that the nation owes to them some permanent recognition of their patriotism and their valor, and ample and permanent provision for those of their survivors who have received disabling and honorable wounds in the service of the country; and that the memories of those who have fallen in its defence shall be held in grateful and everlasting remembrance.

RESOLVED, That we approve and applaud the practical wisdom, and unselfish patriotism and the unswerving fidelity with which Abraham Lincoln has discharged, under circumstances of unparalleled difficulty, the great duties and responsibilities of the presidential office; that we approve and indorse, as demanded by the emergency and essential to the preservation of the nation and as within the provisions of the Constitution, the measures and acts which he has adopted to defend the nation against its open and secret foes; that we approve, especially, the proclamation of emancipation and the employment as Union soldiers of men heretofore held in slavery; and that we have full confidence in his determination to carry these and all other constitutional measures essential to the salvation of the country into full and complete effect.

RESOLVED, That we deem it essential to the general welfare that harmony should prevail in the national councils, and we regard as worthy of public confidence and official trust those only who cordially indorse the principles proclaimed in these resolutions, and which should characterize the administration of the government.

RESOLVED, That the government owes to all men employed in its armies, without regard to distinction of color, the full protection of the laws of war; and that any violation of these laws, or of the usage of civilized nations in time of war, by the rebels now in arms, should be made the subject of prompt and full redress.

RESOLVED, That foreign immigration, which in the past has added so much to the wealth, development of resources, and increase of power to this nation,—the asylum of the oppressed of all nations,—should be fostered and encouraged by a liberal and just policy.

RESOLVED, That we are in favor of a speedy construction of the railroad to the Pacific coast.

RESOLVED, That the national faith, pledged for the redemption of the public debt, must be kept inviolate, and that for this purpose we recommend economy and rigid responsibility in the public expenditures, and a vigorous and just system of taxation; and that it is the duty of every loyal State to sustain the credit and promote the use of the national currency.

The Baltimore Convention

RESOLVED, That we approve the position taken by the government, that the people of the United States can never regard with indifference the attempt of any European power to overthrow by force, or to supplant by fraud, the institutions of any republican government on the Western Continent; and that they will view with extreme jealousy, as menacing to the peace and independence of their own country, the efforts of any such power to obtain new footholds for monarchical governments, sustained by foreign military force, in near proximity to the United States.[26]

The third resolution in favor of a constitutional amendment prohibiting slavery was the outgrowth of an earlier suggestion by Lincoln that such a plank should be included in the platform.[27] The sixth resolution was also of considerable importance; like the admission of the Missouri radical delegation it was an attempt to placate the Unconditional branch of the party. The person or persons against whom the resolution was directed remained a matter for conjecture. It was generally felt the resolution was aimed specifically at Montgomery Blair whose trenchant denunciations of the Unconditionals had made him absolutely *persona non grata* to them.[28] The reference may have also been directed against the other conservative members of the cabinet, Gideon Welles and Edward Bates. Welles insisted that though public opinion believed the resolution was directed at Blair it was actually aimed at Seward.[29] The eleventh resolution was regarded as a compromise. The Unconditionals had wished to make it another censure upon Lincoln and Seward, but the conservatives had assumed the President and his cabinet were in accord and headed the resolution to the effect that they approved the decision "taken by the Government, that the people of the United States can never regard with indifference the attempt of any European power to overthrow by

[26] Edward Stanwood, *A History of the Presidency*, 301–303.

[27] Garrison and Garrison, *William Lloyd Garrison*, IV, 113, 117. Garrison said the announcement of the third resolution created the greatest demonstration at the convention.

[28] Nicolay and Hay, *Abraham Lincoln: A History*, IX, 70.

[29] William Smith, *The Francis Preston Blair Family in Politics*, II, 267; Welles, *op. cit.*, II, 174.

force, or to supplant by fraud, the institutions of any republican government on the Western Continent."[30]

A resolution which was conspicuously missing from the platform was one favoring the confiscation of rebel property. This idea had been urged most emphatically before Congress by Representative Julian, and it had found its way into the platform of the Radical Democracy, although repudiated by Frémont. The National Grand Council of the Union League of America, which had met the day before the convention, also adopted a resolution favoring such a course. At the party's national convention the question had been presented before the subcommittee which was working on the resolutions and it had originally reported favorably on including such a plank. In the full committee, however, the resolution encountered such opposition from the conservatives led by McKee Dunn of Indiana that it was ultimately rejected.[31]

The following day the convention was ready to proceed with the business of picking the candidates. Lincoln's renomination was already a certainty, but it was not accomplished without considerable delay, irregularities in procedure, and drama. The Unconditionals made one last attempt to voice their dissatisfaction, and Lincoln's friends somewhat ludicrously vied with each other for the honor of presenting his name. According to reporter Noah Brooks some of the delegates almost flew at each other's throats in their anxiety to have the honor of nominating Lincoln. Simon Cameron, Henry Raymond, Governor William Stone of Iowa, and Lincoln's friends Burton Cook and Thompson Campbell all struggled with each other to make the nomination.[32]

[30] Nicolay and Hay, *Abraham Lincoln: A History*, IX, 71.

[31] Clarke, *op. cit.*, 257. S. Holtslander to Lincoln, June 10, 1864, Robert T. Lincoln Papers. This interesting letter insisted that the confiscation plank in the Cleveland platform was part of an attempt to accuse Lincoln of increasing the cost of the war by refusing to embark upon a course of confiscation.

[32] Speer, *op. cit.*, 283–84; Brooks, *Washington in Lincoln's Time*, 154; Brooks, "Two War-Time Conventions," *The Century Magazine*, Vol. XLIX (March, 1895), 724–25. It had been agreed that Thompson Campbell would present Lincoln's name; however, before this could be done Cameron sent a paper to the clerk with instructions to read it. When this was done it was discovered that it was a resolution calling for the renomination of Lincoln and Hamlin. Lincoln's nomination was then rushed through. Actually Cameron was playing a clever game. He had come to the convention as one of Lincoln's emissaries to nominate Johnson, but he did not want it to appear that either he or Lincoln was opposed to Hamlin. He intro-

The Baltimore Convention

When the roll call was taken each state cast a unanimous ballot for Lincoln until the clerk reached Missouri. John Hume rose and cast the twenty-two votes of his state for Grant. The reaction to this move was instantaneous; one of the Missouri delegates later recalled that he feared the angry delegates would throw the entire Missouri contingent into the streets.[33] When the clerk finishing calling the roll, Hume again arose and moved that the nomination be declared unanimous. Lincoln was adjudged to have 506 votes and was duly nominated. The delegates promptly went into paroxysms of delight; flags were waved, the air filled with flying hats, and the brass band added to the din with a lively rendition of "Yankee Doodle." It was a long time before the chairman was able to restore order, for the delegates continued to emit sporadic outbursts of what the administration press termed "hearty" and "spontaneous" cheering for their champion.[34]

When the celebration had subsided the convention turned its attention to the last remaining task—the selection of Lincoln's running mate. To fill this position there were many available candidates, including Hamlin, Andrew Johnson, Daniel S. Dickinson, and Joseph Holt. Circumstances seemed to dictate the selection of a War-Democrat such as Johnson or Dickinson. This move would do more than anything else to demonstrate the inclusive character of the Union party, and the selection of the former would make a favorable impression abroad by having a candidate from one of the reconstructed states.[35]

duced this resolution which he knew would not carry in that form, and thereby created the illusion that he wanted Hamlin too.

[33] Walter B. Stevens, *loc. cit.,* 110–11.

[34] *Albany Evening Journal,* June 9, 1864.

[35] Dudley, *loc. cit.,* 509; McClure, *Our President,* 184–85; James H. Glonek, "Lincoln, Johnson and the Baltimore Ticket," *Abraham Lincoln Quarterly,* Vol. VI (March, 1951), 255–71. Glonek disagreed with the old view that Lincoln engineered the nomination of Johnson. He maintained that the nomination of Johnson actually came about because of the situation in regard to Massachusetts and New York, and that Lincoln took no hand in the affair. It seems strange to the present writer that Lincoln, who took such an active part during the party's convention, could not have said something about his preferences for vice-president. It is quite true that the hostility of Sumner for Seward, and the fear in New York that Seward might be forced from the cabinet if Dickinson was chosen, proved to be the determining factors in the selection of Johnson. Yet this does not prove that Lincoln refused to express any preference as to candidates or that he did not have emissaries actively working at the convention for Johnson.

Lincoln & the Party Divided

Lincoln, as has been seen, made some overtures to Benjamin Butler. At the same moment, however, while Cameron was approaching the General in Virginia, Lincoln sent Daniel E. Sickles to Nashville to investigate Johnson as a possible alternate choice. The Tennessean was a lifelong Democrat, and a border state man. He was a staunch supporter of the Union and a recognized friend of labor. There had been many rumors of the tyranny of his administration in Tennessee, and it was primarily to study this situation that Lincoln sent Sickles to Nashville. After learning that these accusations were unfounded, Lincoln decided to have the former tailor on the ballot with himself, and forces were set in motion to secure this objective.[36]

Shortly before the convention met, Lincoln spoke to Simon Cameron and Alexander McClure suggesting that these two men as members of the Pennsylvania delegation should work for the selection of Johnson. The President also saw fit to mention to Abram Dittenhoefer that he preferred Johnson, while S. Newton Pettis later insisted that when he spoke to Lincoln about his preferences for the vice-presidential nomination, the Chief Executive replied, "Governor Johnson of Tennessee."[37] William Seward, Henry Raymond, and James Lane were apparently also aware of Lincoln's desires. On another occasion he mentioned his choice to Ward Lamon and Leonard Swett. "Lincoln, if it were known in New England that you are in favor of leaving Hamlin off the ticket it would raise the devil among the Yankees," cautioned Swett. Finally, however, he yielded and consented to go to Baltimore to work for Johnson. He asked Lincoln if it were permissible to tell the delegates that he desired to have Johnson on the ticket. Lincoln replied that it was not, but added, "I will address a letter to Lamon here embodying my views which you and McClure and other friends may use if it be found absolutely necessary; otherwise it may be better that I shall not appear actively on the stage of this theatre."[38]

[36] Robert Winston, *Andrew Johnson: Plebeian and Patriot*, 253–54; *Frank Leslie's Illustrated Weekly*, April 9, 1864; R. H. Mayburne to Trumbull, January 20, 1864, Trumbull Papers.

[37] Dittenhoefer, *op. cit.*, 83; Pettis to McClure, July 20, 1891, in McClure, *Lincoln and Men*, 111–17, 470–71; Alexander McClure, *Lincoln as a Politician*, 18–19.

The Baltimore Convention

McClure and Cameron performed their work effectively among the Pennsylvania delegates; only Thad Stevens objected to the selection of a candidate from a "damned rebel province."[39]

There was also the New York delegation to consider for there was much support being given her native son Daniel S. Dickinson, who was the choice of the Unconditionals led by Lyman Tremain. Before the convention Chauncey Depew and W. H. Robertson called on Seward who informed them Lincoln preferred the selection of Johnson. At the first meeting of the delegates, Hamlin and Dickinson had the greatest support. Weed was anxious to prevent the selection of Dickinson, for his election would have forced the resignation from the cabinet of William Seward, who was another New Yorker. Weed and Raymond had engineered the admission of the delegations from Tennessee, Louisiana, and Arkansas in return for a promise to oppose Dickinson.[40]

Raymond apparently was willing to see Hamlin renominated, but he swung over to Johnson when he learned that Massachusetts would not support Hamlin. Senator Sumner was trying to drive Seward from the cabinet by forcing the nomination of Dickinson and at the same time hoping to send Hamlin back to Maine to take the senatorial seat from Sumner's old enemy William Fessenden. With Raymond's help the Johnson movement gained headway in the New York delegation, and it was finally decided to give him thirty-two votes, Dickinson, twenty-eight, and Hamlin, six.[41]

The Illinois delegation was undecided which way to jump. Many men had approached Nicolay to learn whether the President had given him some instructions on the vice-presidential matter. The secretary could only reply that as far as he knew Lincoln was

[38]Lamon to McClure, August 16, 1891, in McClure, *Lincoln and Men,* 109, 446; Speer, *op. cit.,* 284.

[39] McClure, *Our Presidents,* 186; Milton, *The Age of Hate,* 55; J. B. Bingham to Johnson, June 26, 1864, Andrew Johnson Papers. Cameron introduced the resolution calling for the renomination of Lincoln and Hamlin knowing that it would be tabled. This was done to remove the responsibility for Hamlin's defeat from his shoulders and to protect Lincoln.

[40] Chauncey Depew, *My Memories of Eighty Years,* 60–61; Van Deusen, *op. cit.,* 307–308; Hamlin, *op. cit.,* 464–69, 480–81; Milton, *The Age of Hate,* 46–48; Alexander, *op. cit.,* III, 94.

[41] The first vote was Hamlin, 20; Dickinson, 16; Tremain, 6; Johnson, 8.

not committing himself to anyone.[42] Swett, who was a member of the delegation, sought to protect Lincoln by declaring for Joseph Holt, a War-Democrat from Kentucky. Burton Cook, head of the delegation, turned toward Swett and eyed him doubtfully; he suspected that Lincoln's old friend was double-dealing, and he asked Nicolay to inquire confidentially of Lincoln whether Swett was to be trusted. Lincoln's assurances failed to convince Cook, and he hurried to Washington for a personal interview. Lincoln reassured him and he left the capital under the impression that the President really hoped to see Hamlin rechosen.[43]

Senator Morrill, who was acting as Hamlin's manager, did not realize his man would be beaten. The day before the convention opened Hamlin seemed to be definitely ahead.[44] On the first ballot, taken on June 8, Johnson surprised many by polling 200 votes to Hamlin's 150, while Dickinson ran third with 108. At the correct psychological moment Horace Maynard of Tennessee arose and delivered a rousing speech in favor of Johnson. According to Burton Cook and Theodore Tilton, this speech did more than anything else to sway the delegates toward the Tennessean. Governor William Stone of Iowa also jumped to his feet and cast the sixteen votes of his state for Johnson. In doing so, he completely disregarded the delegation's spokesman, Daniel Chase, and also the fact that the majority of the delegates from Iowa opposed Johnson. Before Chase could get the floor to denounce Stone's move, Kentucky announced the change of its vote to Johnson and the irresistible tide had begun.[45] As state after state swung to Johnson, it became apparent that nothing could check the torrent; Tremain of New York moved that his selection be made unanimous, and it was so done.

Lincoln had secured his wish; Johnson was to be his running mate. McClure, Cameron, Swett, Lamon, and Raymond had done their work well. Raymond's biographer gave him most of the

[42] Nicolay to Charles Hamlin, March 3, 1897, in Hamlin, *op. cit.*, 471; McClure, *Lincoln as a Politician*, 20.

[43] McClure, *Lincoln and Men*, 109; Milton, *The Age of Hate*, 44–45; Nicolay and Hay, *Abraham Lincoln: A History*, IX, 72–73.

[44] Lamon to Lincoln, June 7, 1864, Robert T. Lincoln Papers; Nicolay to Hay, June, 1864, in Helen Nicolay, *Lincoln's Secretary*, 207–208.

[45] Hamlin, *op. cit.*, 471–72, 476–79.

credit for having maneuvered matters so that Johnson's name was presented at the right moment. Gurowski noted a widespread rumor in Washington that Raymond had been the real master-mover at the convention and was to be rewarded for his services with the French legation. Most of the blame, however, fell upon men who were not guilty. Both William Seward and Gideon Welles were suspected of being the culprits who had deprived Hamlin of his renomination.[46]

As for Lincoln, he seemed greatly pleased by the selection.[47] Among the Republicans who had opposed the President the reaction to Johnson's nomination was varied. George Stearns wrote that Johnson's presence on the ballot would reconcile him to accepting Lincoln. James Blaine, who came from Hamlin's state and might consequently have been disappointed at the choice, believed that Johnson's nomination had added strength to the ticket. George Julian, on the other hand, voiced the feeling of many when he said that Johnson was a poor choice because "he did not reside in the United States" and did not subscribe to the principles embodied in the platform.[48]

With the convention's work finished, the delegates headed for home. Some stopped off briefly at the capital to pay their respects to Lincoln. The Missouri delegation visited him, and he made some facetious remarks about what they had done at Baltimore. The atmosphere was cleared between them; Lincoln realized what had lain at the bottom of their conflict, and one of the Missourians was later able to remark, "We never had any further occasion to complain about the control of the federal patronage in Missouri so long as Mr. Lincoln lived."[49]

The entire convention had aroused little attention; the public mind had been prepared for the results by the previous action of the legislatures and the local meetings. "Except the nomination for Vice-President, the whole proceedings were a matter of course,"

[46] Augustus Maverick, *Henry J. Raymond and the New York Press,* 168; Seitz, *Lincoln the Politician,* 422–23; Gurowski, *op. cit.,* III, 254; Welles, *op. cit.,* II, 47.

[47] S. Newton Pettis to Johnson, June 10, 1864; Lincoln to Johnson, June 11, 1864, Andrew Johnson Papers.

[48] George Stearns to Johnson, June 9, 1864, Andrew Johnson Papers; Blaine, *op. cit.,* I, 522; Julian, *Political Recollections,* 243; Clarke, *op. cit.,* 258.

[49] Walter B. Stevens, *loc. cit.,* 111.

Lincoln & the Party Divided

wrote Welles, while Lincoln's secretary, Hay, noted in his diary that it had been a very quiet affair. "Little drinking—little quarreling—an earnest intention to simply register the expressed will of the people and go home."[50] Gurowski, on the other hand, saw the convention in a different light. He wrote:

> It would be interesting to make analytical statistics of the Baltimore Convention. Then it would be found out how many officeholders, postmasters, contractors, lobbyists, expectants, pap-editors, composed it. Then find out how many bargains were made in advance, how many promissory notes were delivered, and similar facts, and the true character of that convention would be understood.[51]

Although the selection had been unanimous and the cheering long and allegedly spontaneous, there were some who detected that beneath the surface were smoldering embers of discontent. Edward Bates said that the nomination had been made as if the real purpose were to defeat Lincoln, while Andrew Johnson was not reassured to learn that such men as Henry Davis, Thad Stevens, and Henry Blow were dissatisfied with the ticket and hoped for its defeat.[52] It was apparent that there were still dangerous shoals and breakers ahead.

The convention had hardly adjourned when a movement was underway, propelled primarily by the depressing military news from Virginia, to remove Lincoln from the nomination. Bates was right; on the horizon of the sunny sky a small cloud appeared which was soon to grow to menacing proportions. There was danger that some of the dissatisfied might yet achieve their desire to replace Lincoln with an Unconditional.

[50] Carpenter, *op. cit.,* 163; Welles, *op. cit.,* II, 47; Dennett, *Lincoln and the Civil War,* 186.

[51] Gurowski, *op. cit.,* III, 253

[52] Beale, *op. cit.,* 374–75; J. B. Bingham to Johnson, June 26, 1864, Andrew Johnson Papers.

) VIII (

A Slight Shift
in the Balance

O N THE FIRST of March, Grant emerged from the West to
assume command of the entire Union Army for the purpose of leading it to victory over the indomitable Lee. Old
"Unconditional Surrender" was selected to occupy the position
which had in turn been incompletely filled by McDowell, Mc-
Clellan, Pope, Burnside, Hooker, and Meade.

As the ground south of Washington began to dry out sufficiently to make military operations possible, a new call was sent out
from Lincoln; more fuel was needed for the furnace of war, the
gaps in the squadrons along the Potomac had to be filled. Seven
hundred thousand troops were requested. Lincoln had entered
upon the war for the Union resolved to win; there could be no
retreat now, but Grant was the last hope. The President, that
sapient appraiser of popular reaction, knew the people were tired
of the blood bath and the drafts. One more defeat and it was all
over; the election would go to a Copperhead, and the Balkaniza-
tion of the United States might begin.

After thorough preparation the Union Mars chariot began to
roll across the Rapidan on May 4 and swung southeast as it went
into the Wilderness. It was here that Lee struck with the full force
of his army amid a tangle of shrubs and bushes which made it impossible for the Northerners to make use of their superiority in
men or materiel. For the next few days the Union forces were submitted to Lee's merciless harrying, but the stubborn advance con-

105

tinued, with the wounded pouring back to Washington and re-placements streaming to the front in an uninterrupted torrent. Then came the ordeal of Cold Harbor. Ugly rumors drifted into the capital and into the press hinting at the unanticipated slaughter being conducted by "Butcher" Grant. There had been nothing like it in Virginia since the earlier campaigning of McClellan, the "Chickahominy Gravedigger." While Grant's columns were sweating slowly, inexorably forward, word began to arrive from Georgia. The news was not likely to produce paroxysms of joy throughout the North, but it did indicate that the methodical William Sherman was halfway to Atlanta, moving forward with his western half of the pincers which Grant was trying to close about the Confederacy.

Because of the news from Grant's army a pall of gloom settled down over the North that threatened to force Lincoln out of the White House. The popular support which he had worn like a mantle in the midst of his enemies became threadbare and tattered. The Unconditionals renewed their fusillade against him, while many dissident voices were heard calling for another convention and another candidate. Once again the long-suffering President made vicarious atonement for the horrors of the war, while the Democrats and the Unconditionals heaped abuse upon him.

As the gloom thickened throughout the North during June, momentous developments occurred in Virginia which were des-tined to bear important fruit. Just as Sherman was moving ahead relentlessly but unspectacularly in Georgia, so the balance also moved in Grant's favor in the East, but few realized it at the moment. June was the month for Lee to deliver his *friedensturm,* but instead he committed a serious error. By brilliant maneuvering Grant managed to elude Lee and moved his army across the James River, so that he was placed in a position to begin operations against Petersburg. This move was overshadowed, unfortunately, by a Confederate raid executed against the capital by Jubal Early. It was a humiliating experience for the North and a shock to most of the people of the North, who were surprised to learn that the Confederacy, which they believed to be tottering on the brink of destruction, could still muster enough troops for a lightning dash into Maryland. Lee, however, paid a dear price, for while Early galloped north, Grant slipped across the James. The success of Grant's crossing would ultimately mean incalculable harm to the Confederacy, and no one knew it better than Lee. But though the military balance had shifted in Grant's favor, the people and the politicians failed to realize it, and they denounced Lincoln and the war as failures.

As the military news seemed to grow more depressing, Lincoln was confronted also with a cabinet crisis. After an unpleasant exchange over the selection of personnel in the New York Custom House, Chase again offered his resignation. This time, contrary to Chase's expectation, Lincoln saw fit to take him at his word.[1] Though there was a momentary protest from some of the Unconditionals, Lincoln's appointment of Senator Fessenden of Maine as Chase's successor pacified most of them.[2]

Chase's departure from Lincoln's official family was undoubtedly not anticipated by the Secretary, but now that he was out of office he was free to renew openly his quest for the nomination. He made some short visits to New York and Boston to discuss the impending canvass with his friends.[3] There seemed to be little possibility, however, that many people would wish to espouse his cause, for among the American voters there was a tendency to feel that he had deliberately unshouldered the heavy financial burdens confronting his department, that he had quit at a critical moment.

Another story rife in Washington at the time was that Chase had left the cabinet to become the Democratic nominee. Frémont, it was rumored, contemplated waiving his nomination in the Secretary's favor. Several Democratic senators had spoken to Chase prior to his resignation and had indicated their desire to make

[1] Schuckers, *op. cit.,* 505–509; Maunsell B. Field, *Memories of Many Men and Some Women,* 296–300; Chase to Cameron, July 11, 1864, Cameron Papers; Chase to Nettie Chase, July 5, 1864, Chase Papers (Library of Congress); Francis Blair, Sr., to Francis Blair, Jr., July 4, 1864, in William Smith, *The Francis Preston Blair Family,* II, 271; Hugh McCulloch, *Men and Measure of Half a Century,* 186; Welles, *op. cit.,* II, 62–63; Chase to Stanton, June 30, 1864, Stanton Papers; Dennett, *Lincoln and the Civil War,* 199.

[2] Dennett, *Lincoln and the Civil War,* 199–202; Carman and Luthin, *op. cit.,* 269; William Salter, *The Life of James W. Grimes,* 265; Welles, *op. cit.,* II, 93–94; Seward, *op. cit.,* III, 230.

[3] Donnal V. Smith, *op. cit.,* 148.

him their nominee if he were not in Lincoln's cabinet, and on July 6 he wrote in his diary that he would support any man they nominated (perhaps hoping he might become that man) if they would "only cut loose from slavery and go for freedom and the protection of labor by a national currency."[4] Chase apparently would not only swap horses but was willing to exchange streams as well.

Lincoln had more serious problems, however, than Chase's renewed interest in the Presidency. The most immediate concern of the President was the renewal of the struggle with the Unconditionals over reconstruction. After his December proclamation Lincoln took the initiative and organized new state governments first in Louisiana and later in Arkansas. The Unconditionals viewed these developments with considerable alarm, for they had long suspected that Lincoln contemplated erecting a new conservative party based on a fusion of all elements hostile to their program. They believed that as part of that plan he was seeking to create two or more pseudo states out of a few counties so that he could carry several Congressional votes in his pocket.

The Unconditional leader from Maryland, Henry W. Davis, had forced through the House of Representatives a bill which embodied the Unconditionals' partial conception of a reconstruction policy. Ben Wade carried the measure through the Senate. The Wade-Davis bill, as it became known, provided for immediate emancipation and the acceptance of the Thirteenth Amendment as a *sine qua non* for readmission into the Union. Before delegates could be received in Congress from the seceded states, a majority of the people in each state would have to subscribe to an ironclad oath. Yet, even in this form, the bill was not a full-blown version of the Unconditionals' ideal. No provisions were incorporated in it for Negro suffrage. No reference was made to Stevens' and Sumners' pet "state suicide" and "conquered province" theories. It contained no clauses calling for confiscation or punitive action. The whole purpose underlying the bill was to deter Lincoln from welcoming the prodigals back prematurely. James Blaine later explained the current Unconditional attitude: "It was commonly

---

[4] Beale, *op. cit.,* 381; William Smith, *The Francis Preston Blair Family,* II, 270; Warden, *op. cit.,* 627.

regarded as a rebuke to the course of the President in proceeding with the grave and momentous task of reconstruction without waiting the action or invoking the counsel of Congress."[5]

Lincoln's subsequent pocket veto of the measure, which was speedily followed by a proclamation in which he explained his reasons for doing so, angered the Unconditionals. "What an infamous proclamation," said Thad Stevens as he gave vent to the increasing hostility toward the President among the Unconditionals.[6]

Within a few days Lincoln was forced to take another step which further jeopardized his chances for re-election. The military disasters in May and June necessitated the issuing of a proclamation calling for an additional 500,000 troops, all deficiencies on each state's quota to be made good by a draft beginning September 5. The prospect of a draft on the very eve of the state elections in Indiana, Ohio, and Pennsylvania filled many with forebodings of defeat. The announcement shocked the people, for the administration had said the earlier calls would be the last. Democratic leaders did not lose this opportunity to show the incompetence of an administration which threw away lives so recklessly and then blandly asked for another half-million. In the old Northwest there were open threats of violence and resistance to the new order.

The clamor to end the war increased. Horace Greeley was still making life unbearable for Lincoln. He insisted that the President should undertake peace negotiations with some Confederate agents vacationing at Niagara Falls, Canada. Lincoln surprised Greeley by empowering him to conduct these negotiations, and the editor set off much against his will bearing Lincoln's terms for peace: the abolition of slavery and the restoration of the Union. Greeley botched the negotiations, and the Confederate agents proved to have no power to conclude peace. The whole affair ended in a fiasco, much to Greeley's embarrassment and displeasure.[7] While this *opéra bouffe* was being acted out, Lincoln dispatched Greeley's friend James Gilmore and Colonel James Jacquess to visit Jefferson Davis in Richmond. The two erratic visionaries set out with

[5] James A. Woodburn, *Life of Thaddeus Stevens*, 316–17; Blaine, *op. cit.*, II, 42; Williams, *op. cit.*, 318–21; Dennett, *Lincoln and the Civil War*, 204–206.

[6] Thad Stevens to Edward McPherson, July 10, 1864, McPherson Papers (MSS in Library of Congress).

[7] Nicolay and Hay, *Abraham Lincoln: A History*, IX, 184–200.

high hopes of ending the conflict, but, like Greeley's excusion to Niagara, their mission was doomed to failure.[8]

Through these missions, however, Lincoln accomplished one important result. He silenced many of the critics who insisted that the South was eager for peace and would yield if given fair terms. The Jacquess-Gilmore mission especially brought back conclusive proof that this was not so. Jefferson Davis had told the envoys that nothing short of independence would satisfy the Confederacy. Those who loved the Union had no choice after this but to fight to the finish.

The gloomy situation on the military front and the prospects of another draft produced a mounting feeling of war weariness; Lincoln's stock began to go down, and the Unconditionals regained hope that perhaps they could force him from the race and substitute a man of radical stripe.[9]

The Unconditionals decided to force Lincoln from the nomination by detaching most of his support in an open bolt and then concentrating on another candidate. Following an interview with Weed, Forney, and others, Representative James Ashley of Ohio wrote to Butler at Fortress Monroe, "They all agree with singular unanimity that such a movement as we talked of ought to be made at once. . . . I did not say to any of them that I knew your views on the subject, but suggested to them that it was probable you and your friends would go into such a movement." Ashley enclosed a call for a convention in New York on August 17 at Cooper Institute. The call was addressed to all who favored the abolition of slavery, the one-term principle, the enlistment of Negro troops, and a vigorous prosecution of the war; and to those who opposed arbitrary imprisonment by executive decree.[10]

[8] Gilmore, *op. cit.*, 240–44.

[9] J. B. Bingham to Johnson, June 26, 1864, Andrew Johnson Papers; Charles Cleveland to Chase, July 1, 1864, Chase Papers (Pennsylvania); Stanton to Lincoln, July 14, 1864, Stanton Papers. Russell Everett to Cameron, August 23, 1864; G. Coontz to Cameron, August 15, 1864, Cameron Papers. John Sherman to William Sherman, July 24, 1864, Sherman Papers. Herbert to Butler, July 4, 1864; Mason Weld to Butler, July 26, 1864; Edgar Conkling to Butler, July 18, 1864, in Marshall, *op. cit.*, IV, 464, 512, 546–47. Theodore Pease and James Randall (eds.), *Diary of Orville Hickman Browning*, 1850–1864, 676.

[10] J. H. Ashley to Butler, July 24, 1864, in Marshall, *op. cit.*, IV, 534–36.

A Slight Shift in the Balance

Butler's chief of staff, James Shaffer, wrote from Washington, "If the War Democracy will go to Chicago ... and split off from balance of their party and nominate you *on your own platform* ... the way is clear." Henry W. Davis, Shaffer reported, was busy writing a protest against Lincoln, and he proposed that this protest should be held up until after August 9, when Butler would have been endorsed by the War-Democracy. "Then have Davis come out with his paper," he continued, "and have other leading Republicans come out and call a mass meeting at New York, or elsewhere, to endorse the action of War Democracy, and I think it will settle the matter."[11]

Out in Cincinnati Edgar Conkling was formulating a plan to unite the War-Democrats and Frémontites behind Butler. "Prompt action on the part of your friends," he assured Butler, "will set the ball in motion, and all of Lincoln's office-holders can't stop it. . . . Let War Democrats nominate you with the understanding that Frémont will retire, and advise his friends to unite in you, and they too will immediately receive more than enough support from men like myself to settle your selection." Most Republicans, he told the General, were Lincoln men "from pure necessity" and were eager to "get a competent, loyal President, in the place of our present imbecile incumbent."[12]

Lincoln's opponents failed to co-ordinate their attacks. The Wade-Davis manifesto appeared on August 5 instead of four days later as Butler's men had desired. The document was a derogatory, malevolent denunciation of the Chief Executive. It accused him of trying to control the electoral votes of the reconstructed states and called upon all loyal party men to repudiate him.[13] Rumors were flying that these two Congressional leaders intended to follow up the protest with an appeal for Lincoln's impeachment. Lincoln's friends were vehement in their denunciations of the manifesto, but Lincoln took the whole incident with his custo-

[11] Shaffer to Butler, July 23, 1864, in *ibid.*, IV, 513.
[12] Conkling to Butler, July 18, 1864, in *ibid.*, IV, 510–11.
[13] *New York Tribune*, August 5, 1864; S. S. Cox, *Three Decades of Federal Legislation*, 341. Cox points out that it would have been impossible for Lincoln to have gotten the southern states to cast their electoral votes without the consent of Congress, and so these accusations were groundless.

mary aplomb.[14] "It is not worth fretting about," he reassured one of his friends.[15] Lincoln's self-assurance may have been a guise to conceal his worry over the affair, but he may have seen what the politicians in Washington did not see—that the manifesto had not had its desired effect upon the public. James Garfield, for example, found it expedient to spike a rumor in his Ohio district that he had helped write it. Benjamin Wade was universally denounced throughout Ohio and his name stricken from the list of speakers in that state. Henry Davis became so unpopular in Maryland that he was later defeated for re-election. Many years afterward Albert Riddle recalled that "everywhere, North, East, South, and West, the masses were with Mr. Lincoln. No President was ever more cordially sustained by the people." On the other hand, he recollected that "thinking Union men were quite unanimous in sustaining Mr. Wade and Mr. Davis, as was the majority of both Houses of Congress."[16] It seemed to be the same old story; Lincoln was supported by the people and opposed by the Unconditional political leaders.

As far as Lincoln's re-election was concerned, the politicians in Washington, like Dante's lost souls, had abandoned all hope. Even the President was disconsolate and admitted to Schuyler Hamilton, "You think I don't know I am going to be beaten, *but I do* and unless some great change takes place *badly* beaten."[17]

[14] J. K. Herbert to Butler, August 6, 11, 1864, in Marshall, *op. cit.*, V, 8–9, 35–37; Welles, *op. cit.*, II, 95–96; Montgomery Blair to D. H. McPhail, August 12, 1864, Blair Papers.

[15] Carpenter, *op. cit.*, 145; Welles, *op. cit.*, II, 98; William Barton, *The Life of Abraham Lincoln*, II, 293; Ward Lamon, *Recollections of Abraham Lincoln, 1847–1865*, 188–89.

[16] Theodore Smith, *op. cit.*, I, 378–79; Welles, *op. cit.*, II, 121–22; Riddle, *Recollections of War Times*, 305.

[17] Herbert to Butler, August 6, 11, 1864; N. G. Upham to Butler, August 12, 1864, in Marshall, *op. cit.*, V, 9-10, 35–37, 43–44. Nicolay and Hay, *Abraham Lincoln: A History*, IX, 250; Gurowski, *op. cit.*, III, 304–305, 315; Frank Howe to John Andrew, August 12, 1864, in George Smith, "Generative Forces of Union Propaganda" (Ph.D. dissertation), 415; J. F. Morse to Chase, August 2, 1864, Chase Papers (Library of Congress); Mellen to Chase, August 13, 1864, Chase Papers (Pennsylvania); Francis Lieber to Sumner, July 3, 1864, in Frank Friedel, "The Life of Francis Lieber" (Ph.D. dissertation), 629; Leonard Swett to his wife, August [?], 1864, in Ida Tarbell, *The Life of Abraham Lincoln*, II, 200–201; Welles, *op. cit.*, II, 103; Raymond to Cameron, August 19, 21, 1864, Cameron Papers; H. H. Elliott to Welles, August 31, 1864, Welles Papers.

A Slight Shift in the Balance

As the portents became gloomier, the National Executive Committee of the Union party assembled in New York on August 22; the chairman, Henry Raymond, penned Lincoln a lengthy report of the discussion. He assured Lincoln that, according to Elihu Washburne, Simon Cameron, and Oliver Morton, it was impossible to carry Illinois, Pennsylvania, and Indiana. According to his own analysis New York would be lost by at least 50,000 votes. He blamed the situation on the lack of military success and the fear that peace was impossible unless slavery was abolished. Raymond suggested that Lincoln state publicly that the abolition of slavery was not a *sine qua non* for peace, and make some overtures toward Richmond for ending the war.[18]

The infectious despair had spread even to the President, who on August 23 took steps to chart his future course of action, which he predicated on the assumption that he would be defeated. He carefully wrote a brief note in which he pledged co-operation with his successor to win the war between the time of the election and the inauguration. This note was folded, sealed, and given to the cabinet members for their signature. John Hay caught the sickness, too, and began to despair; he wrote to Nicolay, "If the dumb cattle are not worthy of another term of Lincoln, then let the will of God be done, and the murrain of McClellan fall on them."[19]

On August 25, Raymond and his committee paid a personal visit to Washington to urge upon Lincoln his acceptance of the recommendations made in the editor's letter. In the light of what had occurred at Niagara Falls and the fruitless visit of Jacquess and Gilmore to Richmond, Raymond's suggestion seemed wholly unfeasible, and Lincoln finally convinced the committee that to begin peace overtures would have serious and costly consequences. Lincoln was careful to reveal none of his anxiety over his impending defeat; after a few smiles and probably a few of his customary stories, he dismissed the committee, which, according to Nicolay, "went home encouraged and cheered."[20]

18 A. G. Fuller to Richard Yates, August 3, 1864, in William Hesseltine, *Lincoln and the War Governors*, 377. Raymond to Lincoln, August 22, 1864; Weed to Seward, August 22, 1864, in Nicolay and Hay, *Abraham Lincoln: A History*, IX, 218–19, 250.

19 Dennett, *Lincoln and the Civil War*, 237–38; Hay to Nicolay, August 25, 1864, in William Thayer, *The Life and Letters of John Hay*, I, 212–13.

20 Nicolay and Hay, *Abraham Lincoln: A History*, IX, 221.

If Raymond and his friends went home hopeful, the extremists who were busily engaged trying to force Lincoln from the nomination did not. As early as August 6 a group of malcontents assembled in Hamilton, Ohio, to consider the possibility of prevailing upon Lincoln and Frémont to withdraw so that a new convention could be held at Buffalo on September 22. The calls which emanated from this meeting failed to bear fruit, and a second series was then issued on September 3 for a meeting at Buffalo. This seemed to arouse no better response than the first.[21]

Although the Ohio meetings failed, they did give rise to more gatherings of the same sort in New York, where a movement was started in favor of a convention in Cincinnati late in September. Colonel Shaffer reported to Butler that many concurred in this plan "to get a Call prepared, hold it until the Chicago Convention meets, and if that Convention nominates a Peace Man or adopts a Peace platform, then ask the War Democracy to join and issue the Call." Shaffer had a two-hour interview with Weed, who told him," "Lincoln [could] be prevailed upon to draw off." George Wilkes, the firebrand editor of *Wilkes' Spirit of the Times,* and Ohio politician Tom Ford were also agreed that Lincoln should sacrifice himself to save the party. Lincoln's old friend Leonard Swett, Shaffer claimed, intended to visit Washington "to tell Lincoln that it is the judgment of all the best politicians in this city and elsewhere, that he can't carry three states, and ask him to be prepared to draw off immediately after the Chicago Convention." Greeley declared, "We must have another ticket to save us from utter overthrow. If we had such a ticket as Grant, Butler, Sherman, with Admiral Farragut for Vice., we could make a fight yet." Even the reliable John Forney expressed his willingness to sacrifice Lincoln to save the election.[22]

In compliance with the appeals being voiced on every hand for a new convention, a group of malcontents arranged a meeting at the home of New York Mayor George Opdyke on August 18. The Opdyke meeting was propelled by such journalistic leaders

[21] Donnal V. Smith, *op. cit.,* 148–49; *New York Herald,* August 6, 1864.

[22] Shaffer to Butler, August 17, 1864, in Marshall, *op. cit.,* V, 67–69; Henry L. Stoddard, *Horace Greeley, Printer, Editor, Crusader,* 227; *Washington Chronicle,* August 16, 1864.

A Slight Shift in the Balance

as Greeley, Parke Godwin of the *Evening Post,* Theodore Tilton, and George Wilkes; and such political luminaries as Wade, Davis, Governor John A. Andrew of Massachusetts, Charles Sumner, and David D. Field. Altogether, about twenty-five men were present at this conference. Convinced that "none of the Candidates for the Presidency already presented can command the united confidence and support of all loyal and patriotic men," they urged all who agreed with this conviction to attend a convention at Cincinnati on September 28 "to concentrate the Union strength on some one candidate who commands the confidence of the country even by a new nomination if necessary." Each man who attended this meeting was given a stack of these calls with instructions to send them to prominent men throughout the country, who in turn were to be instructed to send their replies to John Austin Stevens, Jr., so that arrangements could be made for a second meeting at the home of David Dudley Field on August 30.[23]

The Opdyke meeting may have been engineered primarily in the interest of Chase. The former Secretary's interest in the Presidency seemed as yet to be very much alive; there were many observers who reported this to be the case.[24] He had a representative at the Opdyke meeting. Many of the men who were most active in New York and who attended the meeting were treasury agents or very good friends, including Opdyke and John Stevens. The fact that they chose Cincinnati, Chase's home town, seems to be somewhat significant; and the two earlier calls emanating from Butler County, Ohio, where Cincinnati is located, were both signed by L. D. Campbell, who was a Chase supporter. By the process of elimination he seems to be the only possible candidate they could have endorsed. Both Lincoln and Frémont were out of the question, and Butler probably was, too, in view of the fact that John Andrew, who was one of the most influential men at the meeting and, according to Shaffer, the author of the call, was a political

[23] J. K. Herbert to Butler, August 27, 1864; Shaffer to Butler, August 29, 1864, in Marshall, *op. cit.,* V, 116–17. Henry G. Pearson, *The Life of John A. Andrew: Governor of Massachusetts, 1861–65,* II, 159–61. The call is reproduced in the *New York Sun,* June 30, 1889.

[24] Barnes, *op. cit.,* 445; George S. Merriam, *Life and Times of Samuel Bowles,* I, 413; Welles, *op. cit.,* II, 120.

opponent of Butler's for many years.[25] Thus only Chase and Grant were left as possible Union nominees, and the latter's commitments in Virginia and his oft repeated assertions that he would not run for political office during the war, seemed to leave Chase as the only man who was willing and able to run.

While the calls for the new convention were being distributed, steps were taken to secure the withdrawal of Lincoln and Frémont so that all obstacles in the way of a new convention would be removed. About August 20 a group of abolitionists in Boston addressed a letter to Frémont concerning the possibility of his withdrawal. Frémont's reply indicated that he could not take this step without consulting the party which had nominated him, but he assured them he was ready to do whatever seemed best and would abide by the decision of a new convention.[26] Lincoln made no formal statement concerning his willingness to withdraw and permit a new convention to meet.

Replies began pouring into John Stevens' hands. There were many dissenting voices raised, but a sufficient number endorsed the proposed meeting that it could be held at Field's home on August 30.[27] George Wilkes, who was present at the session, wrote later that all the delegates "came to the conclusion that it was useless and inexpedient to attempt to run Mr. Lincoln in the hope of victory against the blind infatuation of the masses in favor of McClellan."[28] They resolved to go through with their original plan for a convention at Cincinnati; a committee was appointed to wait upon the President for his approval. In anticipation that Lincoln would refuse to leave the race, it was decided to meet anyway "to settle whether the friends of the country should nominate a new candidate (probably Grant) or continue for Lincoln."[29] It was also decided that Greeley, Godwin, and Tilton were to send out joint letters to the loyal governors asking three questions: (1)

25 Shaffer to Butler, August 29, 1864, in Marshall, *op. cit.,* V, 116.
26 McPherson, *op. cit.,* 425–26; Bartlett, *op. cit.,* 121.
27 There are many letters concerning this meeting reproduced in the *New York Sun,* June 30, 1889.
28 Wilkes to Washburne, August 31, 1864, Washburne Papers.
29 Lieber to Sumner, August 31, 1864, in Friedel, "The Life of Francis Lieber" (Ph.D. dissertation), 630; Herbert to Butler, August 27, 1864, in Marshall, *op. cit.,* V, 117–18.

A Slight Shift in the Balance

Can Lincoln be re-elected? (2) Can your state be carried for Lincoln? (3) Should there be another candidate? Other letters of similar vein went to prominent editors and men in public life.[30] The meeting received one rude blow, however, when John Andrew refused to attend. He had been most active at the Opdyke meeting, but now he announced that he would support Lincoln. In reading accounts of the Jacquess-Gilmore mission in the press, he had learned that Lincoln had insisted upon emancipation as one of the terms of peace; this satisfied him and he abandoned the movement to shelve Lincoln.

By September 1, Lincoln's personal popularity was apparently at such a low ebb that Gurowski could write with much certitude, "Out Lincoln . . . is to be the war cry."[31] Were the prospects as black as Lincoln and the Unconditionals believed? In the absence of an accurate yardstick to appraise popular opinion in 1864, a definite answer is impossible. It may well have been, however, that even though morale was quite low in August, Lincoln would have won the election. Richard Smith of the *Cincinnati Gazette* wrote during the depth of gloom, "I think we shall be able to rally our people around the *cause* and elect Mr. Lincoln even as it is."[32] There is undoubtedly much truth in his statement for Lincoln was only a symbol of a unified country, and although his personal prestige may have been tarnished by the misfortunes of the summer, the people would still have voted for him solely because he was the candidate of the Union cause. Regarding the foment in Washington over the coming election, Noah Brooks later noted that "to some degree although not to the extent that Washington politicians believed, the country was responsive to the excitement which prevailed at the capital."[33]

The excitement and doubt concerning the outcome of the election may, as Brooks maintained, have been felt largely by the politicians rather than by the people as a whole. The politicians had been out of touch with the popular will before, especially when they insisted earlier in the year that Lincoln was not desired

[30] Pearson, *op. cit.*, II, 161–63.

[31] Gurowski, *op. cit.*, III, 329.

[32] Smith to [John Stevens?], August 27, 1864, in *New York Sun*, June 30, 1889.

[33] Noah Brooks, *Washington in Lincoln's Time*, 130–31.

for another term. They may have been completely out of touch again with what the people actually thought.

In the absence of a political poll the best way to appraise the grass-roots opinion in 1864 is through the local press. Carl Sandburg pointed out that during the summer the small-town Union editors, who were closest to the people and knew their wishes, never faltered in their support of Lincoln.[34] These editors were the spokesmen of the people. Their stand behind Lincoln seems to indicate that the people were also behind him. They knew the dislikes, prejudices, and thoughts of their subscribers, and they always reflected the thought of the population they served. The people supported only the papers which expressed their views; any editor who was out of step with the thought of his community soon found himself out of business. Therefore, when the small-town editors retained their loyalty for Lincoln during the dark months of 1864, when all of the Washington observers were predicting his defeat, they were merely reflecting the continued loyalty of the people.[35]

Whatever antipathy may have been felt toward Lincoln and the acrimonious attacks of the Unconditional leaders melted away during the first week of September with an almost miraculous suddenness, which would seem to indicate that the hostility toward the President was actually not as extensive as many believed. The military situation changed abruptly with the remarkable victories of Sherman in Georgia and paved the way for one of the most astounding denouements in history.

In the meantime, however, the Democrats assembled in Chicago for their own convention.

[34] Sandburg, *op. cit.*, II, 591.

[35] William Zornow, "The Attitude of the Western Reserve Press on the Re-election of Lincoln," *Lincoln Herald*, Vol. L (June, 1948), 35–39, is an examination of the Union papers in this highly Republican section of Ohio. All the small-town papers continued to support Lincoln.

) IX (

A Resurgent
but Bewildered Democracy

HE DEMOCRATIC PARTY, which assembled at Chicago on
August 29 to nominate its candidate for the Presidency,
was ebullient over its rival's discomfiture, but the prospects
of victory were blighted somewhat by the same factious spirit that
weakened the Unionists. With the formation of the National
Union party in 1862, great segments of the Democratic party had
been absorbed into this new creation. The liquidation of the Democratic party seemed to have been so thorough that Sumner proudly
announced on April 24, 1862, "The Democrats have disappeared!
This is the greatest act of the administration."[1] Governor Horatio
Seymour and politico Fernando Wood of New York urged upon
their party the maintenance of a clear-cut opposition to Lincoln
in order to delay the complete absorption of the Democracy. The
smashing victories gained in 1862 at the polls served notice that
the Democratic party was very much alive, and these victories revived hope that the party would win in '64.

The party, however, was being placed more and more in an
untenable position. On the one hand stood Lincoln and the Republicans, calling upon all loyal men to join the Union party. This
stand instantly made it appear that anyone who did not join preferred disunion, a position closely bordering on treason. "Loyalty
to Republicanism," said George Julian, "was ... accepted as loyalty
to the country."[2] The existence of this situation explains why the

[1] Edward Pierce, op. cit., IV, 68.
[2] Julian, Political Recollections, 244. The Loyalty For the Times: A Voice From
Kentucky, April, 1864, 3.

119

administration was able to make such effective use of the treason issue during the canvass.

Many Democrats accepted the offer to join forces with the new party, and this group which supported wholeheartedly the admin·istration's war effort became known as "War-Democrats." Their position seemed so closely identified with the administration's that Judge Miller of Ohio could say with much certitude, "There is no real difference between a War Democrat and an Abolitionist— They are links of one sausage, made of the same dog."[3]

Occupying the middle ground was a large group which believed that the restoration of the Union should be the paramount aim of the war and which had supported the government to achieve this objective. This group could not endorse Lincoln's administration, as the War-Democrats had done, because of the President's alleged arbitrary, unconstitutional acts. Many of them did not believe that abolition should be included among the peace terms, for they felt that insistence upon emancipation had no effect other than to prolong the conflict unnecessarily. Horatio Seymour was one of the chief spokesmen of this group, which was often erroneously called the Copperhead faction. These men were not Copperheads *per se;* they merely opposed emancipation and the high-handed methods adopted by the government, such as the suspension of habeas corpus and the suppression of newspapers. They claimed that the prolongation of the war and the unconstitutional methods used to conduct it were undermining the democratic form of American government. Peace negotiations should be started at once, they averred, or as soon as practicable, on the basis of a Southern acceptance of the restoration of the Union.[4]

Actually this majority of the Democratic party was so much in harmony with the war policies of the administration (exclusive of the slavery question and the arbitrary acts) that there was often talk of fusion. Chase was suspected of intending to angle for the Democratic nomination. There is some evidence to show that Frémont hoped to win the Democratic nomination. There were

[3] Matilda Gresham, *Life of Walter Quintin Gresham,* 1832–1895, I, 290.

[4] Stewart Mitchell, *Horatio Seymour of New York,* 298, 337, 339, 361–62; Henry Conkling, *An Inside View of the Rebellion: An American Citizen's Text-book,* 22.

Resurgent, Bewildered Democracy

Democrats at Cleveland trying to obtain the selection of Grant earlier in May; and after the Baltimore convention Governor Andrew, who resented the "snap nomination," secretly met with Seymour to discuss the possibility of finding a new candidate.[5] All this activity would certainly indicate that the moderate Democrats could not have been so far removed from the Unionists on matters of policy.

The dilemma of the moderates was complicated by another factor. While the Union party and the War-Democrats flanked them on one side, on the other stood a smaller but very loquacious minority of ultra-peace advocates, the radical or Copperhead wing of the party. Their spokesmen were clamoring for peace. A significant number had taken a position favoring peace even with the recognition of a divided country. These men often urged youths to resist the draft and soldiers to desert; they sought in every way to embarrass the war effort. Many of them were probably traitors; some actually had delusions of erecting a Northwest Confederacy which would be closely allied with the Southern.

The Democrats were faced with the necessity of reconciling these different positions. Since their party represented many divergent groups, ranging from those who advocated an all-out war effort to those who wanted to continue the war but conform to the Constitution, and from those who wanted an armistice as soon as possible and a negotiated peace based on a recognition of the Union to those who wanted peace at any price, there was much difficulty in selecting a candidate or writing a platform to reconcile all of them. Seymour and many of the moderates wanted a civilian candidate, while others wanted a military leader such as George McClellan. Whichever way they turned, the Democrats were acutely aware of the smarting jabs from the horns of the dilemma they had to face; how could the war and peace factions be harmonized? Two alternatives seemed to present themselves, and neither was satisfactory. "They must nominate a Peace Democrat on a war platform, or a War Democrat on a peace platform," predicted the White House sage to Noah Brooks.[6] Lincoln's customary foresightedness proved to be correct again, for the delegates

[5] Stewart Mitchell, *op. cit.*, 364–65; Pearson, *op. cit.*, II, 157–58.
[6] Brooks, *Washington in Lincoln's Time*, 180.

121

ultimately selected the latter alternative, but instead of reducing the dilemma, they succeeded only in becoming impaled on both its horns.

Despite the strong desire to select a civilian, the only man who seemed to possess a sufficiently large following to merit consideration was the "young Napoleon," George Brinton McClellan. "Little Mac" had burst upon the amazed public with dazzling suddenness when he was made the commander-in-chief of the Union Army in November, 1861, at thirty-four years of age.

McClellan's chief claim to a lasting niche in history was as a forger of thunderbolts, for it was he who transformed the ragged bands of volunteers into the superb fighting machine which was destined to become the Army of the Potomac. It was unfortunate that the American Carnot, once having performed this great service, remained upon the stage too long, and his glory was tarnished during the timorous vacillating Peninsular Campaign. It was his great tragedy that once having forged the thunderbolt he failed to hurl it effectively.

Though McClellan's career as a soldier ended with only a partial victory at Antietam, he was not disgraced. Those who came after him had to undergo the humiliation of Fredericksburg and Chancellorsville, and until Grant arrived in 1864 no general in the East shone any brighter than "Little Mac." As for his defeats on the peninsula, his friends explained them away on the ground that a jealous administration had failed to give him proper support because Lincoln feared him as a presidential rival.[7] Like Butler and Frémont the Democrats' champion was also cast in the role of a martyr.

As a possible presidential nominee McClellan had great support from some influential Democrats and among the soldiers. In New York his previous railroad connections with the Ohio and Mississippi Railroad stood him in good stead with Erastus Corning, president of the influential New York Central, and Dean Richmond, vice-president of the same line. In New Jersey, where he resided after his removal from the military command, he was supported by the officers of the Camden and Amboy Railroad,

[7] *Chicago Times*, June 10, 12, 14, 18, July 4, 1864; Hiram Ketchum, *General McClellan's Peninsular Campaign*, 67–68.

which was also a powerful political influence in the state. During a visit to Boston in 1863 he made many important contacts with the residents of Beacon Hill. Among the soldiers his popularity was proverbial. It was only from the Copperheads that talk of his nomination received much opposition. The peace faction was naturally hostile to a military figure, and it doubly suspected McClellan because he commanded the troops which had arrested the members of the Maryland Legislature in 1861 when the federal government was making every effort to keep that state from joining the Confederacy. The Copperheads described him as the candidate of the "bloated Aristocrats," the railroad magnates, and the "great unwashed of the Celtic persuasion."[8]

According to Sandburg, McClellan's interest in the Presidency dated from July 7, 1862, when he wrote his celebrated Harrison Landing letter to the Chief Executive.[9] This letter may have been written with an eye to the Presidency, but if it was, McClellan showed a surprising lack of interest in politics until late in 1863.[10] The General kept aloof from political currents until October of that year, when he wrote a letter to Charles Biddle endorsing the candidacy of Judge George W. Woodward for the governorship of Pennsylvania. "Little Mac" intended his letter only as a personal gesture, but actually it made him the most popular candidate for the Democratic nomination.[11]

This letter, which placed McClellan squarely in the presidential race, was a restatement of his views of 1862. The policies expressed in both letters became the General's personal platform during the campaign and won him the support of the majority of the Democratic party. He desired the war to continue till the Union was restored. He had no quarrel with the executive's assuming more

[8] Arthur Cole, *The Era of the Civil War, 1848–1870,* 232; William S. Myers, *General George Brinton McClellan: A Study in Personality,* 405–29; Edward Kirkland, *The Peacemakers of 1864,* 112–15.

[9] Sandburg, *op. cit.,* III, 244. McPherson, *op. cit.,* 385–86.

[10] S. S. Cox to McClellan, May 31, 1863, McClellan Papers (MSS in Library of Congress); McClellan to Weed, June 13, 1863, in Barnes, *op. cit.,* 428–29. McClellan refused Cox's request that he run for governor of Ohio in 1863 against Vallandigham, and he refused to accept Weed's invitation to join in a movement to get the Democrats to support the administration. This would indicate his lack of interest in politics at that time.

[11] Myers, *op. cit.,* 427–28; Dudley, *loc. cit.,* 506.

power during the struggle; in his Harrison Landing letter he had urged Lincoln to direct the entire civil and military policy of the country against the rebellion. The point where he and the Democrats parted company with Lincoln's party was as to how that power was to be used. The Democrats insisted that there should be no interference with slavery, no arbitrary arrests, no martial law in pacific areas, no confiscation, and no punitive measures against the vanquished. These were the essential planks in the conservative Democrats' platform as well as McClellan's It was inevitable that they would turn to him as their nominee, and the Woodward letter clinched his case.[12]

McClellan's hope of becoming the Democratic nominee almost ran aground on the shoals of Copperhead opposition. His friends tried to get him to issue a declaration of principles which would placate the peace men, but the General continued to maintain the position favoring a vigorous prosecution of the war which he had taken in his Harrison Landing and Woodward letters.[13] His relations with the Copperheads, therefore, would determine to a large extent his success in winning the nomination.

Before the convention finally assembled, the moderate Democrats in Ohio, the bailiwick of the peace men and Vallandighamites, got the state party convention to support McClellan. In addition, he was also assisted by the powerful faction in New York led by August Belmont, Manton Marble, and Dean Richmond.[14]

On January 12, Democratic party leaders journeyed to August Belmont's residence to arrange for the national convention. They chose Chicago and selected Independence Day for the date of the opening session, despite considerable opposition from other party leaders, who approved of neither the time nor the place. As a

[12] Marble to McClellan, November 11, 1863; John Shenk to McClellan, November 2, 1863, McClellan Papers. Dennett, *Lincoln and the Civil War*, 143–44. These indicate the importance of the Woodward letter in making McClellan the most popular Democratic candidate.

[13] Myers, *op. cit.*, 439.

[14] A. Norton to McClellan, February 28, 1864; George Morgan to McClellan, March 28, 1864, McClellan Papers. J. Arnold to Marble, March 29, 1864; Cox to Marble, May 2, 1864; Cox to Marble, December 5, 1863, Marble Papers (MSS in Library of Congress). Hiram Ketchum to Samuel F. B. Morse, January 23, 1864, Morse Papers (MSS in Library of Congress). Charles Mason Diary, February 21, 1864 (MSS in Library of Congress). Porter, *op. cit.*, 192–93.

matter of fact, the previous evening a group of fifty Democratic congressmen had met at the capital and designated Cincinnati as their choice of location.[15] The peace men did not want the meeting held in July. They wanted an autumn date, because they thought that if the summer military campaigns failed, they could better succeed in nominating a peace man. Cox called Marble's attention to this situation in June when he wrote that delaying the convention "affords the radical movement a chance to jerk McClellan, and they are at it. . . . There is no denying that since Grant's failure, or seeming failure, there is an increase of the peace sentiment—irrespective of consequences."[16]

As the summer progressed, the unpropitious military situation seemed to grow darker with each communiqué. A general spirit of dejection and futility pervaded the entire North. Democratic leaders yielded to both the pressure of the peace men and a quite understandable desire to capitalize on their opponents' growing misfortune and decided to postpone the convention till as late as possible. August 29 was the date finally selected. The reaction to this move was varied, but most party members seemed to feel like Carle Goodrich of Ohio, who wrote that they were "all silent and all damned non-plussed."[17]

The situation among the Democrats was further complicated by the sudden reappearance in Hamilton, Ohio, of Clement Vallandigham, who quitted his Canadian exile despite the explicit injunction of the federal government not to do so. The district convention in Hamilton selected him as a delegate to the national convention. Lincoln made no move to apprehend the exile, for he undoubtedly saw at a glance that the wily Ohioan's return would in the long run prove more embarrassing to the Democrats than to the administration. One of McClellan's friends observed prophetically, "Vallandigham's advent will I fear give serious trouble. It will at all events compel a decided platform of action before the

15 *National Intelligencer,* January 14, 15, 1864.

16 Cox to Marble, June 20, 1864; McClellan to Marble, June 25, 1864; Dean Richmond to Marble, June 16, 1864; William Cassidy to Marble, June 11, 1864; J. M. Baldwin to Marble, September 5, 1864, Marble Papers.

17 Carle Goodrich to Marble, June 27, 1864; Cox to Marble, n.d.; Thomas Seymour to Marble, June 15, 1864; J. Warren to Marble, June 17, 1864; William Cassidy to Marble, n.d., Marble Papers.

meeting at Chicago."[18] It was precisely a platform of action which the wavering McClellan could not offer his party, and consequently Vallandigham was free to organize his peace advocates against the conservatives.[19]

With Vallandigham back in harness, the opposition to McClellan's nomination quickened throughout Ohio, New York, and Pennsylvania. In Philadelphia the peace faction printed and distributed in adjoining states a circular urging the party to renominate either Pierce or Fillmore.[20] In New York the strong clique of peace men was trying to force McClellan to accept the Ultra doctrines of Alexander Long of Ohio, who had openly espoused the cause of peace even at the cost of the Union.[21] All this served as an additional indication that McClellan would encounter a storm before his nomination was accepted.

As the military situation deteriorated during July, there was the usual agitation and pressure to restore McClellan to military command. Francis P. Blair, father of the two obstreperous brothers, Frank and Montgomery, realized that this situation might be turned to good account. If McClellan were amenable to an offer of restoration to active duty, his bid for the Democratic nomination would be thwarted. Apparently without revealing his intentions to the Chief Executive, Blair departed for New York to lay his plans before McClellan's managers. A meeting between the two men was arranged, and Blair tried to get McClellan to make himself the center of the loyal Democrats by asking Lincoln to restore him to command and thus disclaim any desire for the nomination. McClellan gave a vacuous reply implying that he had no aspirations for the White House.[22]

[18] [?] to McClellan, June 16, 1864, McClellan Papers.

[19] Dennett, *Lincoln and the Civil War*, 193. Fernando Wood told Lincoln that "he could do nothing more politic than to bring Val[landigham] back" and assured the President that there would be two Democratic candidates in the field ere long.

[20] Amasa Parker to McClellan, July 24, 1864; James Hall to McClellan, July 18, 1864, McClellan Papers.

[21] Cox to Marble, July 25, 1864, Marble Papers.

[22] James Rhodes, *History of the United States from the Compromise of 1850 to the Final Restoration of Home Rule at the South*, IV, 507; *National Intelligencer*, October 5, 1864; Meyers, *op. cit.*, 433–35; Nicolay and Hay, *Abraham Lincoln: A History*, IX, 246–49; H. J. Eckenrode and Bryan Conrad, *George B. McClellan: The Man Who Saved the Union*, 269. Draft of a letter to Blair, n.d., McClellan Papers.

Resurgent, Bewildered Democracy

During the weeks of August preceding the assembling of the national convention there were no indications that the peace men had given up their opposition to McClellan. George Morgan, the General's adviser from Mount Vernon, Ohio, told him early in the month that it looked as if rival candidates would be presented at the convention by the peace element from Ohio, New York, and Pennsylvania. He told him that Samuel Cox had returned home for the purpose of talking with Vallandigham, and he urged the General to write a letter in favor of an armistice to lure the Ultras into his fold.[23] Another friend from St. Louis wrote in a similar vein, "I feel justified in saying that the Democratic and conservative party in the west will require an almost straightout peace platform for their presidential candidate, and opposition to Mr. Lincoln's *emancipation* proclamation, and to *confiscation* except by and under the constitution." Even Cox urged him to write a letter pledging to use "all rational methods at every honorable chance for peace." The Congressman further maintained that "the *ne plus ultras* of our party will take Peace and Union, if we don't insist on war in our platform." Vallandigham was adamant; the best he would concede to Morgan and Cox was that he would support McClellan if he won the nomination but that he would not speak in the canvass, which would have made his support rather hollow and ineffectual. The equally influential Samuel Medary, editor of the Columbus, Ohio, *Crisis,* was, according to Morgan, completely "incorrigible" and refused to accept the General under any circumstances.[24]

While Morgan, Cox, and others urged him to declare for an armistice to win the Ultras, others pressed McClellan to support the prosecution of the war. "If the ring of battle is not in the Presidential campaign platform, if the cry is for Peace, Peace, and some Vallandigham or Kin is associated with you (for Vice-Presi-

[23] Morgan to McClellan, August 4, 1864, McClellan Papers. McClellan later remarked, "Morgan is very anxious that I should write a letter suggesting an armistice! If these fools will ruin the country, I won't help them."

[24] Harrison to McClellan, August 1, 1864; Morgan to McClellan, August 14, 17, 1864; J. W. Fitch to Morgan, August 10, 1864; N. Capen to McClellan, August 17, 1864; W. H. English to McClellan, August 16, 1864; A. C. Niven to McClellan, August 17, 1864, McClellan Papers. Cox to Marble, August 7, 1864, Marble Papers.

dent) then our cause is lost," despaired one correspondent.[25] his father-in-law, Colonel R. B. Marcy, told him that John Douglas of Illinois claimed that the fight in the convention would be over the platform and that if the Ultras succeeded in forcing the meeting to adopt a peace plank, the party would be defeated. He urged McClellan not to accept under those circumstances.[26]

McClellan refused to make any further statements of policy after the Woodward letter in October, 1863. In June, 1864, he spoke at West Point during the dedicatory ceremonies for a new monument and reaffirmed the necessity for a restored Union, but he said no more. He did yield, however, to the entreaties of his friends to have some official representative at the convention who would be empowered to express his views if trouble arose.[27] And from the way the peace men acted, there did not seem to be the slightest doubt that such would be the case.

[25] S. L. Mershow to McClellan, August 12, 1864; John Hasting to McClellan, August 10, 1864; Joel Parker to McClellan, August 27, 1864, McClellan Papers.

[26] R. B. Marcy to McClellan, August 12, 1864, McClellan Papers.

[27] Harrison to McClellan, August 12, 1864; E. W. Cass to McClellan, August 18, 1864; [?] to McClellan, August 21, 1864, McClellan Papers.

) x (

The Chicago Fiasco

IT WAS a strange crew which trooped aboard the Democratic ark at Chicago on August 29, and Gideon Welles, who surveyed the proceedings from Washington via the press, drew a depressing picture of the delegates, "extreme partisans of every hue,—Whigs, Democrats, Know-Nothings, Conservatives, War men and Peace men, with a crowd of Secessionists and traitors to stimulate action—all uniting as partisans, few as patriots." In the face of such a motley opposition, he predicted, "I do not think that anything serious is to be apprehended from the Convention."[1]

The two paramount problems to be considered at Chicago were the selection of a candidate and the drafting of a platform. McClellan was already the most obvious choice for the nomination. He had great popularity with the War-Democrats, he had a strong following among the moderates, and could probably swing many of the independent votes, too. Much was made of his appeal to the fighting man. In the actual convention McClellan was nominated with scarcely any opposition, but before the first session took place on August 29, the delegates were gathered in many secret conclaves, the political cauldron was bubbling, as the peace men launched a movement to put forward the name of Governor Horatio Seymour.

Seymour had desired the Presidency for a long time. He was

---

[1] Welles, *op. cit.*, II, 120, 132. For the President's reaction to the forthcoming convention see Dennett, *Lincoln and the Civil War*, 193.

a bitter opponent of Lincoln's administration because he thought that Lincoln had yielded too often to the Unconditionals in order to win their support for his re-election. He could not stand McClellan, either, because he was a military man and in 1861 had participated in the arrest of the Maryland Legislature. This act led Seymour to rank the General in the same category as Lincoln— a menace to American civil liberties.

The launching of the Seymour boom at the preconvention caucuses was largely the work of Fernando Wood. Seymour had no great affection for the New York Copperhead leader or for the cause he represented, but he made no effort to prevent the use of his name by men whom he despised. Wood probably had no interest in Seymour, but was using him largely to kill off McClellan's chances. During the convention Wood was alleged to have remarked, "I don't care five cents for Seymour: he is only a convenient tool just now." There were high hopes among the anti-McClellan men that New York might be induced to give a complimentary vote for Seymour on the first ballot and thereby prevent the General from receiving the two-thirds vote necessary for nomination. Many delegates from Ohio were also actively working to induce others at the convention to cast a complimentary vote for Seymour.[2]

The first meeting of the New York delegation ended in a stalemate. When the anti-McClellan men learned on August 28 that the New York delegation had failed to make a decision on the candidate, their hope of having Seymour chosen revived. It was discovered that delegates from at least sixteen states personally favored the Governor as a compromise candidate between the peace and war factions, but they were all from delegations acting under the unit rule and were, therefore, powerless to act alone. McClellan's men kept fighting. An informal poll taken late in the evening of August 27 revealed that the General had 175 votes, or more than enough to assure his nomination on the first ballot. By Monday morning, August 29, it became apparent that the McClellan forces could not be checked. Seymour announced on

[2] The complete story of the Seymour boom at the preconvention caucus is told in William F. Zornow, "McClellan and Seymour in the Chicago Convention of 1864," *Journal of the Illinois State Historical Society*, Vol. XLIII (Winter, 1950), 282–95.

The Chicago Fiasco

Sunday that no more attention was to be given to his name. The New York delegation voted to support McClellan.

After the convention adjourned, George Mason wrote to Mc-Clellan and commented on the "honorable bearing" of Seymour throughout the convention. He advised the General that had the Governor been willing to have permitted the use of his name, Mc-Clellan's chances would have been less certain.[3] It is true that Seymour did not permit the use of his name after the opening of the official session on the twenty-ninth, but there can be little doubt that he did permit the peace men to use it in the preconvention meetings. Some of his confidential friends explained later that he had been playing a game to outwit Fernando Wood. Seymour, they maintained, knew that Wood and the Ultras were merely using him to defeat McClellan, but he allowed the Copperheads to use his name to prevent their going to someone else. It was Seymour's hope to turn the peace men to McClellan at the proper time. "He was afraid that if he withdrew his name at the start they would concentrate on some other man who would make mischief, and therefore he allowed his name to be used to prevent it," explained the Governor's partisans.[4] If such were his intentions, he neglected to reveal them to anyone in the New York delegation. Belmont, Tilden, and Richmond, the leaders of the New York delegation, were convinced that Seymour was in earnest about wanting the nomination and not merely seeking to mislead Wood and the Copperheads. Until Sunday, August 28, when he announced his withdrawal, Seymour was undoubtedly a serious contender for the Democratic nomination. He withdrew only after it was conclusively proved that he had no chance of securing the nomination. To show his dissatisfaction with McClellan, he threw his vote away on another nominee, but like all good party men he supported the General wholeheartedly after the nomination became official.

It has often been maintained that there was a bargain between the peace and war factions whereby the nomination of McClellan was bought by permitting the peace men to write the platform.[5]

---

[3] Morgan to McClellan, September 1, 1864, McClellan Papers.

[4] *New York Herald*, August 30, 1864.

[5] Kirkland, *op. cit.*, 133; Blaine, *op. cit.*, I, 527; Wood Gray, *The Hidden Civil War*, 183–84.

131

Lincoln & the Party Divided

The peace men, on the contrary, were never reconciled to accepting McClellan as the nominee, if one judges by the vehement opposition they offered to his selection both before and after the convention. If any bargains had been made, it does not seem possible that the peace faction would have opposed him so desperately. It seems much more reasonable that the Ultras came to the convention fully determined to capture both nominations and to write the platform, and that when they failed to accomplish this three-fold goal, they sulked, Achilles-like, in their tents.

The composition of the platform was the first official act of the convention. Vallandigham made a strong bid for the position of chairman of the Resolutions Committee, but he was finally overridden through the efforts of Samuel Tilden, August Belmont, William Cassidy, editor of the *Albany Argus,* and other New York leaders. Tilden's group succeeded in securing the election of James Guthrie of Kentucky by a vote of thirteen to eleven. Even though Vallandigham was defeated for the chairmanship, he still wielded great power on the committee, and according to his own testimony, "wrote the second, the material resolution of the Chicago platform, and carried it through the sub-Committee and the General Committee, in spite of the most desperate, persistent opposition on the part of Cassidy and his friends, Mr. Cassidy himself in an adjoining room laboring to defeat it."[6] This last statement should put the quietus on the assertion that there was a bargain permitting the Ultras to write the platform.

There were, in all, six resolutions presented to the assembly by the committee, but the second was the most significant. It resolved that:

This convention does explicitly declare, as the sense of the American people, that after four years of failure to restore the Union by the experiment of war, . . . justice, humanity, liberty and the public welfare demand that immediate efforts be made for a cessation of hostilities, with a view to an ultimate convention of the States, or other peaceable means, to the end that

[6] Vallandigham to the editor of the *New York News,* October 22, 1864, in McPherson, *op. cit.,* 423.

The classic likeness of the President
made by Mathew B. Brady

The Chicago Fiasco

at the earliest practicable moment peace may be restored on the basis of the Federal Union of the States.[7]

This famous "war failure" plank was adopted with great enthusiasm by the convention. The delegates apparently were not aware that they were offering the South an armistice with no *quid pro quo,* and that Davis's government would regard the whole thing as the equivalent of a Southern victory. It is difficult to understand why Samuel Tilden, who had fought so hard to make Guthrie chairman of the committee, did not speak out more emphatically against this plank. DeAlva Alexander, in his history of New York politics, suggested that Tilden held back because he feared that a fight over the platform might shatter the party as it had done in 1860, and that he further hoped McClellan's letter of acceptance might be worded in such a way as to act as an antidote to Vallandigham's poisonous platform.[8]

We do know that there were serious fights in the sessions of the Committee on Resolutions over the wording of the second plank. Vallandigham called attention to these efforts to defeat his resolution, but he added, "The various substitutes never at any time received more than three votes." He did modify his position slightly, but refused to accept the moderate's version completely. Amasa Parker claimed that the moderates wished to word the second resolution to read that "immediate negotiations ought to be commenced for the purpose of attaining peace on the basis of a restoration of the Union," but Vallandigham refused to assent to this version.[9]

After the adoption of the platform the convention proceeded to consider the nominations. This affair had already been settled shortly before the sessions began on August 29. On the first ballot McClellan polled 174 votes (one less than he received on the unofficial poll on Sunday); Thomas Seymour, 38; Horatio Seymour, 12; Charles O'Conor, 1/2; with 1 1/2 blank. This was amended to give McClellan 202 1/2 and Thomas Seymour 28 1/2, whereupon Vallan-

[7] McPherson, *op. cit.,* 419.
[8] Alexander, *op. cit.,* III, 110, 113; Nicolay and Hay, *Abraham Lincoln: A History,* IX, 256–57; Stewart Mitchell, *op. cit.,* 366–68.
[9] Parker to McClellan, September 5, 1864, McClellan Papers.

digham moved that the nomination be made unanimous. It was so done. While the states were casting their ballots for "little Mac," the peace men made it clear that they were not as yet fully resigned to accepting him as the candidate. Benjamin Harris of Maryland and Alexander Long of Ohio attempted to deliver speeches against him, while other delegates kept shouting for Seymour.[10] The die was cast, however, and the nomination of McClellan went through.

If the Ultras had been bested by the nomination of McClellan, they regained some of their lost advantage on August 31 when the Ohio Copperhead George H. Pendleton was selected as the vice-presidential nominee. On the first ballot Guthrie received 65½ to Pendleton's 55½, but on the second ballot New York swung its votes to the Ohio politico and the other states followed suit; whereupon he was nominated unanimously.

When the convention adjourned, there was still no indication that the peace men were reconciled to the nomination of McClellan. As he was leaving the convention, Vallandigham told one of the delegates that "he would keep quiet, withdraw his meetings, and with Medary and others have some tall cussing."[11] The cause was not entirely lost even then for the Ultras. There was some possibility that McClellan would reject the nomination. He had written before the convention that he would accept "unless it be coupled with conditions distasteful to [him]."[12] The second resolution might be just such a condition.

The Ultras earnestly hoped that McClellan would refuse the nomination because of the platform and thus make inevitable the selection of a peace man at a new convention. In fact, a resolution proposed by Charles Wickliffe of Kentucky and adopted by the convention declared that it would not adjourn *sine die* because it was possible that "circumstances may occur between now and the

[10] Brooks, *Washington in Lincoln's Time,* 184–85; *Official Proceedings of the Democratic National Convention Held in* 1864 *at Chicago,* 39, *passim;* Stewart Mitchell, *op. cit.,* 368–69; Eckenrode and Conrad, *op. cit.,* 271–72.

[11] Cox to Marble, September 19, 1864, Marble Papers. L. Edgerton to McClellan, September 3, 1864; John Douglas to McClellan, September 5, 1864, McClellan Papers.

[12] J. Lawrence to McClellan, August 31, 1864 (quoting McClellan), McClellan Papers.

4th of March next which will make it proper for the Democracy ... to meet in convention again." The convention could be convoked again at the discretion of the National Committee. There was much speculation among the Unionists over the import of the Wickliffe resolution, and they were inclined to suspect some diabolic plot or conspiracy on the part of the Democrats. Actually the correct explanation seems to be that the peacemen fully expected that McClellan would refuse the nomination and a new convention would be necessary. All eyes turned toward McClellan as he laboriously composed his letter of acceptance, or as the Ultras hoped, letter of rejection.

It took McClellan more than a week to write his letter of acceptance, and during that time he was constantly buffeted by the conflicting currents of party opinion. From several sources letters came to the General informing him of the hostility of the peace men who had nominated him only when it proved to be impossible to prevent his selection. "Mr. Wickliffe's resolution . . . ," said John Douglas, "was only done in the expectation that you would not accept that platform and this was the only method that the people could be driven from their enthusiasm for you, viz, kill you and then renominate one of the *Seymours*." George Train quipped, "As you are a railway man, General, you know that it is dangerous to stand on the platform." From all over the North came similar letters urging him to reject the platform and write his own.[13]

On the other hand, Vallandigham urged him not to come out too strongly for war or it would cost him two hundred thousand votes in the West.[14] In the face of such conflicting advice McClel-

[13] Douglas to McClellan, September 5, 1864; William Flagg to McClellan, Septembzer 11, 1864; George Curtis to McClellan, September 1, 1864; W. A. Stephens to McClellan, September 2, 1864; George Train to McClellan, August 31, 1864; John Day to McClellan, August 31, 1864; William Gray to McClellan, September 1, 1864; Hiram Ketchum to McClellan, September 1, 1864; Sidney Brooks to McClellan, September 1, 1864; Samuel Barlow to McClellan, September 2, 1864; William Daves to McClellan, September 2, 1864; E. Farreni to McClellan, September 2, 1864; Isaac Wister to McClellan, September 3, 1864; L. Edgerton to McClellan, September 3, 1864; Key to McClellan, September 4, 1864; W. Aspinwall to McClellan, September 4, 1864; D. Barnes to McClellan, September 5, 1864; F. Anderson to McClellan, September 6, 1864; John Whiting to McClellan, September 6, 1864; John Dix to McClellan, September 8, 1864, McClellan Papers.

[14] Vallandigham to McClellan, September 4, 1864, McClellan Papers.

lan wavered, and according to Charles Wilson, who has analyzed the various drafts of his letter of acceptance, he shifted his ground twice.[15] At the outset McClellan rejected all thought of an armistice in any sense. From this point he shifted to a pseudo-Ultra position and supported an armistice with no *quid pro quo*. Unlike the true Ultra, however, he believed that if the negotiations, which were to follow the cessation of hostilities, broke down, the war should be resumed. Overwhelmed by the pressure of his friends, he speedily departed from this unnatural position and, as one Republican wag asserted, "straddled the crack." On September 3 he was advised by Belmont that he should word his letter to indicate that "cessation of hostilities can only be agreed upon after we have sufficient guarantee from the South that they are ready for a peace under the Union." Probably influenced by such advice, the General rewrote his letter to assert that Southern recognition of the Union must be a preliminary to the cessation of hostilities:

> So soon as it is clear, or even probably, that our present adversaries are ready for peace, upon the basis of the Union, we should exhaust all the resources of statesmanship practiced by civilized nations and taught by the traditions of the American people, consistent with the honor and interests of the country, to secure peace, re-establish the Union, and guarantee for the future the constitutional rights of every State. The Union is the one condition of peace—we ask no more.[16]

This was no peace-at-any-price declaration. McClellan maintained that "no peace can be permanent without Union." He did not mention "war" in the letter, however, an omission undoubtedly prompted by the fact that many friends had advised him not to do so. In his letter McClellan angered the Ultras by speaking indirectly of the possibility of resuming the war in the event armistice negotiations failed and also by attaching conditions to his armistice offer. At the same time he betrayed the War-Democrats, who were opposed to an armistice in any sense.

[15] Charles Wilson, "McClellan's Changing Views on the Peace Plank of 1864," *American Historical Review*, Vol. XXXVIII (April, 1933), 498–510.

[16] McPherson, *op. cit.*, 421.

The Chicago Fiasco

Several of McClellan's friends hailed his letter of acceptance as a masterful document, but among the Ultra faction there was a general tendency to deprecate his action.[17] The general opinion among the Ultras was that the letter had placed him on the same platform with Lincoln. One peace journal wrote that the principles of the peace party had ceased to exist.

> The question then will be only as to how the war is to be carried on [said the editor] and not as to the unconstitutionality of the war. If the work of blood is to go on, Abe Lincoln is, no doubt, as efficient in its prosecution as General McClellan would be, while the policy of military necessity would be urged by the latter as well as the former, to justify whatever violations of the Constitution might be deemed expedient.[18]

The Ultra faction everywhere seemed to be in revolt against the letter.[19]

On September 14 a group of about fifty peace men assembled at the St. Nicholas Hotel in New York to consider the possibility of choosing another candidate. Benjamin Wood of the *New York News* and James McMaster of the *Freeman's Journal* were the moving spirits of the gathering.[20] The Copperhead leader Fernando Wood was not present at this abortive meeting, for two days previously he had written pledging support to McClellan.[21] In Ohio there were other indications that the peace faction would not accept McClellan after his letter was published. Vallandigham had already cancelled his speaking tour, and Alexander Long was calling for a new convention. Medary's *Crisis* failed to carry Mc-

17 R. B. Marcy to McClellan, September 8, 1864; Benjamin Rush to McClellan, September 9, 1864; Amos Kendall to McClellan, September 10, 1864, McClellan Papers. Robert Winthrop, *A Memoir of Robert C. Winthrop*, 235.

18 *Metropolitan Record* in *Albany Evening Journal*, September 14, 1864; *Chicago Tribune*, September 10, 1864; Mrs. Butler to Butler, September 14, 1864, in Marshall, *op. cit.*, V, 133–34; *New York News* in *Albany Evening Journal*, September 14, 1864.

19 Justin Morrill to Sumner, September 8, 1864, Morrill Papers (MSS in Library of Congress); Morgan to McClellan, September 16, 1864, McClellan Papers.

20 Wood Gray, *op. cit.*, 200–201; Kirkland, *op. cit.*, 137.

21 Fernando Wood to Frank McElroy, September 12, 1864, in *Albany Evening Journal*, September 15, 1864.

Clellan's name at its masthead. Medary was interested in the proposed peace bolt, but a fatal malady was already sapping his eagerness for the fight.[22]

While the meeting was in progress in New York, similar consultations were taking place in Ohio between Vallandigham and the chief leaders of the Sons of Liberty, an esoteric society over which he was the presiding officer. Efforts were made to induce the radical portion of the Ohio state ticket to withdraw and to have a new convention at Cincinnati. Before the month was out, however, Vallandigham had been approached by party leaders and induced to back McClellan. In his speeches he eulogized McClellan as a general and executive, but denied that he expressed the sentiments of the Democratic party.[23]

A few of the most vociferous die-hards among the Ultra faction resisted the appeals to close party ranks. In accordance with the suggestions made in New York and also at certain conferences in Ohio, a meeting was arranged in Cincinnati on October 18 and 19 under the auspices of William Corry and Alexander Long of Ohio, William Singleton of Illinois, and Lafe Develin of Indiana. About fifty delegates were present from Ohio, Indiana, Illinois, and Iowa. Resolutions were adopted declaring the war unconstitutional and imploring the Democrats to repudiate McClellan and select a new candidate. A nomination was offered to Long, who wisely declined it. Time for such a project was already running out, and when Long refused, the whole affair expired in its own insignificance.[24]

For better or worse, the Democrats had to begin their cam-

[22] *The Crisis,* September 9, 1864; *Chicago Tribune,* September 9, 1864; Riddle, *Recollections of War Times,* 295; Lansing to McClellan, September 26, 1864, McClellan Papers; Cox to Marble, September 21, 23, 1864, Marble Papers.

[23] Morgan to McClellan, September 16, 1864; D. Vorhees to McClellan, September 15, 1864; Amasa Parker to McClellan, September 16, 1864; George Pendleton to McClellan, September 27, 1864, McClellan Papers. Washington McLean to Marble, September 13, 1864, Marble Papers. *Cincinnati Commercial* September 26, 1864; James Vallandigham, *The Life of Clement L. Vallandigham,* 367.

[24] *Cincinnati Convention, October 18, 1864, for the Organization of a Peace Party upon State-Rights, Jeffersonian Democratic Principles and for the Promotion of Peace and Independent Nominations for President and Vice-President of the United States.* Wood Gray, *op. cit.,* 200–201.

paign with a platform proclaiming that "immediate efforts be made for a cessation of hostilities, with a view to an ultimate convention of the States" and a candidate running on a plank insisting that "the re-establishment of the Union in all its integrity is and must continue to be the indispensable condition of any settlement." The platform and the letter failed to clarify precisely where the Democracy stood, and there was much truth in an amusing appraisal written by Robert Schenck of Ohio, who said:

> The truth is that neither you nor I, nor the Democrats themselves, can tell whether they have a peace platform or a war platform; a peace ticket or a war ticket. Perhaps it may be explained in this way; that it is either one or the other, or both or neither; but upon the whole it is both peace and war, that is peace with the rebels but war against their own government.[25]

Actually there does not seem to be much doubt that with a few exceptions the overwhelming majority of the party wanted the restoration of the Union, but the question was whether the South was to acknowledge before the armistice that the Union was to be restored or whether the belligerents would lay down their arms first, without any condition attached, and then an "ultimate convention" would be called. McClellan's letter was in tune with the former view. The wording of the platform, especially the lack of reference to a *quid pro quo* and the unfortunate expression "ultimate convention" created the rub. Had the Confederacy obtained an armistice without any prior conditions attached, it would have achieved a victory. It was absurd to believe that under these circumstances a convention could have been called subsequently to arrange a reunion, and when the call failed, it was unlikely that the dispirited, demoralized North would have resumed hostilities.[26]

McClellan either saw or was shown that such a settlement was impossible and entirely incompatible with his previous training and public utterances. He, therefore, made the restoration of the

[25] *Letters of Loyal Soldiers.*
[26] *Harper's Weekly*, September 24, 1864; *The Great Surrender to the Rebels in Arms*, 5.

Union a condition for the cessation of hostilities, and by assuming this position, placed himself on the same platform with Lincoln.[27]

[27] James Randall, "Has the Lincoln Theme Been Exhausted?", *American Historical Review,* Vol. XLI (January, 1936), 288. There is a letter in the Andrew Johnson Papers (unsigned, undated) stating that Lincoln and McClellan held similar views and describing the struggle as merely the traditional rivalry of the "outs" to get "in" so that they could "fatten on [treasury] drippings." There is much truth in this despite its oversimplification.

) XI (

The Balance Shifts Back

THE PROSPECTS of Lincoln's re-election began to brighten almost immediately after the promulgation of the Chicago platform, for most of the Union party leaders and the Unconditionals were inclined to view it as treasonable.[1] From all directions came evidence that the platform had greatly enhanced Lincoln's chances of re-election, and various Unconditional leaders began to declare that in view of what had taken place at Chicago there was no alternative but to support the President.[2] Many staunch Democrats, too, were inclined to suspect their own party's loyalty and hastened to pledge their support to the administration.[3]

The Chicago platform put the quietus on the proposed new convention that had been planned at the Opdyke and Field meetings. There was still some talk on the subject, but the Democratic convention had made such a move unlikely.

Events were rapidly shaping in Georgia to prove that the Democrats' "war failure" plank was a palpable lie. Jefferson Davis replaced the careful Joseph E. Johnston, commanding the troops in

[1] Welles, op. cit., II, 129–30; Harper's Weekly, September 10, 1864.

[2] Bingham to Johnson, September 16, 1864, Johnson Papers; A. Taft to Wade, September 8, 1864, Wade Papers; W. B. Thomas to Chase, September 18, 1864, Chase Papers (Library of Congress); Sumner to Richard Cobden, September 18, 1864, in Moorfield Storey, Charles Sumner, 273–74; Daniel Dickinson to Cass, September 26, 1864, in John R. Dickinson, Speeches, Correspondence, etc., of the Late Daniel S. Dickinson, II, 658–59; Swett to his wife, September 8, 1864, in Tarbell, op. cit., II, 202–203.

[3] Frank Geise to McPherson, October 10, 1864, McPherson Papers.

Lincoln & the Party Divided

Georgia, with the more fiery John B. Hood. Abandoning the delaying tactics of his predecessor, Hood prepared to deliver a heavy blow against the more powerful Sherman at Atlanta. It was a desperate throw by a gambler who was risking all on one last chance. If Sherman could be shaken or driven back, it was almost certain that Lincoln would never be re-elected, and March 4 would find a Democrat in the White House. If the gambler failed, there would be no recourse but a Confederate evacuation of Atlanta and the re-election of Lincoln would be certain. The gambler threw and lost; Lincoln heard on September 3 that Atlanta had capitulated. The balance was swinging; the Democrat threat began to recede, and within a few weeks the dissenters were "all making tracks to Old Abe's plantation,"[4] as Bennett had predicted.

The victory at Atlanta was, therefore, the turning point of the canvass of 1864. Those who were discussing the possibility of another convention realized that it was now an impossibility.[5]

Though Lincoln seemed now a certain winner, there were still many fences to be mended, rivals to be placated, and prodigals to be welcomed back into the fold. After Hood's defeat, John Murray Forbes, a prime mover in the demand for a new convention, suggested a meeting in New York of certain men from the West who would take it upon themselves to organize the campaign and advise Lincoln. He especially feared that Lincoln might be induced by Raymond and others to begin negotiations with the South, feeling that Davis might be willing to listen to terms after the victory in Georgia. Governor Andrew, who had refused to attend the conference at David Dudley Field's home, agreed with Forbes that since Lincoln's re-election seemed certain, some of the "men of motive and ideas [should] get into the lead," assume control of the "machine and 'run it' themselves." He, too, was afraid that the President might yield to the saccharine persuasions

---

[4] *New York Herald*, August 24, 1864.

[5] Henry Elliott to Welles, September 5, 1864, Welles Papers; R. David to Joseph Holt, September 6, 1864, Holt Papers (MSS in Library of Congress); Butler to his wife, September 5, 1864, in Marshall, *op. cit.*, V, 125; G. B. Sedgwick to [John Stevens?], September 7, 1864, in *New York Sun*, June 30, 1889; H. W. Davis to [John Stevens?], September 4, 1864, in *New York Sun*, June 30, 1889; G. B. Sedgwick to Forbes, September, 5, 1864, in Sarah F. Hughes (ed.), *Letters and Recollections of John Murray Forbes*, II, 101.

of Raymond and others who were talking about offering the South terms; and to forestall such action, he arranged for a meeting in New York on September 12. Letters were written to the governors of Indiana, Illinois, and Ohio, urging them to join him in Washington so that the four could "rescue" Lincoln from "those who for the want of political and moral courage, . . . are tempting and pushing him to an unworthy and disgraceful offer to compromise with the leaders of the rebellion."[6]

There was no large meeting in New York on September 12 as planned, but there had been a great deal of personal consultation and written exchanges during the preceding week. The forces of opposition were melting away before the sun of Lincoln's revived popularity. Those who did gather in New York on the appointed day were a whipped lot, and the projected Cincinnati convention was abandoned ingloriously. George Wilkes wrote to Butler, "If we could only get a convention together we could make it the master of the situation, in despite of the Lincoln influences. . . . I confess, however, the prospect now looks very slim." In order to save the face of the conspirators, Wilkes suggested that, since the convention could not be assembled, they might "call mass meetings in every state, and request the people to inscribe their preferences on their ballots, by way of instructing the President how to form a Government. . . . This will enable us, here, to get gracefully out of the failure of the . . . Convention."[7]

The machinations, nevertheless, were finished; J. A. Willard wrote to Stevens that he concurred on abandoning the project; while Weed, who had kept an eagle eye on the whole sorry procedure, wrote to Seward a few days after the requiem was sung in New York for the departed spirit of the Cincinnati convention:

The conspiracy against Mr. Lincoln collapsed on Monday last [September 12]. It was equally formidable and vicious, embracing a larger number of leading men than I supposed possible. Knowing that I was not satisfied with the President, they came to me for cooperation, but my objection to Mr. Lincoln

[6] Pearson, *op. cit.*, II, 164–69.
[7] Wilkes to Butler, September 15, 1864, in Marshall, *op. cit.*, V, 134–35.

is that he has done too much for those who now seek to drive him out of the field.[8]

Governor Andrews, Forbes, and their colleagues bearing letters from Governors Yates and Brough hastened to Washington and implored Lincoln to listen to no more talk of peace while the rebellion was tottering.[9]

Although the threat of a new convention had expired as Sherman's veterans swung through the gates of Atlanta, there was still the problem of John Frémont's divertive Radical Democracy, which was very much alive. The next task was to inter it with the remains of the Cincinnati convention, and forces had been set in motion early in August with that objective in mind.

There never seemed to be any doubt that Frémont could hope for anything more than to create an embarrassing diversion within Lincoln's party. According to the Pathfinder's biographer, his personal papers nowhere contain the slightest indication that he expected to be elected. In fact, he had been hesitant about accepting the nomination. His lack of confidence and enthusiasm is understandable, for, according to Chittenden, "the nomination of Frémont fell upon the country so dead, that he probably had no friend who did not deeply regret that it had been made."[10]

The question naturally arises why Frémont accepted a nomination which carried with it such little chance of success. There are two possible explanations: he was merely working out a personal grudge against Lincoln or he regarded the Cleveland nomination as a steppingstone to something better. His friends were certain that he contemplated fusing his party with the Democrats and becoming the candidate of that group.[11] The fact that in his

---

[8] Willard to [John Stevens?], September 15, 1864, in *New York Sun,* June 30, 1889; Weed to Seward, September 20, 1864, Robert T. Lincoln Papers; Pearson, *op. cit.,* II, 171.

[9] Pearson, *op. cit.,* II, 171.

[10] Allan Nevins, *Frèmont, Pathmarker of the West,* 573; L. E. Chittenden, *Personal Reminiscences,* 1840–1890, 314–15.

[11] *Boston Transcript,* June 6, 1864; Gurowski, *op. cit.,* III, 251; *Indianapolis Gazette,* June 13, 1864; *Indianapolis Journal,* June 13, 1864; *Albany Evening Journal,* June 7, 1864; J. B. Bingham to Johnson, June 26, 1864, Andrew Johnson Papers; *Westliche Post in Harper's Weekly,* June 23, 1864; *Ohio State Journal,* June 8, 1864; *New York Times,* June 12, 28, 1864; *National Anti-Slavery Standard,* June 18, 1864.

The Balance Shifts Back

letter of acceptance he discreetly suppressed any reference to his earlier role in the emancipation controversy in Missouri and repudiated the confiscation plank was taken as evidence that he was seeking to placate the Democrats.[12] Frémont's relations with the Democratic party provides one of the most tantalizing and unscrutable aspects of the election of 1864. Some of his friends are known to have approached McClellan with an offer of support if Frémont were given the secretaryship of war or his old command in Missouri. As late as August, Frémont was alleged to have declared his willingness to withdraw from the race if McClellan was nominated. At the Democratic convention Caspar Butz urged his selection, and one of his former officers, Justus McKinstry, was there carrying a written pledge from Frémont to declare for an immediate armistice and a convention of the states. Frémont apparently hoped to win the party's nomination on the strength of this letter, but when he failed to do so, McKinstry was instructed "to make any arrangement which the Democrats determined to be best in regard to running or withdrawing from the Presidential contest."[13] McClellan was in no mood to come to terms with the Pathfinder.

Frémont failed to obtain the Chicago nomination, he failed to weaken Lincoln's chances of re-election, and he failed to come to terms with McClellan. There was nothing to do but withdraw from the race. Senator Chandler had been working since August to secure precisely that result.

Chandler spoke to both Wade and Davis, who agreed they would support Lincoln if Montgomery Blair was removed from the cabinet, and the President accepted their terms. Having performed the all-important task of reconciling Lincoln and the Unconditional faction led by Wade and Davis, Chandler next proceeded to attempt some negotiations with Frémont.[14]

[12] William Zornow, "Some New Light on Frémont's Nomination at Cleveland in 1864," *Lincoln Herald*, Vol. LI (October, 1949), 21–25.

[13] Myers, *op. cit.*, 443–44; Bartlett, *op. cit.*, 124. McClellan to Samuel Barlow, March 16, 1864; Max Langenschwarz to McClellan, August 10, 1864; R. B. Marcy to McClellan, September 13, 20, 1864, McClellan Papers. Barlow to Marble, August 24, 1864, Marble Papers.

[14] In fact some negotiations had been undertaken much earlier. Edgar Conkling to Butler, July 18, 1864; Mason Weld to Butler, July 26, 1864, in Marshall, *op. cit.*, IV, 510–11, 546–47.

Lincoln & the Party Divided

The Chandler-Frémont negotiations have provided much grist for the historical mill, with many interpretations often diametrically opposed. Earlier accounts connected closely the Frémont and Blair withdrawals as the outcome of a bargain arranged by Chandler. The most recent conclusion is that "Chandler was undoubtedly responsible for the immediate moves which led to both the removal of Blair and the withdrawal of Frémont, but there is little except hearsay evidence to show that there was any direct connection between the two events."[15]

Chandler went to New York and with the capable assistance of George Wilkes arranged some interviews with Frémont. He apparently offered Frémont a high command in the army and also mentioned that his tormentor Blair would be replaced. The removal of Blair was a secondary matter, for that would have occurred regardless of what Frémont said or did, because of the promises made to Wade and Davis. Frémont had had an earlier visit from Chase and Henry Wilson, who offered him a cabinet post and the dismissal of Blair if he would withdraw and support Lincoln. Despite the advice of some of his friends to do so, Frémont refused to withdraw after this earlier visit, and there is no evidence to indicate that he was any more amenable toward Chandler's offer.[16]

Frémont's withdrawal may have been hastened by the Chandler interview, but it probably came as a result of a realization that his position was hopeless. His plans to gain the Democratic nomination had gone awry. The military victories in September seemed to place him in opposition to Lincoln and cost him the support of the abolitionists. He could not scramble back on a war platform. He had renounced the position of his own party, and he was

[15] Charles R. Wilson, "New Lights on the Lincoln–Blair–Frémont 'Bargain' of 1864," *American Historical Review*, Vol. XLII (October, 1936), 71–78; Rhodes, *op. cit.*, IV, 529; Winfred Harbison, "Zachariah Chandler's Part in the Re-election of Abraham Lincoln," *The Mississippi Valley Historical Review*, Vol. XXII (September, 1935), 267–76; Bartlett, *op. cit.*, 128–29; Nevins, *Frémont, Pathmarker of the West*, 578–81; *Zachariah Chandler: An Outline Sketch of His Life and Public Services*, 273–77; Charles Moore, "Zachariah Chandler in Lincoln's Second Campaign," *The Century Magazine*, Vol. XXVIII (July, 1895), 476.

[16] Marcy to McClellan, September 23, 1864, McClellan Papers; Nathaniel Sawyer to Frémont, September 13, 1864, Johnson Papers.

spurned by the opposition. There was nothing left to do but withdraw, and he did so on September 22. The slurring comments which he made against Lincoln's administration in his letter of withdrawal seem to indicate that no "deal" had been made with Chandler.

The withdrawal of Frémont and his fellow nominee, Cochrane, convinced Lincoln that the psychological moment had arrived to fulfill his promise to Wade and Davis. On September 23, Blair resigned and went back to Maryland to enter the canvass for Lincoln. Everyone gave Chandler proper credit for having resolved a difficult situation, while the Michigan senator held a private "celebration" and in a most unaccustomed manner was actually "very complimentary to everybody."[17]

The good news of Atlanta had scarcely been made known when the victory snowball gained additional momentum. Sheridan smashed back the advancing Confederates at Winchester, while Farragut turned his guns successfully upon the enemy at Mobile. The malcontents began trooping back aboard Lincoln's bandwagon. While Wade and Davis were placated by a pledge that Blair would be removed, others joined because they saw that it was futile to resist Lincoln further. Senator Wilson of Massachusetts and Lyman Trumbull of Illinois entered the canvass early in September. Edward Everett, who had opposed Lincoln in 1860, was won over, while Sumner, now fully reconciled to having the Rail Splitter again, urged all former supporters of the old Bell-Everett ticket to follow their leader's example. Even Thad Stevens declared from the rostrum, "Let us forget that he [Lincoln] ever erred, and support him with redoubled energy." Representative George Boutwell of Massachusetts, Daniel Dickinson, Whitelaw Reid, and Anna Dickinson, all former opponents of Lincoln's re-election hastened to attest their newly discovered devotion. General Grant was induced to write a letter which could be construed as an endorsement for the Chief Executive's re-election. Salmon Chase hastened to Washington for a long, secret session with Lincoln. When he went to Ohio to enter the canvass,

---

[17] Rothschild, *op. cit.,* 326; William Smith, *The Francis Preston Blair Family,* II, 286–87; Gurowski, *op. cit.,* III, 359; J. K. Herbert to Butler, September 26, 1864, in Marshall, *op. cit.,* V, 167–68; Welles, *op. cit.,* II, 156–58.

many insisted that Lincoln had offered him the chief justice-
ship as bait.[18]

Lincoln did not neglect important newspaper editors. Greeley
swung back to Lincoln's side after the President apparently made
some vague promises about the possibility of making him postmaster general. He offered James Gordon Bennett of the *Herald*
the position of minister to France. Although Bennett refused the
offer, he, nevertheless, soon brought his paper over in favor of
Lincoln. John Murray Forbes was given credit for persuading
William C. Bryant to desist from his attacks on Lincoln and to
bring the *Evening Post* back into the Union fold.[19]

From all sides the dissident leaders hastened to renew their
fealty to Lincoln's administration. Every effort was being expended
to defeat the allegedly treasonable Democratic party. The Unconditionals, however, had renewed their loyalty with crossed fingers,
for most of them intended to revive the struggle after the vicissi-
tudes of the canvass were safely behind them. Colonel Shaffer
voiced the feeling of the majority when he wrote to Butler a week
before the canvass closed, "I promised Tremain that after the
smoke of election was well cleared away that I would go to New
York with a number of our live men and arrange for a general
attack front and rear on Lincoln." There was no doubt that, once
Lincoln was safely inaugurated, the conflict over reconstruction
and the Negro would be resumed with all its intensity.

---

[18] Charles Bartles to Trumbull, September 1, 1864, Trumbull Papers; Charles
Sumner, *Works,* IX, 68–69; Alphonse Miller, *Thaddeus Stevens,* 146–47; Richard
Current, *Old Thad Stevens: A Story of Ambition,* 203–204; Stevens to Morrill, Oc-
tober 7, 1864, Morrill Papers; George Boutwell, *Speeches and Papers Relating to
the Rebellion and the Overthrow of Slavery,* 347. Whitelaw Reid to John Stevens,
September 24, 1864; D. S. Dickinson to John Stevens, September 23, 1864; Chase to
John Stevens, September 20, 1864, all in *New York Sun,* June 30, 1889. *New York
Independent,* September 8, 1864; Butler to his wife, September 9, 1864, in Marshall,
op. cit., V, 128; Welles, *op. cit.,* II, 140–41; Herbert to Butler, September 26, 1864, in
Marshall, *op. cit.,* V, 167–68; Schuckers, *op. cit.,* 511; Charles Schmidt to Chase,
August 28, 1864, Chase Papers (Library of Congress); Grant to Elihu Washburne,
August 16, 1864, in *Appleton's Annual Cyclopedia for 1864,* 134.

[19] Don Seitz, *Horace Greeley,* 266–70; Dennett, *Lincoln and the Civil War,*
215; Weed to Bigelow, April 26, 1865, in John Bigelow, *Retrospections of an Active
Life,* II, 520; McClure, *Lincoln and Men,* 80–82; Seitz, *The James Gordon Bennetts:
Father and Son,* 191–95; Pearson, *op. cit.,* II, 164.

) XII (

Democrats and Traitors:
Twin Cherries on One Stem

T HE CHICAGO convention paved the way for the introduction of the domestic treason issue into the presidential canvass. It was probably inevitable that the issues involved in the election of 1864 should grow out of the all-important national endeavor to bring the war to a successful conclusion. The issue of domestic treason became the one most exploited by the Unionists during the campaign.[1]

Actually only a very small number of Democrats could be accused of treason *per se*. Many expressed their dissatisfaction with the administration's policies by individual comment and others saw fit to express theirs through quasi-secret societies. These expressions of antagonism to the war effort brought forth charges of disloyalty from the supporters of the administration. Such accusations were leveled not only at those who actively opposed and resisted the war effort but also at those who merely voiced protestations against the conduct of the war.

The forces of opposition to the administration found a cooperative medium in the secret politico-military societies founded in many states, especially those of the old Northwest. Undergoing reorganization from time to time, these forces were variously des-

[1] William Zornow, "Treason as a Campaign Issue in the Re-election of Lincoln," *Abraham Lincoln Quarterly*, Vol. V (June, 1949), 348–63; William Zornow, "Campaign Issues and Popular Mandates in 1864," *Mid-America*, Vol. XXXV (October, 1953), 195–216.

ignated as the "Knights of the Golden Circle," the "Order of American Knights," the "Order of the Star," and in and after 1864, as the "Sons of Liberty." The formal structure of these societies was both political and military in character. Lodges or temples were co-ordinated into political subdivisions under a hierarchy of officials with military titles. These societies were universally suspected of plotting against the government.

Since a blind partisan spirit dampened and even extinguished the patriotism of many Democratic leaders, and since the membership of the secret societies, allegedly carrying on disloyal or treasonable enterprises, came mainly from the ranks of the Democratic party, the issue of treasonable attitudes and activities supplied political capital for the Union party throughout the war.

The election year had scarcely dawned when the treason issue appeared in Congress. Since a formal canvass could not be undertaken until the parties had held their nominating conventions, had selected their candidates, and had formulated their platforms upon which to wage the campaign, congressmen were content to introduce the treason issue into the deliberations of the legislative body. During April an attempt was made to expel the Ultra leader, Alexander Long, from the House of Representatives. The whole affair generated much heat, with the congressmen dividing along party lines over the desirability of expelling the outspoken Ohioan. The newspapers speedily joined the fray, and in the course of the debates and editorializing an attempt was made to form a link in the public mind between Long, the whole Democratic party, and the odious term "treason."[2]

In June the issue was reheated and served up to the electorate by the publication of General William S. Rosecrans' report on the activity of secret societies in Missouri. The report alleged that the societies were plotting to overthrow the national government and establish a Northwest Confederacy. The newspapers were quick to open an attack on the Democrats. "There is nothing in the

[2] *Congressional Globe*, 38 Cong., 1 sess., 1499–1503, 1506–19, 1533–57, 1577–1606, 1618–35. For newspaper comment on the treason issue see: *Boston Post*, April 13, 1864; *Washington National Republican*, April 14, 1864; *Cleveland Leader*, April 16, 1864; *Chicago Tribune*, July 27, 1864; *Boston Daily Journal*, August 22, 1864; *Chicago Times*, January 19, 1864; *Cleveland Plain Dealer*, July 28, 1864; *The Crisis*, June 22, 1864.

Democrats and Traitors

record of treachery that can compare with this," observed an Ohio journal. "There is nothing in the history of conspiracy that equals the Democratic conspiracy in the bloodiness and villainy of its deliberate designs." And the *Chicago Tribune* noted that "an organized military conspiracy within the Democratic party of the North now exists, determined to array the whole Democratic party of the North in arms against the Government."[3] Such accusations were difficult to disprove, and all the Democrats could do was deny their guilt in most emphatic terms.[4]

Prior to the Chicago convention the accusations of treason remained more general than specific except in the case of the Rosecrans report. The deliberations at Chicago and the platform adopted, however, provided the opposition with a definite point for attack. Throughout the remainder of the campaign the Unionists assailed their opponents' convention and platform as treasonable.

The charges which the Unionists hurled at the convention and platform centered on four lines of attack. The first accusation was rather general and consisted of characterizing as treasonable all the speeches, deliberations, and activities of the Chicago convention. "Treason to the government has for hours at a time cascaded over the balconies of the hotels, spouted and squirted, and dribbled, and pattered, and rained on our out of doors listeners and pedestrians," reported the *Chicago Tribune*. Greeley's paper commented that each speaker "seemed to try his best to outdo the last in going to the furthest limits of treasonable speech." That every man at the convention was a "black hearted traitor" was the considered opinion of the *New York Times*.[5]

Such sweeping accusations could hardly have swayed many of the electorate. More direct and specific charges of treason were

[3] *Cincinnati Daily Gazette*, July 29, August 6, 24, 1864; *Chicago Tribune*, August 9, 1864; *Boston Daily Journal*, July 2, 30, 1864.

[4] James Vallandigham, *op. cit.*, 360; *Cleveland Plain Dealer*, July 29, August 1, 1864.

[5] *New York Tribune*, September 2, 1864; *Chicago Tribune*, August 31, 1864; *New York Times*, September 24, 1864; John Brough, *The Defenders of the Country and Its Enemies. The Chicago Platform Dissected. Speech Delivered at Circleville, Ohio, September 3, 1864*, 8; Gerrit Smith, *Gerrit Smith on McClellan's Nomination and Acceptance*, 14.

marshaled to prevent a Democratic victory at the polls. The second accusation directed against the Democrats was that their sympathy toward the Confederacy was apparent in their unwillingness to censure it in the platform. One Unionist organ cried, "It is a significant fact, too, that the speakers at the convention were men who have ... been noted as rebel sympathizers. ... It is likewise noticeable that not one word has been uttered in condemnation of the rebellion."[6] In denouncing the proceedings at Chicago for failing to condemn the rebellion, the Unionists hastened to point out that there had been no hesitation in attacking the administration. The *Philadelphia Press* commented on Seymour's keynote speech: "The speech made by Horatio Seymour ... is characteristic of the man and his party—not one word in denunciation of the rebellion, but hundreds in hatred of the Union." Governor Brough explained the failure to condemn the rebellion by charging that "the leaders of the Chicago Convention were the aiders and abettors of the Southern men who brought the rebellion upon us, and have been their sympathizers from that time to the present."[7]

The third point of attack on the platform insisted that it had been actually written at the instigation of Southern agents. In editorials and speeches the Unionists maintained that prior to the convention Democratic leaders went to Niagara Falls to confer with rebel agents and from this meeting emerged the platform adopted at Chicago. A Boston reporter wrote on the opening day of the convention, "The tone of the Convention to-day renders it certain that the programme agreed to at Niagara Falls between the Southern envoys and leading Democrats will be adopted here." "The Chicago Convention was really managed by a conclave of emissaries and diplomatists who have been rusticating at Niagara. ... These rebels and their Northern friends actually ... prepared the platform," claimed another writer. The *New York Tribune* insisted, "It [the platform] was concocted by Rebels in Richmond ... was agreed to by disloyal politicians of the North in a con-

[6] *Cincinnati Daily Gazette*, August 30, 1864; *New York Times*, September 7, 1864; *Philadelphia Press*, September 1, 30, 1864; *Cincinnati Daily Gazette*, October 18, 1864; *New York Herald*, September 28, 1864.

[7] *Philadelphia Press*, August 31, 1864; *New York Times*, September 10, 1864; Brough, *op. cit.*, 8; *New York Tribune*, October 24, 1864; *Cincinnati Daily Commercial*, September 12, October 19, 1864.

Democrats and Traitors

ference with Rebels at Niagara Falls—and was taken to Chicago and adopted by a convention expressly chosen to adopt it."[8] Other speakers, apparently unwilling to go along with these accusations, insisted that the platform had been written by the Sons of Liberty, the secret society suspected of being treasonable.

The fourth point of attack was directed along the line that the convention was merely a phase of the well-laid plans of the secret societies to rebel against the government. Some insisted that the party intended to rebel if it lost the election on the ground that there had been military interference at the polls. The *Boston Daily Journal* examined the platform editorially and found it composed of "hard words" which threatened "armed resistance to the government . . . in a certain contingency." Others claimed that the Democrats hoped to see the Union forever split. They are "ready to barter the integrity of the Union for the sake of political power," proclaimed the *New York Tribune.* "There were not twenty men in the Chicago convention who sincerely believed in the Union, or who made any demonstrations of regard for the Union that were not intended to swindle and deceive the people," trumpeted the *Philadelphia Press.*[9] In leveling their accusations of treason at the convention and platform, the Unionists proclaimed that the Democrats were unpatriotic, if not treasonable, to the Union. By these assertions they hoped to discredit the Democracy in the eyes of loyal voters and to enhance their own chances of victory.

The Democrats were hard pressed to find a means of replying to such accusations. The defense of their party revolved mainly around protestations that the Democracy was not a disunion party, but one whose chief aim was the restoration of the union. "The paramount aim of the Democratic party is to restore the Union," declared the *New York World,* and this theme was belabored in the press and on the stump alike.[10] Democrats were quick to

[8] *Boston Daily Journal,* August 30, September 29, 1864; *New York Tribune,* September 7, 22, 23, 1864; *New York Times,* September 7, 23, 1864.

[9] *New York Tribune,* September 8, 1864; *Philadelphia Press,* September 9, 23, 1864; *The Chicago Copperhead Convention,* 4; *Boston Daily Journal,* September 15, 1864; *Cincinnati Daily Gazette,* September 18, 1864; *New York Times,* September 23, 1864; Charles Drake, *Speech of Charles D. Drake Delivered Before the National Union Association at Cincinnati,* October 1, 1864, 15.

[10] *New York World,* September 1, 1864.

point out, with justification, that their platform was no different from Lincoln's program as outlined in his "To Whom It May Concern" letter.[11]

The Democrats apparently hoped to counterbalance their disadvantageous position on the treason issue by charges against the Unionists based on alleged violations of civil liberties. Placed on the defensive by the treason issue, the Democrats found it increasingly difficult to reply to these accusations. To complicate matters further, the charges that the Democrats were involved in a secret conspiracy came to the front again during August and the remainder of the canvass. Prior to the events which transpired in August, the Unionists' accusations were rather vague and indefinite; however, thanks to Governor Oliver Morton, they were soon able to present the voters with what appeared to be more tangible proof of Democratic perfidy.

Morton had received abundant proof during August that the possibility of his re-election to the governorship of Indiana was fading rapidly. The gloom of despair settled down over the state, and the embittered Democrats made no secret of the fact that they intended to call him to account at the polls. After every possible alternative for reviving the party's hopes seemed to prove fruitless, Morton decided to return once again to the time-honored strategy of domestic treason. This device had been applied with excellent results in the preceding elections. Once the bogy of treason was put on parade the fires of partisanship quickly rekindled.

In reviving the domestic treason issue in August, Morton not only rendered invaluable help to his own re-election, but greatly aided the national canvass as well. Many of the Democrats denounced the revival of the treason issue as the work of a desperate politician, but many others realized that a small faction of extreme peace men was playing into Morton's hands. These men had gone beyond the bounds of good sense in their attacks upon the state and the national administration, and it was easily possible for a

[11] *Cleveland Plain Dealer*, September 2, 22, 1864; *New York World*, September 26, 27, 28, 1864; *Boston Daily Journal*, September 19, 1864; Henry Clinton, *Speech of Henry L. Clinton of New York at Patchogue, Long Island, October 1, 1864*, 1, 20.

shrewd politician like Morton to convince the voters that the position occupied by these Ultras was the position occupied by the party as a whole.

By means of several spies and turncoats, Morton and General Henry C. Carrington, military commander in Indiana, kept a close check on the Sons of Liberty in their state.[12] On July 30, Morton and Carrington published a report on the activities of the secret societies in the *Indianapolis Daily Journal,* that was later issued in pamphlet form for circulation as campaign literature. No treasonable evidence was presented in the document except for the editorial comments of Carrington and the distortions which the Union press was willing to make in the wording and interpretation of the report. Union editors, often with tongue in cheek, wrote of their horror at learning of this most diabolic conspiracy against the safety of the country. It was about that time that Harrison Dodd, grand commander of the Sons of Liberty in Indiana, played into Morton's hands and also those of the national politicians by engineering an absurd scheme which seemed to be the final proof of the Unionists' assertions.

Dodd and some of his friends planned to liberate Confederate prisoners at Camp Morton, seize the arsenal, and raise a general insurrection throughout the state. Presumably they intended to create some kind of a Northwest Confederacy. The coup was to take place on August 16. Through his spy, Felix Stidger, Morton learned most of the facts about the conspiracy, and he sat back waiting for Dodd to complete his scheme.

The Grand Commander continued to apprise others of his plans, one of whom was J. Bingham, editor of the *Indianapolis State Sentinel* and chairman of the state central committee. Bingham was flabbergasted at Dodd's plans, and in a solemn meeting on August 5 the party leaders exacted an oath from Dodd and his companions that they would abandon such an irrational scheme. August 16 came and went with no repercussions; the revolt was

---

[12] Kenneth M. Stampp, "The Milligan Case and the Election of 1864 in Indiana," *The Mississippi Valley Historical Review,* Vol. XXXI (June, 1944), 41–58. Benn Pitman (ed.), *The Trials for Treason at Indianapolis,* 80 ff.; Felix Stidger, *Treason History of the Order of Sons of Liberty.*

a failure. No overt act was committed, and the Sons of Liberty and the party were in no way implicated in Dodd's scheme.[13]

Morton was not so easily bilked. His agents raided Dodd's office and seized some weapons and a great deal of personal correspondence which linked many prominent Democrats with the Sons of Liberty. Dodd was subsequently arrested as he returned from the Chicago convention and placed on trial for treason on September 22 at Indianapolis.

Throughout the trial the prosecution could never advance its evidence against the Sons of Liberty and the Democratic party beyond mere rumor and hearsay. The absence of conclusive proof, however, did not deter the Union leaders from continuing their accusations of Democratic treason. The press carried full reports of the trial as it unfolded, and Carrington, presiding Judge Alvin Hovey, and Morton continued to make speeches to drive home the point that the Sons of Liberty was a treasonable society in which the majority of the members were Democrats. The message of Democratic perfidy was carried over the nation. The wavering were won to the cause. The apathy of August gave way to a bustling activity, as the voters turned out to hear stump orators haranguing about treason. Gustave Koerner, who was campaigning for Lincoln, wrote that it was useless to speak unless one chose as his text the time-honored one of domestic treason. Audiences were loath to listen to anything else.[14] "The exposé of the Sons of Liberty is tearing the ranks of the Democracy to flinders," wrote a Unionist in Indiana. "McClellan stock is not quoted at all. McDonald [gubernatorial nominee in Indiana] stock is fast going down."[15] Edward Bates wrote in his diary that "even matters of the gravest intrinsic importance are, just now, viewed and acted upon only in their relations to the pending elections—e.g. the prosecution of Dodd et al (*Sons of Liberty!*) in Inda."[16] There could be no doubt that the Unionists were finding the Dodd trial an excellent bit of political capital.

[13] Stampp, "The Milligan Case and the Election of 1864 in Indiana," *The Mississippi Valley Historical Review*, Vol. XXXI (June, 1944), 50.

[14] Gustave Koerner, *Memoir of Gustave Koerner, 1809–1896*, II, 434–36.

[15] W. H. Terrell to General Wilder, September 6, 1864, in Stampp, "The Milligan Case and the Election of 1864 in Indiana," *The Mississippi Valley Historical Review*, Vol. XXXI (June, 1944), 55.

[16] Beale, *op. cit.*, 422.

Democrats and Traitors

While the trial was in progress, Dodd managed to escape from his cell window and flee to Canada. The Unionists hailed his flight as conclusive proof of his guilt and continued to hammer away in their effort to identify the Democratic party with the forces of treason. Other members of the Sons of Liberty, Lambdin P. Milligan, Horace Heffren, Andrew Humphreys, and John C. Walker, were taken into custody to undergo a similar trial at a propitious moment.

The Dodd trial had no sooner ended than Judge Advocate General Joseph Holt issued a report on October 16 further exposing the activity of the secret societies. This report was based to a large extent on information supplied by Rosecrans, Carrington, Morton, and Colonel Sanderson, who had been investigating the organizations for many months. The Holt report served as a convenient device to keep the public aware of the nature and magnitude of the treason being committed by the Democratic party. A special edition was prepared and circulated as campaign propaganda.[17] "If there is a prudent, a thoughtful, a patriotic man in this country who thinks of voting for McClellan, we pray him to study the astounding testimony in the treason trial at Indianapolis," said the *New York Tribune*. "There is no longer room for a doubt of its nefarious purposes. The evidence in the trial of Dodd . . . is overwhelmingly conclusive," echoed the *Boston Daily Journal*. In speaking of the Sons of Liberty, the same paper observed, "The members of the organization unquestionably all call themselves Democrats." So the link was formed in the public mind between the Democracy and treason.[18]

Against this attack the Democrats had no defense and merely revealed their impotence by the billingsgate denunciation they

---

[17] *Report of the Judge Advocate General on 'The Order of American Knights', Alias 'The Sons of Liberty': A Western Conspiracy in Aid of the Southern Rebellion. New York Tribune*, October 17, 1864. One of Holt's friends wrote that his "report came out at a most auspicious moment and is doing a world of good." R. W. Williams to Holt, October 26, 1864; E. Dennis to Holt, October 24, 1864; D. Hooper to Holt, November 4, 1864; S. Pooley to Holt, November 5, 1864, Holt Papers.

[18] *New York Tribune*, October 3, 4, 1864; *Chicago Tribune*, October 8, 1864; *Albany Evening Journal*, October 5, 1864; *Boston Daily Journal*, October 12, 24, 1864; *Ohio State Journal*, October 17, 1864; *Cleveland Daily Leader*, October 17, 1864; *Harper's Weekly*, October 29, 1864; *Detroit Advertiser and Tribune*, August 24, 25, 29, September 9, 1864.

poured upon Sanderson, Carrington, and the others.[19] Some Democrats sought to defend themselves by ridiculing the report and the trial. The *Boston Post* sarcastically remarked, "Mr. Holt—for some time—has turned his attention to inventing Democratic conspiracies." The *New York World* scoffed at his report of a "rigamarole meal-tub plot" as "monstrously absurd." The *Cincinnati Daily Enquirer* labeled it as a "cold blooded piece of campaign propaganda printed and circulated at public expense."[20]

In addition to the exposé of the activities of the Sons of Liberty in Indiana and of Dodd's conspiracy, other plots were revealed during the late summer to facilitate Unionist victories in the state and national canvass. The *Chicago Tribune* reported a plot to liberate 6,000 prisoners from Camp Douglas near Chicago. The chief spy in the Camp Douglas drama testified that the 150 most influential men in the Sons of Liberty in Illinois paralleled the list of the 150 most prominent men in the Democratic party. Many claimed that Democratic party meetings were in reality sessions of the secret order and that campaign funds were actually being collected for the purpose of buying weapons. In Ohio a conspiracy led from Canada by John Y. Beall for the purpose of liberating Confederate prisoners on Johnson's Island and capturing the *U.S.S. Michigan* on Lake Erie was alleged to have been hatched by the Sons of Liberty and the Democrats. A rumor spread that Confederate agents were gathering in Canada to burn Detroit in the event the Democrats lost the election.[21]

In addition to attacking the Democratic party as an organization and trying to stigmatize it as treasonable, the Unionists

---

[19] *The Crisis*, August 10, 1864; *Detroit Free Press*, August 2, 1864; *Chicago Times*, September 7, 1864.

[20] *Boston Post*, October 17, 1864; *New York World*, October 20, 1864; *Cleveland Plain Dealer*, October 24, 1864; *Ohio State Journal*, October 29, 1864; *Cincinnati Daily Enquirer*, October 16, 20, 1864; *Madison Patriot*, November 3, 1864; *Chicago Times*, September 16, 1864.

[21] *Chicago Tribune*, November 8, 9, 1864; *Chicago Times*, November 8, 9, 1864; Arthur C. Cole, *The Era of the Civil War*, 310–11; I. Winslow Ayer, *The Great Northwestern Conspiracy in All Its Startling Detail*, 111–12. H. Rossman to C. A. Dana, October 13, 1864; H. Rossman to Holt, September 29, 1864, Holt Papers. William Zornow, "Confederate Raiders on Lake Erie: Their Propaganda Value in 1864," *Inland Seas*, Vol. V (Spring, 1949), 42–47 (Summer, 1949), 101–105.

Democrats and Traitors

also directed some of their heaviest fire against McClellan and Pendleton. There was an oft repeated rumor that McClellan had visited Lee shortly before the battle of Antietam. Some insisted he had volunteered his services to the Confederacy; others claimed he had given ammunition to Lee during the battle of Antietam. There was another story that he had hidden away safely aboard a gunboat during the cannonading at Malvern Hill. In comparing McClellan to the peace men, Gerrit Smith noted, "It is true that their treason is more open and noisy than his, but his is nevertheless as real and earnest as theirs."[22] Pendleton came in for a share of the venom too. A pamphlet was prepared to acquaint the voters with the full range of his treason. "George H. Pendleton . . . ," declared the document, "has persistently pursued in Congress that course most calculated to encourage the armed enemies of the country, and to foster secession and treason of all kinds and grades." Pendleton's career was set forth in the most damning light. He was labeled "the Great Dodger" because, the Unionists said, whenever a bill was being discussed or voted upon in Congress which would be beneficial to the Union, Pendleton dodged into the cloakroom to avoid having to vote for it!

What hurt the Democrats most in attempting to defend their party against the charge of treason was that many of their own members turned on them and joined the attack. The War-Democrats, who were campaigning for Lincoln, always made it clear that they were not proud of the treason-ridden Democratic party. They urged all other Democrats who loved the Union to support Lincoln. As John Dix said, "We can have no companionship with this infidelity to the country, and to the Democratic party. We repudiate the action of the convention as untrue to all the obligations of duty, and as a misrepresentation of the feelings and opinions of those for whom it assumed to speak." Hiram Walbridge added,

[22] Emile Bourlier to the Union League of Philadelphia, September [?], 1864, Western Reserve Historical Society MSS; Edgar Conkling to Holt, November 7, 8, 1864, Holt Papers; *New York Tribune*, August 30, September 7, 16, 1864; *New York Times*, September 8, 1864; Gerritt Smith, *op. cit.*, 12. Lincoln apparently doubted McClellan's loyalty. See: Dennett, *Lincoln and the Civil War*, 218–19; Benjamin F. Wade, *Facts for the People. Ben Wade on McClellan and Generals Hooker and Heintzelman's Testimony; Sights and Notes by a Looker-on in Vienna;* George Wilkes, *"McClellan" Who He is and "What He has Done" and Little Mac: "From Ball's Bluff to Antietam."*

Lincoln & the Party Divided

"For myself I can read the Chicago platform no otherwise than as a white flag of surrender to the rebels."[23] There were many Democrats in 1864 who were convinced that their party was tainted with treason and who sought to entice their fellows away from supporting it. They appealed to the latter by taking to the stump for Lincoln and by assembling in New York in a body to protest against the proceedings at Chicago and to repudiate them in the name of all loyal Democrats.

During the canvass the attack on the platform and the "war failure" plank was probably misdirected, for it assumed disloyal intentions on the part of those who had framed the document. Actually such was not entirely the case, for even most of the peace men wanted an armistice as a preliminary step toward an ultimate convention and a reunion of states. The majority of the party stood with McClellan on a platform calling for a vigorous prosecution of the war and for peace only after the South had accepted reunion.

The implication that the Democrats were involved with the secret societies in some diabolic conspiracy against the government was the most damaging thrust of all. Any Democrat who did not support the administration was indiscriminately lumped with the Copperheads. What was a Copperhead? In answer to that question Benjamin Butler compared one to a combination of Benedict Arnold and Judas. Another wag defined a Copperhead as a rebel posing as a Democrat. Republican syllogisms constructed around the words Copperhead, Democrat, traitor, and rebel were presented *ad nauseam*. It is not difficult to sympathize with Allen Thurman of Ohio, who at the Democratic state convention of 1862 lamented, "Never since God made this world has any party been so infamously treated as has the Democratic party since this war began. Though you give your flesh and blood to put down rebellion, if you do not favor abolition you are denounced as a rebel sympathizer."[24]

[23] *Ohio State Journal*, November 5, 1864; *New York Tribune*, November 2, 1864; *Harper's Weekly*, October 22, 1864; *Cleveland Daily Leader*, November 4, 7, 1864; Dickinson, *op. cit.*, II, 659–60; Henry Conkling, *op. cit.*; Morgan Dix, *Memoirs of John Adams Dix*, II, 93; *Letters of Loyal Soldiers*, 4; William Swinton, *The War for the Union from Fort Sumter to Atlanta*.

[24] *Madison Patriot*, May 4, 1863; John S. Hare, "Allen G. Thurman: A Political Study" (unpublished Ph.D. dissertation, Department of History, Ohio State Univer-

Democrats and Traitors

As indefensible as the attacks on the Democrats' platform and convention, and the insinuations that they were engaged in treasonable enterprises, may be, the charges against McClellan and Pendleton reached the nadir of campaign strategy. In the long run, however, if one can believe Edward Bates, the denunciation of McClellan as a traitor hurt the Unionists more than it aided them. Bates noted that "these charges of treachery and treason, not well established by proof, do but take off the edge from other accusations which cannot be defended, thus, discrediting the best founded objections against him, and exciting a popular sympathy for him as a persecuted man."[25]

The accusation of treason was the most decisive issue presented in the campaign. Thurlow Weed, who was probably a competent authority on judging the various factors involved in the campaign, wrote that "the disloyalty of the Democratic party . . . worked its own over-throw. Mr. Lincoln is to be re-elected (if at all) on the blunders and folly of his enemies."[26]

More important than the fact that the treason issue was the most used and probably most decisive issue of the campaign of 1864 is the fact that the opprobrium of treason was to hang upon the Democratic party for twenty years. The "Great Conspiracy" of 1864 was the warp in the fabric of the "Bloody shirt." Daniel Dickinson, writing in August 1864, when the specter of domestic treason was beginning to stalk the canvass, said concerning the Democratic party, "Now it has the taint of disloyalty, which whether true or false will cling to it, like the poisoned shirt of Nessus, for a century."[27] His was a most prophetic observation.

sity, 1933), 123. Frank Klement, "Middlewestern Copperheadism: Jeffersonian Democracy in Revolt" (unpublished Ph.D. dissertation, Department of History, University of Wisconsin, 1946), 210.

[25] Beale, *op. cit.,* 423 .

[26] Weed to John Bigelow, October 19, 1864, in Bigelow, *Retrospections of an Active Life,* II, 221–22.

[27] Dickinson to Colonel Willard, August 15, 1864, in Dickinson, *op. cit.,* II, 656.

XIII

The Democratic Response

WHILE THE Union party was succeeding so completely in fixing the stigma of treason upon its political opponents, the Democrats were hard pressed to uncover an issue which they could inject into the campaign to counteract these damning allegations. The whole campaign resulted in a general obscuring of issues. The voting public went to the polls in November with no clear issues before it. The false emphasis which the Union press and speakers continued to place upon the "war failure" plank beclouded the basis facts of the campaign. Actually, Lincoln and McClellan were agreed on nearly all fundamental points except emancipation. Had the Democrats won the election, they would have been under the leadership of a man whose previous training, public utterances, and letter of acceptance made it clear that he would accept no peace with the Confederacy except on the basis of a prior recognition of the Union.[1] This fact was reiterated by leading party spokesmen on innumerable occasions. In speaking of the Chicago convention, Seymour remarked, "I have seen much of political gatherings, but never before did I attend a convention so absorbed by one single idea—to save our Union and to save our country." Even Copperhead Pendleton insisted the party was pledged to "the restoration of peace on the basis of the Federal Union of the states."[2]

[1] George McClellan, *West Point Oration*, 6.
[2] Thomas Cook and Thomas Knox, *Public Record . . . of Horatio Seymour*, 241.

The Democratic Response

Many Unionist editors knew the true situation and fearing that their readers realized McClellan was committed to a restoration of the Federal Union, hastened to add that the General would not really be the master of his party but would yield the scepter to the Copperheads. "The imbecility of McClellan will surrender it [the country] to the traitors' hands," said one Unionist. Another opined that neither McClellan nor the War-Democrats would "have any hand in shaping the policy of the party," but that would be done by Vallandigham, "a southerner by birth and a traitor by profession." Sumner remarked that McClellan could no more become separated from the platform than the Siamese twins could be sundered.[3]

The editors insisted that the Copperheads were ready to destroy the Union for the sake of peace. Here again they beclouded the facts of the campaign, for most of the Copperheads did not wish to see the Union shattered. To be sure, there was a leaven of such wild fanatics within the Democratic party, but they constituted a decided minority. Although they clamored for peace, the majority of the Copperheads also stood for an armistice and an "eventual convention" of the states to discuss reunion. They may not have been able to achieve such an aim, especially after the fighting had been suspended, but that does not detract from the fact that they sincerely believed the Union could be restored only by an armistice and negotiation.

The voters in 1864 went to the polls with no clear conception of what the issues were before them. They had read and been told incessantly that a vote for the Democrats was a vote for Jeff Davis and disunion. To the average Northerner, who had seen his friends and family march off to the war and who had himself borne the myriad hardships of the crisis, it was unthinkable that such sacrifices would lead only to disunion and dishonor. Not only did he hear that the Democrats were actually in league with the enemy, but at the critical moment in the canvass came the glorious vic-

McPherson, *op. cit.*, 422; George Comstock, *Let Us Reason Together, Speech Delivered at the Brooklyn Academy of Music*, 2; Robert Winthrop, *Speech of Honorable R. C. Winthrop at the Great Ratification Meeting in Union Square, New York, September 17, 1864*, 6–7.

[3] John Hamilton, *Coercion Completed or Treason Triumphant*, 24; Charles Bristed, *The Cowards' Convention*, 3.

tories in Georgia. There was no need to make an appeal to reason, for it would have been lost in the excitement of the moment. There were no forward-looking issues in the campaign.[4]

Since it became apparent late in the canvass that victory was in sight, it seems likely that the question of reconstruction would have become one of the principal issues of the campaign, but such was not the case. The prospect of having reconstruction introduced as an issue was none too pleasant for the Unionists; it was a question which had already seriously weakened their party. "I most fear the rock on which we shall split will prove to be reconstruction," said one of Justin Morrill's correspondents as he voiced the fears of many.[5]

The Union party was filled with many small springs of tension which threatened to become uncoiled at any moment. There was the ever present rivalry of Unconditionals and moderates. Many of the former had grown suspicious of Lincoln's designs and were prone to condemn not only his moderate policies but also his practice of rewarding many of his old Whig cronies and former Democrats. There was a faint stirring of nativism among the members who hated to see the party making concessions to foreign voters.[6] Wisdom dictated putting the quietus on the reconstruction question, for there was no point in further aggravating a delicate situation.

A discreet silence on the question of reconstruction was maintained by the Unionists for several months before their convention, and at Baltimore no reference was made in the platform to this troublesome problem. The rallying cry was based on an appeal for all-out co-operation to win the war. There had been a few malcontents who sought to upset the delicate equilibrium by introducing the problem of reconstruction in the Cleveland platform.[7] It was fortunate, indeed, that circumstances prevented this movement from assuming greater proportions; otherwise the party might have divided.

[4] Arthur Cole, "Lincoln and the Presidential Election of 1864," *Illinois State Historical Society Transactions* (1917), 136–37.

[5] W. Swiatt to Morrill, June 2, 1864, Morrill Papers.

[6] Arthur Cole, "Lincoln and the Presidential Election of 1864," *Illinois State Historical Society Transactions* (1917), 132–33.

[7] Lee Norton, *War Election, 1862–1864*, 36–38.

The Democratic Response

The Democrats were aware that reconstruction was the Achilles' heel of the Union party. They sought to bring it into the campaign as an issue, in the hope, perhaps, that it would sunder the opposition. They took the view that the rebellious states were still within the Union and were embraced by the Constitution. The President had no authority to make conditions not fixed by the Constitution as a basis for their recognition as states. His only duty was to execute the laws and subdue the armed power of the rebels. Whenever armed resistance ceased, the states would be restored without condition and without change.

They sought in every way to couple the Democracy with the forces of peace and reunion. They insisted, as was indicated in the previous chapter, that theirs was the true Union party. It was their intention, they claimed, to restore the Union under the old Constitution. The Unionists, according to the Democratic version, were seeking to make the restoration of the Union of secondary importance to the destruction of slavery.[8] They insisted that the Union party, which was seeking to reconstruct the Union on the basis of emancipation and vindictive measures, could never hope to achieve peace. Speaking of the autumn victories, Seymour said, "These victories will only establish military governments in the South, to be upheld at the expense of Northern lives and treasure. They will bring no real peace, if they only introduce a system of wild theories, which will waste as war wastes; theories which will bring us to bankruptcy and ruin. The administration cannot give us union or peace after victories."[9]

The Democrats not only claimed that their opponents were making peace and reunion impossible by insisting upon emancipation and other excessively severe conditions, but also tried to show that by freeing the Negro, they were sanctioning his equality and encouraging racial amalgamation.[10]

[8] George McClellan, *Letter of Acceptance*, 1; *Cleveland Plain Dealer*, October 14, 1864; Joel Parker, *Speech . . . at Freehold, New Jersey, August 20, 1864*, 4; Amasa Parker, *Speech of the Hon. Amasa J. Parker at the Cooper Institute*, 6; Sanford Church, *Speech by Hon. Sanford E. Church at Batavia*, October 13, 1863, 3.

[9] Cook and Knox, *op. cit.*, 253; Winthrop, *A Memoir of Robert C. Winthrop*, 3–4; Belmont, *op. cit.*, 142–44; *Hear Honorable George H. Pendleton*, 5–8.

[10] Sidney Kaplan, "The Miscegenation Issue in the Election of 1864," *Journal of Negro History*, Vol. XXXIV (July, 1949), 274–343; *Cleveland Plain Dealer*, October 14, November 3, 1864; Ketchum, *op. cit.*, 64; John D. Hopkins, *Bible View*

Lincoln & the Party Divided

Not only did they claim that reconstruction based on emancipation would prolong the war and make the Negro the equal of the white man, but they also attacked Lincoln's moderate 10 per cent plan as an insidious scheme to perpetuate his administration in power. George Comstock, for example, complained:

> That I do not misinterpret the design of Mr. Lincoln or the meaning of this extraordinary decree is proved with absolute demonstration by his so-called 'amnesty' or plan of reconstructing the seceding states. . . . Under it the spurious states have sprung into being, whose votes are expected to be given to the author of their existence. Other spurious states are to arise.

Throughout the canvass the Democrats sought vaguely to introduce the reconstruction issue by insisting that the country should be restored solely on the basis of the Constitution. They closely associated emancipation with reconstruction by claiming that the former should not be made a basis for peace or readmission to the Union. They were willing to leave the Negro in bondage and censured their opponents for demanding his freedom on the ground that such a demand was prolonging the conflict and would be detrimental to Northern white labor if carried out. Peace, they maintained, was impossible on such a condition. Furthermore, they claimed, even Lincoln's modest plan of reconstruction was designed for the ulterior motive of assuring his re-election.[11] That the Unionist plan of reconstruction was completely illegal, since neither Congress nor the President had any right to impose terms upon the states contrary to the Constitution, was their main theme.

The Unionists consistently refused to join forces with the Democrats on the reconstruction issue, although the gauntlet was

of Slavery; Samuel F. B. Morse, *An Argument on the Ethical Position of Slavery in the Social System and Its Relation to the Politics of the Day; Lincoln Catechism Wherein the Eccentricities and Beauties of Despotism Are Fully Set Forth,* 27–28; Charles Mason, *The Election in Iowa; Miscegenation Endorsed by the Republican Party; Emancipation and Its Results.*

[11] Comstock, *op. cit.,* 6–7; *Cleveland Plain Dealer,* October 15, 1864; *The Crisis,* October 26, 1864; *New York World,* October 26, 1864; *Address of the National Democratic Committee. The Perils of the Nation. Usurpations of the Administration in Maryland and Tennessee,* 3.

The Democratic Response

thrown to them on several occasions. The question loomed during the summer months within Union party ranks. The conflict provoked over Lincoln's message to Congress and his veto of the Wade-Davis bill was serious, but the important point is that this deep-seated conflict within the party was never allowed to become an issue in the campaign. Conditions in September forced even the wildest to renew their homage to Lincoln, and the Radical Democracy, which might have exploited the question as an issue, conveniently expired later that month.

The voter was never presented with a clear conception of the various modes of reconstruction. At least the campaign speeches, pamphlets, and newspapers gave him no enlightenment on this bothersome question. Since these three media were the average man's source of information on all political questions, it is safe to assume that the majority knew little or nothing of the various phases of the problem. Perhaps the man in the street did not really even care to know, for the war was yet to be won, and victory was the voter's principal concern rather than the problem of a peace which was at least several months removed.

Since the issue of reconstruction was so vaguely presented on the national level by the Union party and was scarcely mentioned at all on the lower electoral levels, popular opinion on this matter could not have been else but confused. The voters did not have an opportunity to express an opinion on this point, since the issue was not clearly presented to them. It is inconceivable that the Unconditionals could later justify their program during Johnson's administration as the fruit of a popular mandate they had been given in 1864.

This confusion did not apply to the question of emancipation, for the issue on this point was introduced on the national, state, and local levels so consistently and so transparently that there was no doubt where the parties stood. In April the Senate had passed a resolution, which was destined to become the future Thirteenth Amendment, and sent it to the House, where it was defeated by sixty-five Democratic votes. Thus emancipation became an issue in the campaign.[12] By taking a stand squarely against emanci-

[12] John B. McMasters, *A History of the United States during Lincoln's Administration*, 507–508.

pation by Congressional or executive action, the Democrats announced to the country that they were opposed to the contemplated Thirteenth Amendment which the Unionists demanded in their platform and which each slave state would have been peremptorily required to adopt.

All branches of the Union party were in agreement that the hated institution would have no place in the reconstructed Union. Both the Baltimore and the Cleveland conventions, as well as the state and many county gatherings of the party, made this point clear in their resolutions. Slavery was the main support of the rebellion and had to be destroyed if peace was to be permanent, they said, as they scoffed at the Democratic contention that peace could be enduringly concluded simply on the basis of the old Constitution. Even Lincoln, who throughout the canvass made no speeches, wrote a statement in which he maintained that the war could not be won without the Negroes' help, which would not be forthcoming "with the express or implied understanding that upon the first convenient occasion they are to be reenslaved."[13] The Unionists made it clear that they intended to further the cause of emancipation and make it an integral part of their reconstruction process.

Since the issue was so clearly cut in this particular case, with the Democrats opposing and the Unionists sustaining the proposed amendment, it is conceivable that the latter party could regard its success at the polls as a popular mandate for such an amendment. The Unionists went no further, however, than to insist that emancipation would be a necessary part of reconstruction and peace. They carefully avoided references to the status of the Negro in the postwar society, for on this point there was no agreement among the segments of the party. Any popular mandate which might have been given by the voters would, consequently, extend only to the desirability of enacting such an amendment and was not to be construed as an expression of popular sentiment on the question of enfranchisement or equality.

13 Sumner, *op. cit.*, IX, 79; Gerrit Smith, *op. cit.*, 9; Bristed, *op. cit.*, 2–3; *Peace to Be Enduring Must Be Conquered*, 1-4; Barton, *op. cit.*, II, 299–300; *Biographical Sketch of Andrew Johnson*, 6-12; Washington Hunt, *Speech of Ex-Governor Hunt at Lockport*, 6.

The Democratic Response

The discussion over abolition was perhaps in reality unnecessary. The Unionists were acknowledging an accomplished fact when they spoke of the desirability of a thirteenth amendment, for by the summer of 1864 the fate of slavery had been sealed. Slavery as an institution probably could not have been continued by the Confederacy even had it been victorious. There was much truth in one Unionist's assertion that the Democrats were defending a corpse.[14]

The war weariness which manifested itself throughout the summer days because of the adverse news from Virginia provided the Democrats with a second issue which they sought to introduce into the canvass. This issue took a variety of forms: (1) the policies of the administration were such as to urge the South to greater resistance, (2) the administration would not make peace because the end of the war would mean its defeat at the polls, and (3) Lincoln would not make peace because it would put an end to the wartime prosperity. Marble's paper claimed that Lincoln "would make no peace now even if he could dictate the terms. Peace and separation would ruin him with the North and prevent his election; peace and reunion would enable the South to participate in the Presidential election, which would be equally fatal to his prospects." Sam Medary noted, "Mr. Lincoln may wish the end—peace and freedom—but he is wholly unwilling to use the means which can secure that end."[15] The Democrats sought to play upon the mounting war weariness throughout the country by insisting that the administration was unwilling to make peace.

According to the Democrats this unnecessary prolongation of the war had many dire consequences for the country, and the blame for these ill effects was to be laid at Lincoln's door. The war was decreasing national wealth, said the Democrats, for the absence of more than one million boys in the army diminished the productive population by one fifth. The war has "already set back the country, as a whole, ten years in its progress, and . . . weakened

14 Hay, *op. cit.*, I, 93.
15 *New York World*, July 22, 1864; *The Crisis*, June 1, 22, 29, 1864; Comstock, *op. cit.*, 2; Belmont, *op. cit.*, 142; Cook and Knox, *op. cit.*, 237–41; Edgar Cowan, *Speech of Honorable Edgar Cowan of Pennsylvania in the Senate of the United States, June* 27, 1864, 15–16; James Gallatin, *Address of Honorable J. Gallatin Before the Democratic Union Association*, October 8, 1864; *Chicago Times*, January 8, March 16, 1864.

us irreparably for future development," lamented *The Crisis*.[16]

Another direct consequence of this prolongation of the war, according to the Democrats, was an enormous increase in the cost of goods. This was a point which every consumer in the North could easily comprehend, for all had felt the unpleasant pinch of wartime inflation. "If Mr. Lincoln's three years' misrule has run up the prices of coal to $15; flour, $16; butter, 60 cents; coffee, 60 cents; clothing to five times its former price—and everything that the people eat, drink, and wear, in a similar proportion—what will be their prices if Mr. Lincoln is reelected?" asked one editor.[17]

Even more vehement were the denunciations heaped upon the President because of the increased national debt. The opposition press was quick to take advantage of the potentialities afforded by the increasing costs of the war and pointed out that such a course was leading to "utter bankruptcy and ruin." According to the Democrats, Lincoln's administration had increased the public debt by $700,000,000, "more than the whole expenses of the government from the Declaration of Independence to March 4, 1861." The writer asked the voters, "Can we afford such a President for four years more?" Democratic propaganda agencies printed for distribution two documents on the question of war debts; one reminded the public that Lincoln had spent more to defeat the South than Europe spent to defeat Napoleon, and the other condemned his administration for not balancing the budget even in wartime.[18]

The events of the late summer deprived the Democrats of every opportunity to capitalize upon the war weariness which had swept the country earlier. The lassitude and the dissatisfaction with the war melted swiftly before the thundering guns of Sherman and Farragut. By September the North was stirring with life and enthusiasm for the cause; it quickened again at news of victory. The sacrifice, the sorrow had not been in vain, and all plunged with renewed spirit into the task of making victory secure. Time passed

[16] *The Crisis*, June 1, 1864.

[17] *The Crisis*, June 1, 1864; *New York World*, September 22, 1864.

[18] *The Crisis*, September 21, 1864; *New York World*, September 24, 1864; James Brooks, *Remarks of Mr. Brooks in the House of Representatives, March 7th*; Thomas P. Kettell, *The History of the War Debt of England. The History of the War Debt of the United States, and the Two Compared*.

the Democrats by, and they found themselves trying to utilize a situation which ceased to exist after September 1. The futile conferences at Niagara and in Richmond also did much to dissipate the issues based on war weariness. For all could see clearly that sweet reasonableness was not to prevail against the South's desire to determine its own destiny. If reunion was to be achieved, it could be done only as the Unionists claimed—by a military victory and by nothing else. McClellan, too, destroyed his party's power to capitalize on this issue when he repudiated the peace plank. He could promise nothing more than Lincoln; the war must go on, for all possibility of a negotiated peace was past, and further talk on that point was useless.

Another issue which the Democrats sought to exploit most thoroughly was the question of civil liberties. Circumstances seemed to dictate the choice of this issue. There was a strong faction within the Union party which had protested Lincoln's violations of civil liberties, and the Democrats probably hoped to aggravate the situation further by introducing the question into the canvass. It was also an issue which would place the Unionists in an embarrassing position, for there was no possible reply they could offer to the charges.

The central theme of the Democrats was that repeated violations of civil liberties were undermining the Constitution, and that if such practices were permitted to continue, the entire pattern of American freedom would be permanently warped or, perhaps, lost forever. The fourth plank of the Democratic platform was a positive statement against "arbitrary arrest, imprisonment, trial and sentence of American citizens in states where civil law exists in full force."

As the issue of civil liberty was developed during the canvass, it blossomed into something broader than a mere attack on Lincoln's arbitrary arrests. The democrats rejected the confiscation acts and conscription and censured Lincoln for interfering in elections and for imposing test oaths upon the citizens of reconstructed states.[19] The Democrats also devoted much attention to Lincoln's

[19] George Curtis, *Honorable George Ticknor Curtis on Constitutional Liberty*, 1, 6; Amasa Parker, *op. cit.*, 2, 7; Comstock, *op. cit.*, 5; *Address of the National Democratic Committee on the Perils of the Nation*, 1–2; Edward Hamilton, *A Republican's View of the Administration Policy*, 10.

Lincoln & the Party Divided

interference with the freedom of the press. The unfortunate incident in 1864 which led to the suspension of the *New York World* and the *Journal of Commerce* gave the Democrats much ammunition to utilize during the summer.[20]

The Democrats concentrated, however, on denunciation of Lincoln's administration for the suspension of *habeas corpus* and arbitrary arrests. Probably about 38,000 persons were arrested during the war.[21] Much could be made of the cases of such prominent men as Clement Vallandigham, but the Democrats were more anxious to concentrate upon arousing the people over the plight of the thousands of anonymous persons who were spirited from their families by Lincoln's felons. Neither age, sex, nor social position and profession protected people from the usurpations of the administration, said the Democrats. Lincoln was accused of arresting a thirteen-year-old boy. Stories were circulated of how clergymen were arrested at their altars, judges on their benches, and even some mourners in a funeral procession. Many of these unfortunate wretches, said the Democrats, went insane after being confined in groups of three in cells which measured a scant three by six feet.[22]

The Democrats hoped to make their greatest appeal to the voters on the civil liberty issue, but failed because they misjudged public reaction. John Sherman wrote to his brother that "all the clamor the Copperheads can make about personal liberty doesn't affect the people, if they can only see security and success. Bad precedents in time of war will easily be corrected by peace."[23] The Union party had been seriously divided over the civil liberty ques-

[20] About one hundred papers were suppressed during the war, and there were many cases where editors were threatened and where postmasters refused to distribute "disloyal" papers. Klement, "Middlewestern Copperheadism: Jeffersonian Democracy in Revolt" (Ph.D. dissertation), 270; Manton Marble, *Freedom of the Press Wantonly Violated. Letter of Mr. Marble to President Lincoln.*

[21] James Randall, *Constitutional Problems Under Lincoln*, 152.

[22] *Mr. Lincoln Arbitrary Arrests: The Acts Which the Baltimore Convention Approves; Ovation at the Academy of Music, July 4, 1863; Reply to President Lincoln's Letter of June 12, 1863;* John Pugh, *Speech of Mr. Pugh to 50,000 Voters Who Nominated Vallandigham and Resolved to Elect Him Governor of Ohio;* Reverdy Johnson, *Reply of Hon. Reverdy Johnson to the Paper Which Judge Advocate Holt Furnished to the President, Urging General Porter's Condemnation.*

[23] John Sherman to William Sherman, July 24, 1864, in Rachel Thorndike (ed.), *The Sherman Letters*, 237; Jacob Cooper, *The Loyalty Demanded by the Present Crisis*, 17.

The Democratic Response

tion, but the regrouping of the party late in September served to quiet opposition to Lincoln on this point. Speakers, writers, and editors sought to justify the violation of civil liberties on the grounds of military necessity. Their defense was, perhaps, a flimsy one, but when news of victory came at last, the people were willing to overlook these violations in their enthusiasm at the approach of peace. Sherman's prediction was coming true; the prospect of peace made them forget bad precedents of wartime.

The revelations of conspiracies and treasonable machinations in the Northwest could not have done else but convince many that Lincoln's government had acted for the public good. His methods may not have been in accord with the letter of the Constitution, but they saved the country from foes without and within, and that is all the voters asked. In addition, although Lincoln's government seized nearly 40,000 persons, his was no police state; the majority were left to enjoy their liberties. While Democratic propagandists and speakers flayed the government for interfering with their rights, Lincoln made no effort to stop them. Such a situation must have given many voters reason to reflect upon the truth of the Democrats' accusations that Lincoln was a power-mad dictator bent on suppressing all opposition.

The Democrats were pointing up a fundamental question which circumstances of the war served, unfortunately, to obscure. They were right in their assertion that there was likelihood of permanent danger inherent in subverting constitutional guarantees. They raised objections to the doctrine of loyalty which "required [them] to acquiesce in silence in the judgment of the public servants as to what the public necessities require."[24] Without an ever vigilant minority, liberties long secured may be lost. Sherman proved to be correct and the Democrats wrong; peace brought a reversal of bad tendencies. But just the opposite could have happened. Given a different executive, a prolongation of hostilities, or a weakening of American resources and institutions, the Democrats' predictions could have proved to be true.

The Democrats replied to the attack on McClellan by turning some heavy fire on Lincoln. They ridiculed his unpolished language, ungainly appearance, and lack of education. His habit of

[24] George Curtis, *The True Conditions of American Loyalty*, 6.

Lincoln & the Party Divided

telling little stories was vigorously denounced. A campaign story given wide circulation was that Lincoln, while riding over the battlefield of Antietam, requested Ward Lamon to sing a rollicking song about Ben Butler. The story was denied by Lamon in private letters, but Lincoln never permitted him to prepare a public statement on the episode.[25]

Since the President was known among the people as "Honest Abe," it was only natural that his honesty should also become a point of attack. The *World* explained, "It is in itself a suspicious thing to find the prefix 'honest' attached to the name of anyone, the most obvious inference being that it is given in *badinage* to some person, whose habits are notoriously the reverse."[26] The accusations of dishonesty reached into Lincoln's own household, and his son Robert was charged with accepting graft.[27]

A host of miscellaneous accusations against Lincoln included charges that he was "reaching for the imperial purple . . . under the baseless and groundless pretence of military necessity," that he had perverted the war aims, that he was an atheist, and that he had prolonged the war by removing from command any general whose exploits threatened to overshadow him.[28]

As they so often did during the canvass, the Unconditionals played into the hands of the Democratic propagandists by drawing similar indictments against their chief. If the Democrats complained that Lincoln had interfered with McClellan's campaigning on the peninsula, the Germans were equally vocal about his mistreatment of Frémont. If the Democrats accused him of desiring to perpetuate his administration, of circumventing the Constitution, and of dishonesty and incapacity, one need only read the Pomeroy Circular, the Wade-Davis Manifesto, Frémont's letter of acceptance, and Wendell Phillip's letter to the Cleveland convention to find identical sentiments expressed. This fact was not lost upon

[25] Lamon, *op. cit.*, 141–46; Paul Angle (ed.), *New Letters and Papers of Lincoln*, 356–59.

[26] *New York World*, September 22, 1864; *Corruptions and Frauds of Lincoln's Administration*, 1; *Address of the National Democratic Committee on the Perils of the Nation*, 3.

[27] *New York World*, September 23, 1864.

[28] Comstock, *op. cit.*, 3; *Harper's Weekly*, October 1, 1864; Raymond, *op. cit.*, 609; *Lincoln Catechism*, 1; *Lincoln's Treatment of Grant. Mr. Lincoln's Treatment of General McClellan. The Taint of Disunion.*

the Democrats, and a pamphlet was distributed showing the voters the low opinions of leading Republicans on their chief.[29]

The issues were joined by both parties with a vehemence seldom exceeded in an American presidential election. Stimulated by the war fever, the canvassers exerted themselves to the utmost throughout the campaign. Dittenhoefer, who participated in the canvass, wrote:

> Night and day, without cessation, young men like myself, in halls, upon street corners, and from cart-tails, were haranguing, pleading, sermonizing, orating, arguing, extolling our cause, and our candidate, and denouncing our opponents. A deal of oratory, elocution, rhetoric, declamation, and eloquence was hurled into the troubled air by speakers on both sides.[30]

The campaign, unfortunately, decided no question except which party was to rule for the next term, and it did not even conclusively settle this point. That temporary creation, the National Union party, was doomed to destruction, for it was not even regarded by all its own members as a bona fide party. There were few occasions when the Unconditionals referred to themselves as Union party men. The closest they came was to call themselves "Unconditional Union" men, but this cognomen referred to their policies and not to their party affiliation. Many of these men did not accept the policies for which the Union party presumably stood. At the same time the Democrats never recognized their opponent as the National Union party. They referred to the opposition as the Republican party; indeed, they could hardly call it the Union party without implying that the Democracy was a disunion party. There was also an unwillingness to admit that many Democrats had found a haven in the Union party ranks; they preferred to regard their party as still unbroken.

The election killed the National Union party, and the Republican party was resurrected after the war.[31] Some former War-

---

29 *Republican Opinions about Lincoln.*

30 Dittenhoefer, *op. cit.*, 87–88.

31 William A. Dunning, "The Second Birth of the Republican Party," *American Historical Review*, Vol. XVI (October, 1910), 56–63.

Democrats maintained their allegiance to the reborn party, but the majority, who had joined the Union party, were shocked by the course of events after 1865 and speedily returned to their pre-war allegiance. President Lincoln and others had dreamed of erecting a new party based on a fusion of the moderate elements of the two older parties, and they had been successful for a time when they could hold these elements together on the platform of winning the war. Lincoln undoubtedly hoped to make this new party a permanent creation; his offer to make Seymour the presidential nominee in 1864 to lure the moderate Democrats closer into the fold bears out this contention, but in such a move he was doomed to failure. There was no program which could have held the groups together for long.

As events finally developed, the Union party vanished after Lincoln's death, and the reborn Republican party fell into the hands of the Unconditional segment. The fruits of victory were garnered by the Radical Democracy and the Unconditional opponents who had lacked the courage actually to bolt the Union party in 1864 but reluctantly accepted Lincoln's leadership because they knew their failure to do so would mean certain defeat at the polls. The 1864 election presents a prime example of an election won by a candidate who represented a party that had no actual existence and whose most important leaders were already planning to embark upon a program diametrically opposed to the one for which Lincoln stood. Once in the saddle after Lincoln's death, these Unconditionals proclaimed that they were armed with a mandate to carry out a Carthaginian peace.

The question naturally arises again whether or not there was such a mandate, and if so, how extensive it was. On the strength of the issues presented by both the National Union and Democratic parties during the campaign, one must conclude that no such all-inclusive mandate could have been given. The Union party won the election because it had a candidate whose popular appeal was, except for the few weeks in July and August, greater than that of any other man who could have been nominated by either party. The military victories achieved during the critical moment of the canvass revived whatever prestige the Chief Executive might have lost during the summer and proved to the voters that the war was drawing to a successful conclusion. The ill-timed war-failure plank and the stupidity of the Democrats, who permitted their Ultras to become involved in activities of seemingly treasonable nature, provided the Union party with its most effectively exploited and most decisive issue.

On the question of reconstruction the issue was so confused that there was no definite choice before the electorate. The Union platform is silent on this point, and the Democrats merely proclaimed that they favored a restoration of the Union and the old Constitution. Had the Democrats had their way, it is possible there would have been a battle over reconstruction, but the Unionists, for reasons already noted, refused to accept the challenge. The issue of civil liberties was important in the campaign, but the voters seemed to be unwilling to call Lincoln to account after it became apparent that the war was drawing to a successful conclusion. In the North there were no ill effects from Lincoln's "usurpations," and the full liberties of the people were restored speedily after the war; only in the South were restraints continued, and this was in perfect accord with the Unconditional doctrine of the "conquered province." The vicious assaults upon the character, intelligence, and integrity of the two rival candidates were regrettable and cruel, but they could hardly be construed as offering a popular mandate on any point. No other significant issues were introduced in the campaign.

The situation was further complicated by the fact that there was a general blurring of party lines on many issues. Many Unionists agreed with the Democrats on the issue of civil liberties, shared their low opinion of Lincoln's character, and denounced his dictatorial tendencies.

Both parties, however, did take positive stands on the emancipation question. The Democrats opposed emancipation by executive, Congressional action, or by amendment, because they believed it would have evil consequences for both races; the Unionists announced that they favored a constitutional amendment abolishing slavery. The voters were given a precise choice, so that a Union party victory did offer a mandate on this point.

Beyond the question of emancipation the voters were deciding merely on two personalities. It was Lincoln who had their affectionate support, and when it became apparent that his administration, despite defeats and mistakes, was leading the North to ultimate victory, and that the Democracy was possibly a treasonable party, there was no question about the final outcome.

XIV

Getting the Issues
to the Voters

TWO INTERESTING aspects of any presidential election are the methods used to collect funds to carry forward the canvass and the projects upon which this money is spent. No previous campaign since the creation of the federal union was attended by such an outpouring of political pamphlets as the election of 1864. This lavish outflow of leaflets was made possible by the collection of unprecedented sums of money for campaign purposes. Aided by wartime prosperity the Union party in particular was able to raise sums of money which would have been unthinkable in earlier elections. Special organizations were created to push forward the propaganda campaign.

One of the most active Union agencies was the Union League of America, which had its inception in 1862 in Tazewell County, Illinois. This society spread rapidly throughout the Northern states, and it was soon joined by other societies known variously as Union Clubs, Strong Bands, National Leagues, Loyal Leagues, and National Union Associations. Their combined membership must have been close to one million, they were secret, and some were of a quasi-military nature.

During the elections of 1863 and 1864, the league performed various functions, but did its best work in the field of disseminating documents and papers. The distribution of campaign propaganda was stimulated by a personal appeal sent out on October 19 by Grand Council President James M. Edmunds and read at all local councils. The members were reminded that the fate of the party was in their hands, and they were urged to do their utmost to assure its success.[1]

The Democrats had comparable organizations in such societies as the Sons of Liberty, Order of American Knights, and the Mc-Clellan Guards. Unfortunately the first two societies became associated with treasonable enterprises and the third unwisely placed itself under a cloud of suspicion by adopting a flag which bore the same colors as the Confederate flag,[2] a fact alone sufficient to link it in the public mind with the forces of disunion.

The work of the party clubs and leagues was augmented by societies charged with the preparation and publication of campaign leaflets. The Society for the Diffusion of Political Knowledge was created by a group of prominent wealthy New York Democrats and intellectuals in February, 1863, under the presidency of Samuel F. B. Morse.

The Unionists were quick to sense the importance of the Democrats' move. During the same month they countered by organizing the Loyal Publication Society for the purpose of supplying the troops with helpful political literature and to counteract the "disloyal" propaganda of the Democrats. Charles King was chosen president. John Murray Forbes was instrumental in helping to form a similar organization known as the New England Loyal Publication Society.[3]

During the three years that it was in existence, the Loyal Publication Society collected $30,000, with which it published a total of 90 different pamphlets and sent out about 900,000 copies of them. During the presidential election it sent out 470,000 documents to various post exchanges, hospitals, newspaper offices, and ladies' societies, as well as 7,000 copies to Europe.

The Democratic society failed to match the profuse output of the opposition. During its existence the society published a total

[1] Hardie "The Influence of the Union League of America on the Second Election of Lincoln" (Master's thesis), 68; William Zornow, "Words and Money to Re-elect Lincoln," *Lincoln Herald*, Vol. LIV (Spring, 1952), 22–30.

[2] [?] to McClellan, July 1, 1864, McClellan Papers.

[3] Frank Friedel, "The Loyal Publication Society: A Pro-Union Propaganda Agency," *The Mississippi Valley Historical Review*, Vol. XXVI (December, 1939), 359–76.

of thirty-nine pamphlets, at least four issued also in a German translation. This output fell short of the ninety documents issued by the Loyal Publication Society, but the literary quality of the articles was much higher.[4] This is quite understandable, for it was not the purpose of Morse and his friends to appeal to the emotions of the American voters but to their intellects.

In the matter of finances the Society for the Diffusion of Political Knowledge also fell short of the amount raised by the Loyal Publication Society. At the end of the first year of operation, the Democratic Society had raised $6,000 and set its sights on a $10,000 goal for the second year. No evidence seems to be available to show whether this amount was ever raised, but even if it were collected, the total was still greatly exceeded by the amount the Unionists raised.[5]

No evidence exists, either, to indicate the total output of pamphlets during 1863–64. According to Manton Marble, one of the founders of the society, it cost fifty dollars to print 1,000 documents. If one assumes that the society's budget for two years totaled $16,000, slightly more than 300,000 documents could be printed—about one-third of the output of the Loyal Publication Society. Undoubtedly the number was actually somewhat larger, for some of the pamphlets were printed at the authors' expense.[6]

The executive committee of the society spent its time obtaining the names of reliable correspondents in as many towns and counties as possible. Nearly seven thousand persons were ultimately on the society's mailing list, representing five thousand towns and villages in fifteen states. Under the frank of several Democratic congressmen, packets of documents were sent to these people, who in turn assumed responsibility for dispersing them to their friends.

Several Democratic state committees instructed their local county agencies to carry on their campaign through the New York society. The county committees were instructed to send mailing lists to the society, which then distributed documents to these people. The local committees were required only to pay for the

[4] Barton, *op. cit.*, II, 288.
[5] Circular No. 7 of the Society for the Diffusion of Political Knowledge, Marble Papers.
[6] Cox to Marble, June 7, 1864, Marble Papers.

paper and for printing the documents. Not only did several county committees use the facilities of the society, but the New York State Central Committee of the National Committee did so as well. This accounts for the fact that only nineteen of the thirty-nine documents printed by the Society for the Diffusion of Political Knowledge were marked with the name of the society; the rest were printed for other organizations.

In the distribution of documents the Unionists far outstripped the Democrats. The Loyal Publication Society printed nearly one million pieces. The Union Executive Congressional Committee, which was founded at the capital and was under the direction of Edwin Morgan and James Harlan, sent out nearly six million documents to various leagues and individuals.[7] Several administration papers such as the *Chicago Tribune* also printed documents at their own expense.[8] The Union League sent out 560,000 copies of its *Union League Gazette* during the campaign. One might hazard a guess that the Union party issued in excess of ten million copies of pamphlets and circulars during 1863–64. Under the direction of James Harlan the Congressional committee blanketed the whole country with leaflets. His biographer did not exaggerate when he wrote that "under his vigorous management large quantities of printed matter found their way to all parts of the North."[9] One of Samuel Morse's correspondents commented on the profusion of Union propaganda:

> I have been aware for a long time that the elections have been carried against us by opinions formed by reading the *Tribune* and kindred prints. At this time immense supplies of reading matter in the shape of speeches and Loyal League documents are flooding the country. You can hardly go into a public office or store but you will see such documents on the table, counters, and even posted up in the shape of handbills. . . . The Loyal Leagues are really affecting public opinion seriously with

[7] Harlan to Washburne, November 19, 1864; H. J. Raymond to Washburne, June 20, 1864, Washburne Papers.

[8] M. Schmitz to McClellan, September 22, 1864; Henry Korpers to A. C. Dodge, n.d., Marble Papers.

[9] Johnson Brigham, *James Harlan*, 186.

their meetings, documents, etc., and I am confident that it
needs immediate action on our part.[10]

It became increasingly difficult to circulate Democratic documents. There was much popular resentment at having "treasonable" literature openly sold, and Secretary Stanton ordered all
Democratic literature barred from the army; it was not until
October 8, 1864, that permission was granted to send documents
to the soldiers, but by then it was too late.[11] If the testimony of
the Democratic papers is to be believed, the distribution of Union
propaganda was often accomplished at the taxpayers' expense. The
National Committee commandeered all available space in the
Capitol, and at least one hundred clerks were sent there from
various governmental departments to address campaign literature.

To supplement the propaganda campaign carried on by
pamphlets and stump orators, the Union party turned also to
colorful personalities of the times and induced some of them to
enter the canvass. Such luminaries as Anna Dickinson, who had
repented of her earlier hostility toward Lincoln, Henry Ward
Beecher, and Frederick Douglass were only a few of the prominent
citizens who entered the field in order to extol the praises of Lincoln and company. Leading military figures were also brought
into the canvass in order to counteract the Democrats' claim that
the army was for McClellan. War-Democrats of national importance were sent into the forefront of the fray to denounce Copperheadism and garner the wavering Democratic votes. Campaign
documents were circulated in German, French, and Dutch trans-
lations, while an additional bid was made for foreign votes by
utilizing such foreign-born leaders as Carl Schurz and Gustave
Koerner, to mention only two.

To distribute leaflets so lavishly and to keep in the field a vast
host of stump orators required large sums of money. Both parties
utilized every conceivable device to fill their coffers for this work.

[10] O. W. Smith to Morse, May 28, 1864, Morse Papers.
[11] C. C. Whittelsey to Belmont, September 9, 1864; H. Seymour to Belmont,
September 26, 1864; C. L. Ward to Marble, n.d.; Charles Mason to Marble, Sep-
tember 28, 1864; George Adams to Marble, September 27, 1864, Marble Papers
Daniel Cameron to McClellan, August 30, 1864, McClellan Papers. Stanton's Order
Book, Stanton Papers. G. Brown to Trumbull, November 5, 1864, Trumbull Papers.

Lincoln & the Party Divided

The Democrats, however, fell far short of the Unionists in this respect. Speaking before Congress in 1908, Democrat William Sulzer of New York estimated that the Union National Committee spent $125,000 to elect Lincoln and the Democrats spent $50,000 in a vain attempt to elect McClellan.[12] Sulzer did not mention the source of his figures. They have been frequently quoted as authentic, but actually possess little validity. It is interesting to note, on the other hand, a contemporary Democratic estimate of what the Unionists spent. Samuel North wrote to Marble that he had learned from an unimpeachable source that "the Republican managers in Philadelphia have on hand a fund of one million dollars."[13] Two days later a second correspondent admitted to Marble that the Unionists were "raising a very large sum of money here [Philadelphia] but it will be nothing like the 'million' mentioned, tho' probably more than half that amount." He went on to explain that all contractors, officeholders, and even laborers in public employ were being assessed.[14]

There is certainly a wide discrepancy between Sulzer's estimate that the Unionists spent $125,000 during the whole campaign and the contemporary estimate that they might spend $500,000 in one city alone. Any attempt to calculate the money spent by both or either party would be at best a hazardous and unnecessary undertaking. What is more important is to discover how the money was collected and on what projects it was spent. Obviously a great deal of money was available, especially for the Union party, and there was a degree of truth in a Democrat's remark that the "Lincoln men were paying out money like water."[15]

Henry Raymond as chairman of the National Union Executive Committee let it be known that all federal officeholders were expected to contribute funds for the campaign.[16] Senator James Lane, who had been placed in charge of the western branch of the National Union Executive Committee shortly after the Baltimore convention, assumed responsibility for collecting funds from the

21 *Congressional Record,* 60 Cong., 1 sess., 6470–71.
13 Samuel North to Marble, September 28, 1864, Marble Papers.
41 Henry Phillips to Marble, September 30, 1864, Marble Papers.
15 C. L. Ward to Marble, n.d., Marble Papers.
16 Carman and Luthin, *op. cit.,* 288–89.

Getting the Issues to the Voters

states west of the Mississippi. In addition to Raymond's committee, Senator Edwin Morgan's Union Executive Congressional Committee was also active in soliciting funds from federal employees, and various state executive committees carried forward the work of raising funds from state employees. Often there was confusion as state committees sought to assess federal employees who had already been approached by collectors representing the national organ of the party.[17]

Another excellent source of money for the Union campaign came from the assessments upon contractors and government suppliers. In Tennessee, for example, each government contractor received a blunt reminder that it was expected that those "who have received the liberal patronage of the government will willingly lend [their] means. . . . [To] those who respond cheerfully to this call . . . the patronage herefore extended to them will without doubt be continued."[18] As early as February a letter was sent to Benjamin Loan stating that after the nominating convention no further government patronage would be extended to newspapers which failed to support the candidate regularly chosen.[19] This practice of extending and withholding patronage and advertising from papers which supported or failed to support the administration was a powerful factor in bringing many of the recalcitrant journals into line.

Federal officeholders, contractors, newspaper editors, and other recipients of federal bounty who failed to make a suitable contribution soon found themselves without positions or without contracts, patronage, and advertising. The work of Raymond's committee was most thorough in this respect, and it was carried out with Lincoln's approval.[20]

During the period of gloom in July and August, campaign collections fell behind. On August 19, Raymond reported, "We are not in funds at present—but hope to have enough for useful pur-

---

[17] Henry Raymond to Cameron, July 17, 1864, Cameron Papers.

[18] W. Crane to Browning, October 19, 1864, Andrew Johnson Papers.

[19] [Stanton] to Benjamin Loan, February 22, 1864, Stanton Papers. Loan was also owner of the *St. Joseph Tribune* in addition to being congressman from Missouri.

[20] Arthur Cole, "Lincoln and the Presidential Election of 1864," *Illinois State Historical Society Transactions* (1917), 134.

poses in time." After Atlanta fell, funds began to pour into the coffers. Some of the cabinet members gave $500 each. In Nashville, Colonel Crane reported that he had raised $20,000 and expected to increase the amount. John Murray Forbes locked himself in a room with several friends and got them to contribute $23,000 before opening the door. And so the money rolled into party head-quarters, and the opposition could only wail:

> The Democrats will enter the coming canvass under the great disadvantage of having to contend against the greatest patron-age and the greatest money-power ever wielded in a presi-dential election. An administration in power has always money in hand as well as swarms of well drilled office-holders to con-duct the canvass; but the Lincolnites will control a thousand dollars where former administrations could not raise ten.[21]

The Union party records of campaign expenditures in New York have been preserved and will serve to give an idea of the projects upon which the money was spent. The committee col-lected $46,775 in the form of contributions ranging from $500 to $2,500. All but $91.34 was spent as follows:

National Union Committee	$10,000	
Henry J. Raymond		$10,000
New York State Union Committee		
L. W. Jerome, Chairman		
For state	10,000	
For city	10,000	
For congressional district	6,000	
State and City	3,521.24	
		29,521.24
War Democrat State Committee		
Peter Cooper, Treasurer		
for Cooper Union meeting	1,000	
Printing and Advertising	500	
Printing General Dix's speech	500	

[21] Raymond to Cameron, August 19, 1864, Cameron Papers; Welles, *op. cit.,* I, 534; Crane to Browning, October 26, 1864, Andrew Johnson Papers; Sarah Hughes, *op. cit.,* II, 90–91; *New York World,* August 25, 1864.

Printing Judge Pierpont's speech	787.42	
Incidentals	250	
		3,037.42
Loyal Publication Society		
Francis Lieber, President		
for distributing documents	1,000	
Union League #2 21 Ward		
A. G. Coffin, Chairman		
For distributing documents to		
soldiers in the field	1,500	
Workingmen's Association		
O. W. Bowne, Chairman	500	
Central Union Lincoln and Johnson Campaign Club		
Through W. M. E. Evarts	500	
Naturalization Fund		
Through Waldo Hutchings		
For naturalizing discharged soldiers		
of foreign birth	500	
Canvassing Seabord Counties of New Jersey		
G. W. Blunt	125	
Balance	91.34	
	$46,775.00[22]	

The campaign funds collected were often put to use aiding newspapers. The case of Edward Sturznickel of Erie, Pennsylvania, was typical. The publisher of a small paper, the *German Spectator,* in Erie, he owed some money to local Democrats, who attempted to foreclose on his property. An appeal was sent to Edwin Morgan's committee. Two other newspapers in Pennsylvania, the *True Democrat* of York County and the *Patriot* of Lehigh County, were in similar financial straits and appealed to the Union Central Committee for aid. An appeal came to Democratic leaders in New York to purchase some papers in Missouri so that the party would have a greater voice in the West.[23] Contri-

---

22 *The Union Campaign Committee Herewith Respectfully Present to the Contributors a Statement of Receipts and Expenditures of the Fund Raised by Them for the Union Campaign of November,* 1864, 1-3.

23 Edward Sturznickel to Cameron, September 14, 1864; E. H. Ranch to Cameron, June 27, 1864; H. Young to Cameron, August 13, 1864, Cameron Papers.

butions from the regular party funds bolstered the assistance being given to papers by government patronage and advertising.

The Democrats assembled their National Executive Committee early in October to prepare for the campaign. A cabinet of the most eminent Democrats was appointed to direct the party until the election. The Executive Campaign Committee was created to direct the collection of funds, to pay for speakers, and to defray the cost of publishing documents.[24]

There is a bit of scattered evidence which indicates how successful the Democrats were in soliciting funds. In Pennsylvania they spent $33,000 during the October canvass. August Belmont paid $15,000 to cover the cost of distributing documents in New Hampshire. But, on the other hand, the Unionists were equally extravagant in that tiny state. James G. Blaine in one letter to Raymond acknowledged having received $3,500, while $10,000 more apparently was delivered to William Chandler and John B. Clarke. Undoubtedly there must have been much more money poured into the New Hampshire campaign. Money flowed freely in Connecticut, too, for Mark Howard wrote to Welles that "too much reliance [was] being placed upon the influence of money loosely scattered." Additional evidence of the vast expenditure going on can be found in the laconic statement of D. N. Cooley, who told Washburne they would have to carry Illinois for Lincoln even if it cost half a million to do so.[25]

In Maryland where Democratic sentiment was quite high, that party was able to triumph in the battle of spending. After the election one of Representative Creswell's friends noted, "By the bountiful supply of money and the admission of votes of rebels and rebel sympathizers we have been beaten by over 700 votes." Another correspondent lamented, "We were not furnished with a single

Edward Sturznickel to McPherson, February 13, 1864, McPherson Papers. B. D. Killian to Belmont, September 10, 1864; H. B. Swarr to Belmont, September 26, 1864, Marble Papers.

[24] Marble to Tilden, September 9, 1864, Plan of the Democratic Campaign, Marble Papers.

[25] H. Phillips to Marble, October 9, 1864, Marble Papers; Mark Howard to Welles, October 28, 1864, Welles Papers; D. N. Cooley to Washburne, October 20, 1864, Washburne Papers; Carman and Luthin, *op. cit.*, 294; Paul Frothingham, *Edward Everett: Orator and Statesman*, 463–64.

dollar to treat our poor Union friends to a social glass. We could get no challengers to stand at the polls, and the return judge would not receive a list of challenged votes, nor did they question anyone. All were permitted to vote."[26] Thousands of dollars were poured out during the struggle to capture the White House and Capitol. Unquestionably much of the money spent found its way into the pockets of repeat voters. Naturalization papers were forged and other irregularities were committed during the struggle. Both parties were undoubtedly equally to blame. When it was all over, the Unionists were able to reap a bountiful harvest from the few crumbs cast upon the waters. They still controlled the executive branch with its veritable flood of patronage and the manufacturers could look forward to several months of contracts, while speculators anticipated prosperous times on the exchange. The Democrats had spent and lost. It would be twenty years before they would reap the fruits of power and place. One can almost sympathize with Manton Marble when he nostalgically wrote to McClellan after the din of battle had subsided, "The half dozen embassies, the two or three collectorships, the fourscore postmasterships, the cotton stealing permits, and fat contracts it would have been my pleasing duty to have solicited at your hands, had the results of Tuesday's election been different, (I make no sinister allusions here and now to your conduct in exciting any hope with a contingent promise to the keepership of the Montauk light house, already promised explicitly to both Barlow and Prime) still repose, all of them, in the hands of our venerated chief magistrate."[27] Marble turned back to his newspaper editing and awaited the dawn of a brighter day.

26 E. Hubbel to Creswell, November 9, 1864; T. Russell to Creswell, November 11, 1864; [?] to Creswell, March 15, 1864, Creswell Papers (MSS in Library of Congress). During the 1863 campaign the Unionists spent $2,500 to buy up about 400 votes in Caroline County, but were unable to repeat this in 1864 because of the Democrats' vigilance.

27 Marble to McClellan, November 13, 1864, Marble Papers.

The October States

THE PRESIDENTIAL election to a large extent depended upon the outcome of the October state elections in Indiana, Ohio, and Pennsylvania. It was generally felt that whichever party carried the October elections in these three states would also emerge triumphant in the presidential election in November.[1] The state elections had been held in New Hampshire in March, and in April Connecticut and Vermont followed suit. Governor Gilmore was re-elected in Vermont, while governors Buckingham and Smith polled the anticipated Union majorities in the other states. The spring elections in these three New England states were not good policital indicators of which way the wind would blow in November. Since they transpired, the nation had passed through the doldrums of despair and defeatism over the slaughter in Virginia. The October elections would, therefore, indicate much more accurately whether the voters had recovered their confidence and would still support the administration.

Kentucky was actually the first state to hold its election after the Union convention. It was a testing ground for the administration. The election was held on August 1 for certain minor county offices and the judge of the court of appeals of the second district. A month before the election, federal troops began to take over the polls, despite Governor Bramlette's protestations. On July 5, Lincoln suspended *habeas corpus* and established martial law. Not-

[1] Dudley, *loc. cit.*, 515.

withstanding the government promise, there was interference three days before the election; the Democratic candidate's name was stricken from the poll books, and some prominent party men were arrested. The Democrats hastened to nominate a substitute candidate and telegraphed his name to the polling places. He was subsequently elected. Later in September, Bramlette wrote to Lincoln protesting such action. The attitude of the Governor and his fellow Kentuckians seemed to indicate that Lincoln's party would encounter much trouble in the state in November.[2]

Prior to Oliver Morton's successful introduction of the domestic treason issue into the campaign, there seemed to be little to indicate that he or Lincoln would fare any better in Indiana. The Democrats were making herculean efforts to drive the hated Morton from office. "Indiana may be as troublesome to Lincoln as South Carolina," was the dismal view taken by one writer, and his sentiments were shared by many.[3] Money was spent lavishly, important politicians and generals were imported into the state to carry on the canvass, but still there were many doubts about the outcome. Morton ultimately requested that enough troops be furloughed home to assure him a majority, and he requested, too, that the draft be delayed until after the election. Lincoln appealed to Sherman to send home some Indiana troops at election time, but the General was reluctant to spare his men at a critical moment. The best Morton could do was to obtain permission to bring home the sick and wounded soldiers. Special agents were at once dispatched from Indianapolis to round up all the disabled soldiers they could find. About nine thousand finally reached home to facilitate Morton's triumph, but since he won by over twenty thousand votes, all the agitation had been superfluous.

Morton's request that the draft be delayed was met by Lincoln's stern refusal. Even after a personal visit to Washington, Morton gained no satisfaction. Sherman had told Lincoln that if the draft did not go off on schedule, the troops at the front might turn on the government.

[2] Coulter, *op. cit.*, 184, 186; Hesseltine, *op. cit.*, 357.

[3] S. Fletcher to Johnson, July 30, 1864; Colfax to Johnson, August 17, 1864, Andrew Johnson Papers. A. Denny to Sherman, August 21, 1864, Sherman Papers. Colfax to Lincoln, August 29, 1864, Stanton Papers. Morton to W. Dunn, August 22, 1864, Holt Papers.

Lincoln & the Party Divided

On the eve of the state election Union party leaders were confident of victory. This confidence was not misplaced, for Morton was re-elected by twenty thousand votes, the state legislature was also captured, and the Union party carried eight of the eleven Congressional seats. This sparkling victory was achieved without a postponement of the draft and with far less than the fifteen thousand soldiers Morton had originally requested. The Democrats denounced the results as completely fraudulent and predicted that McClellan would win easily in November.[4]

While the party was winning in Indiana, it was also meeting similar success in Ohio and Pennsylvania. In the former state the campaign was an anticlimax to the great battle fought in '63 against Vallandigham. Both the politicians and the voters seemed exhausted by those efforts, and the campaign of 1864 was mild by comparison. The Union ticket was carried by 54,000 votes, and the party captured seventeen of the nineteen Congressional seats. The soldier vote was of some importance in achieving these excellent results. The fighting men decided the outcome in three of the Congressional districts.[5]

Victory in Ohio, as in Indiana, was achieved by using the heaviest batteries the Union party could muster. Here the soldier vote was most useful, and it had been closely regulated. There were reports that the polls at Camp Chase were closed when the soldiers showed indications of voting against the administration.[6] The canvass was stimulated somewhat by the presence of national figures such as Andrew Johnson, Salmon Chase, and Supreme Court Justice Noah H. Swayne, who toured the state "preaching the gospel to the heathen."[7]

The Democrats were powerless to prevent a Union party victory in Ohio, and they recognized the inevitability of defeat more

[4] Chase to Sherman, October 2, 1864, Sherman Papers. John Lane to McClellan, October 13, 1864; William Prime to McClellan, October 20, 1864, McClellan Papers. *Indianapolis Sentinel,* October 12, *passim.*

[5] Yager, *loc. cit.,* 582; Porter, *op. cit.,* 126; Eugene Roseboom, *The Civil War Era,* 1850–1873, 429.

[6] Cox to McClellan, October 11, 12, 1864, McClellan Papers; C. V. D. Bang to Marble, October 12, 1864, Marble Papers.

[7] Raymond to Johnson, September 11, 1864; Charles Parrott to Johnson, September 9, 1864, Andrew Johnson Papers. N. H. Swayne to Montgomery Blair, September 26, 1864, Blair Papers.

than a week before the election. One of Belmont's friends wrote on October 3 that there were no chances of carrying Ohio; their only hope was to cut the Union majority to 20,000, and if this could be done there was likelihood that the state could be carried in November.[8] Some blamed the peace men. Vallandigham did "just enough for us to damn us" wrote Cox to Marble, and he further lamented that Medary's paper put up McClellan's name "a little bit and damned him with faint praise."[9] Morgan said that the peace men blamed their party's failure on the letter of acceptance and the war men blamed it on the platform.[10] In any event, the Democrats in Ohio were so demoralized and torn by strife that the Unionists, despite the fact that they were less active than in 1864, easily defeated them.

In Pennsylvania the Unionists carried the election, but by fewer votes than had been expected. After the votes were counted, the Union party controlled sixteen Congressional seats to the Democrats' eight and carried their state ticket by a 13,000 majority. There was much antiadministration sentiment in the eastern part of the state; had it not been for western Pennsylvania, which gave the Union ticket a majority of 15,000 votes, the party would have been defeated. Had it not been for the soldier vote, there would not have been a Union majority of as many as 400 in the state.[11] The closeness of the popular vote depressed Lincoln greatly. After the results were in, Whitlaw Reid could only gasp, "Hasn't *somebody* sold us out there? And would it be a very bad guess to think of Curtin in that connection."[12]

Both parties had made a maximum effort. The Democrats sent over from New York every speaker they could spare and even went so far as to forge naturalization papers to increase their prospective votes.[13] The depressing military news had weakened the administration's popularity in the state, and the draft calls sent

---

[8] J. Green to Belmont, October 3, 1864, Marble Papers.

[9] Cox to Marble, October 8, 12, 1864, Marble Papers.

[10] Morgan to McClellan, October 13, 1864, McClellan Papers.

[11] Norman C. Brillhart, "Election of 1864 in Western Pennsylvania," *Western Pennsylvania Historical Magazine,* Vol. VIII (January, 1925), 29–31.

[12] Reid to McPherson, October 12, 1864, McPherson Papers.

[13] J. Clens to Johnson, October 8, 1864, Andrew Johnson Papers; E. P. Thompson to Cameron, October 14, 1864, Cameron Papers.

it even lower. It was only the introduction of the treason issue and the revival of military fortunes which saved Pennsylvania for the Unionists. During the closing weeks of the canvass, documents were poured into the state and meetings were held in every school district and at every county seat, while broadsides were distributed linking McClellan and the Democrats with Vallandigham and Fernando Wood.[14] With all their work and expenditures of money the Unionists were saved only by the soldiers; Samuel Barlow claimed the Democrats had actually carried the home vote.[15]

The Union party had won the state elections in Pennsylvania, Ohio, and Indiana. But in the first state it had been achieved by the soldier vote; and the Democrats, who knew Morton well, insisted that Indiana had been carried by fraud. The Democrats' reaction to the October vote was varied. Some saw in it a bad omen for the presidential election. "The Democrats are unhappy everywhere, but we have everything to contend with—power, patronage, and unsuspecting men. The Republicans are confident of victory," wrote one of them.[16] Some, on the other hand, were not ready to concede defeat. They pointed to the closeness of the vote in Pennsylvania and the doubtful results in Indiana. William Prime told McClellan that he would certainly carry New York, Pennsylvania, New Jersey, Kentucky, California, Oregon, Maryland, Delaware, and possibly Illinois, Connecticut, Missouri, Michigan, New Hampshire, and Indiana.[17] This would give him 154 electoral votes.

Among the Unionists the outcome of the elections was hailed as a sure indication of what to expect in November. "The victory in Pennsylvania and Indiana assured us of Lincoln's re-election," crowed William Chandler. "The country is to be saved by the intelligence and partiotism of the American people."[18] Lincoln was still gloomy over the prospects, and it is interesting to note that on October 13 he wrote out his own estimate of the November results. He gave himself 120 electoral votes to McClellan's 114. He, like Prime, conceded that the Democrats would carry Penn-

[14] George Miner to Cameron, September 7, 1864, Cameron Papers.
[15] Barlow to McClellan, October 15, 1864, McClellan Papers.
[16] George Smith, MSS diary, October 20, 1864, in Klement, "Middlewestern Copperheadism: Jeffersonian Democracy in Revolt" (Ph.D. dissertation), 306.
[17] William Prime to McClellan, October 20, 1864, McClellan Papers.
[18] Chandler to McPherson, October 13, 1864, McPherson Papers.

sylvania, New Jersey, New York, Kentucky, Maryland, and Delaware; he also included Missouri and Illinois, which Prime had regarded as only probables. California, Oregon, Connecticut, Michigan, New Hampshire, and Indiana he counted in the Unionist column.[19]

Certainly the immediate results of the October elections did not justify the jubilant attitude of the majority of the Unionists. Lincoln's cautious estimate was probably a more accurate appraisal of the true situation during the middle of the month. The October victories, however, unquestionably did much to arouse the enthusiasm of the Union party workers and drove them on to greater activity during the remaining weeks before the national election. Conversely, it could have had no other effect upon the majority of the Democrats than to depress and divide them further. Charges of fraud in Indiana and the closeness of the home vote in Pennsylvania were insufficient to offset the stark fact that their party had suffered defeats in three major states. The October elections proved merely that the balance had shifted again; the doubts of August were now gone, and the fortunes of the Union party were reviving. It was reasonable to expect that they would continue to rise before November.

[19] David H. Bates, *Lincoln in the Telegraph Office*, 277–81. Lincoln wrote out this estimate on October 13 while he was sitting in the telegraph office.

) XVI (

The Month of Decision

THE REMAINING weeks of the canvass passed swiftly, with each
side redoubling its effort to gain a few more wavering votes
and confidently forecasting victory. Despite ominous predictions that armed violence would break out before and during
the election, the citizens trooped to the polls to register their decision without incident.[1] Not even a dismal rain which pelted
down in many states prevented a record number of Northern state
voters from casting their ballots.

Until the very eve of the election many Democrats were confident of complete victory; such astute observers as Morgan and
Cox predicted McClellan's success and said that only fraud could
save the Unionists.[2] On the other hand, the Unionists were just as
certain of victory. Sherman heard from Chase that "there is not
now the slightest uncertainty about the re-election of Mr. Lincoln.
The only question is by what popular and what electoral majorities."[3] This letter had been written early in October, and the
results of the state elections during that month could have no effect
other than to confirm the former Secretary's opinion. President

[1] Dix, *op. cit.*, II, 94.

[2] Morgan to McClellan, November 3, 1864; Cox to McClellan, October 27,
1864; Albert Ramsey to McClellan, October 18, November 7, 1864, McClellan
Papers. E. O. Perrin to Marble, October 31, 1864; J. W. A. to Marble, November
1, 1864, Marble Papers; William Zornow, "Lincoln Voters among the Boys in
Blue," *Lincoln Herald*, Vol. LIV (Fall, 1952), 22–25.

[3] Chase to Sherman, October 2, 1864, Sherman Papers.

The Month of Decision

Lincoln had also dropped his defeatist attitude late in October and summoned F. P. Blair, Sr., into his presence about two weeks before the election. He suggested that McClellan might be induced to withdraw since his election now seemed impossible. "Why should he not act upon it and help me give peace to this distracted country?" inquired the President, and he continued:

> Would it not be a glorious thing for the Union cause and the country, now that my reelection is certain, for him to decline to run, favor my election and make certain a speedy termination of this bloody war? Don't you believe that such a course
> ... would unify public partisan sentiment and give a decisive and fatal blow to all opposition to the reestablishment of peace in the country. I think he is man enough and patriot enough to do it.[4]

Blair bore the President's offer to New York; McClellan was to become commander of the armies and his father-in-law would be made a major general in return for the withdrawal. McClellan, still confident of ultimate success, refused the offer.

The results of the balloting must have struck McClellan and his friends like a bolt from Olympus. President Lincoln was triumphantly re-elected on November 8 with 212 electoral votes to McClellan's 21; only New Jersey, Delaware, and Kentucky saw fit to cast a majority against the Chief Executive. Francis Lieber shouted jubilantly at the momentous victory: "Two days after the Great and Good election of 1864. Behold! For Mac one full-grown pair of states, and also—Delaware."[5] While Senator Sherman wrote to his brother: "The election of Lincoln scarcely raised a ripple on the surface. It was anticipated."[6] His letter betrayed none of the anxiety he had felt a few weeks earlier when he despaired of Lincoln's re-election.

A vigorous campaign had also been fought in each Congressional district, for it would have been pointless to have Lincoln

---

[4] Lamon, *op. cit.*, 205–208.

[5] Lieber to Sumner, November 10, 1864, in Friedel, "The Life of Francis Lieber" (Ph.D. dissertation), 631–32.

[6] John Sherman to William Sherman, December 18, 1864, in Thorndike, *op. cit.*, 241.

returned to the White House without a Union Congress. In some respects the victories scored in this area by the party were more significant than the presidential election. On this level the most significant issue had been the question of a thirteenth amendment and the abolition of slavery. The popular mandate was most decisive. In the Thirty-ninth Congress the National Union party gained twelve congressmen from Ohio, six from Illinois, four from Indiana, three each from New York, Missouri, and Pennsylvania, two from Wisconsin, and one each from Maine, Michigan, New Hampshire, New Jersey, Connecticut, and Nevada; at the same time they lost one each from Delaware and Maryland. The Union party had gained an over-all increase of thirty-seven congressmen. The Thirty-eighth Congress in January, 1865, yielded and passed the amendment.

In the gubernatorial elections the Union party was equally successful. Twelve governors representing that party were chosen by the voters in their respective states. In 1865, Joel Parker of New Jersey would be the only Democratic governor left in the Northern states. The party also controlled most of the state legislatures, and this gave them an opportunity to alter the composition of the United States Senate.

In several states soldiers were permitted to vote in the election. The Unionists were often quick to claim that they alone were responsible for conferring this right upon the fighting men. William Chandler wrote a pamphlet on soldier voting in which he maintained that the Democrats did not "hesitate to oppose by every means in their power, all attempts to confer upon soldiers in the field the right to vote." They did this, he claimed, "simply and solely for the reason that they believe the great majority of the soldiers in the army are not for George B. McClellan and the Copperheads but are for Abraham Lincoln, the Constitution, and the Union."[8]

At first the Unconditionals in Congress feared that McClellan's policies and personal popularity had permeated the army, and as late as January, 1863, a caucus had voted against enfranchising the

[7] Horace Greeley, *The American Conflict*, II, 673; Godwright to Johnson, November 10, 1864, Johnson Papers.
[8] William Chandler, *The Soldier's Right to Vote*, 3-4.

The Month of Decision

soldiers for fear they would vote Democratic. Before another year
had passed, however, they came to feel that education at the front
had progressed enough to entrust the soldiers with the ballot. As
long as the administration could control the soldiers' reading material and could place the election apparatus in the hands of loyal
officers, there was no doubt about the outcome of any vote.[9] Grant
prohibited canvassing among his troops, but Villard wrote "that
no agitation meetings and speeches among the troops in behalf of
the candidates of either party was [sic] allowed before the election
yet so many politicians were serving in the rank and file that considerable quiet canvassing went on nevertheless."[10]

Both parties appealed to the fighting men in their platforms;
such a plank has become a standard fixture of most platforms since,
but it was a new departure in 1864. A second significant development during the canvass of that year was the appearance of veterans' organizations which were politically active. In September,
a Democrat, fearing that the Unionists would not stop short of
intimidation to force the soldiers to support Lincoln, urged Mc-
Clellan to form a veterans' society to offset this possibility. These
clubs, he maintained, would generate enthusiasm, react upon the
soldiers in the field, and contradict the assertion that all soldiers
were for Lincoln.[11] An organization known as the McClellan
Legion grew out of this suggestion, and by October it was deeply
involved in the campaign; to allay the possible accusation of treason, its officers made known that they did not accept Copperheads
as members and repudiated the Chicago platform.[12] The club,
which soon had branches in the principal cities, held regular meetings and staged parades and rallies. The *World* reported that its
influence was "tremendous." The Unionists were quick to realize
the importance of capturing the veteran and soldier vote and
retaliated by organizing the Veteran Union Club.

In seeking to gain the soldiers' support, the Unionists were in-

[9] Klement, "Middlewestern Copperheadism: Jeffersonian Democracy in Revolt"
(Ph.D. dissertation), 250–55; T. Harry Williams, "Voters in Blue: The Citizen
Soldiers of the Civil War," *The Mississippi Valley Historical Review*, Vol. XXXI
(September, 1944), 187–204.
[10] Oswald Villard, *Fighting Years: Memoir of a Liberal Editor*, II, 200.
[11] C. D. Despler to McClellan, September 13, 1864, McClellan Papers.
[12] Henry Liebeman to McClellan, October 8, 1864, McClellan Papers.

finitely more active than their opponents. Medill sent 70,000 copies of his *Tribune* to the army, and many other editors followed suit. Governors sent men into army regiments to protect the soldiers from Democratic contamination. Each governor sought to outdo his neighbor in posing as the soldiers' friend. Many made frequent trips to the front to visit the men and often made it a point to welcome personally regiments home on leave. During the election year the United States Christian Commission distributed about eight million copies of papers and pamphlets (mostly Republican) among camp libraries.[13] Copies of the report on the Peninsular campaign found their way into the camp of the Army of the Potomac in an attempt to discredit McClellan among the men. In certain areas commanding officers prohibited the distribution of Democratic literature. McClellan was asked to supply a list of his friends on the staffs of Sherman, Grant, and Sheridan to whom documents could be sent for dissemination.[14] Many attempts were made to get military leaders to declare themselves in favor of McClellan. At one time or another most of the prominent commanders were alleged to be supporting the young Napoleon. To allow one's name to become linked with his was to lose all chance of advancement. Most officers were quick to declare they were not supporting him, and they may have done so through fear of Stanton. One gets some indication of this from a letter in the Secretary's manuscripts in which the correspondent wrote, "You will perhaps know about the political preferences of the generals whose names I have given you and will know how to apply the remedy better than I do."[15]

Newspapers on both sides maintained that the soldiers would support their candidates. Union papers filled columns with letters from soldiers to relatives and friends emphasizing the army's hatred for Democrats, while the Democrats replied with myriads

[13] Marie L. Rulkotter, "Civil War Veterans in Politics" (Ph.D. dissertation, Department of History, University of Wisconsin, 1938), 7, 15–17. *Chicago Tribune,* January 21, 1864.

[14] Marble to McClellan, n.d., McClellan Papers.

[15] *Harper's Weekly,* November 5, 1864; Edwin Morgan to Stanton, September 15, 1864, Stanton Papers; E. R. Boyle to Sherman, October 21, 1864, Sherman Papers; George Meade to his wife, October 7, November 15, 1864, in George G. Meade (ed.), *The Life and Letters of George Gordon Meade,* II, 232, 242.

The Month of Decision

of letters denouncing Lincoln. The Union party performed its work of propaganda so effectively that on election eve the army seemed to have been completely Lincolnized.[16] The results did not justify the amount of effort, time, and money that had been expended. Shortly before the election General Meade wrote home that "in the army we take but little interest except earnestly to wish the election over."[17] The *New York Herald* concluded, "It seems that the politicians have laid too much stress upon the army vote. That vote will be unexpectedly light."[18]

There were only a few instances in which the soldier vote was decisive. In Maryland, citizens were voting to adopt or reject a new constitution which banished slavery from their soil and withdrew the franchise from those who abetted the rebellion. So important did Lincoln consider this October election that when he heard that Henry Davis was speaking in the campaign, he said, "If he and the rest can succeed in carrying the state for emancipation I shall be very willing to lose the electoral vote."[19] The balloting was very close with 29,536 voting against the new constitution and 27,541 supporting it; but the soldiers saved the day. Including their vote, the final result stood 30,174 for and 29,699 against. Marble, who suspected chicanery, concluded, "Soldiers' votes were 'needed' to secure the adoption of it, and they were cooked up to an exactly sufficient amount."[20]

In determining the outcome of the presidential election, the soldier vote was not a decisive factor. Of the total vote cast in the field, Lincoln received 119,754 to McClellan's 34,291. In such states where soldiers had to return home to vote, definite results are more difficult to obtain. In Connecticut, where Lincoln won by a scant 2,406 votes, the fighting men cast 2,898 for him, thus assuring him victory in that state. Governor Cannon of Delaware insisted that it was the failure to get troops to vote which cost the Union party

16 *Albany Evening Journal*, September 24, 1864; B. Shirley to Holt, October 4, Holt Papers; R. Wann to Mrs. McClellan, November 2, 1864, McClellan Papers.
17 Meade to his wife, September 17, October 11, 1864, in Meade, *op. cit.*, II, 233-34, 244.
18 November 3, 1864.
19 Hay, *op. cit.*, I, 222.
20 *New York World*, October 20, 1864.

a victory in his state.[21] The close results of the October elections convinced Lincoln and his managers that they might not carry Pennsylvania. McClure estimated that he might win by a scant 6,000, but suggested that to play safe 30,000 troops should be sent home from Grant's and Sheridan's armies. Lincoln was hesitant to make such a request from the hard-pressed Grant, but at length troops were obtained from Meade and Sheridan. They could have been better employed at the front, for Lincoln carried the state by 5,712 home votes, but the boys in blue contributed an additional 14,363 to make the victory more conclusive. New York had adopted a law permitting voting in the field. Depew went to the capital to see Stanton to learn the whereabouts of certain regiments from his state so that ballots could be distributed. The Secretary would not impart this information. When he heard of this, Washburne exclaimed: "Why that would beat Mr. Lincoln. You don't know him. While he is a great statesman, he is also the keenest of politicians alive. If it could be done in no other way, the president would take a carpet bag and go around and collect those votes himself." Lincoln paid a personal visit to Stanton after being informed of the incident, and Depew returned to New York with his precious information. "It was the soldiers' vote," said Depew, "that gave him the Empire state."[22]

Only in Connecticut and New York did the soldiers' vote affect the outcome of the election, but even then Lincoln would have carried the popular and electoral vote of the North. Several congressmen owed their seats to the army voters, but even had they not been chosen, the Union party would still have controlled the Thirty-ninth Congress.

There were other ways than to cast ballots, however, that soldiers could be and were used during the election. On election day General Lew Wallace had his troops deployed in Baltimore ostensibly to oversee the voting. So efficient was their work that Lincoln carried the city by five times his opponent's votes, thus being assured of victory in the state. General Butler, upon hearing that there might be trouble on election day, wrote to Stanton, "I pro-

[21] Cannon to Stanton, October 27, 1864, Stanton Papers.

[22] McClure, *Our Presidents*, 196; McClure, *Lincoln and Men*, 200 ff.; Depew, *op. cit.* 53–55; Hesseltine, *op. cit.*, 381.

202

The Month of Decision

pose, unless ordered to the contrary by you, to land all my troops on the morning of election in the city. . . . I have information of several organizations that are being got ready . . . [which] are intending if the elections are close to try the question of inaugurating McClellan and will attempt it if at all by trying how much of an emute [*sic*] can be raised in New York City for that purpose."[23] Troops were at the polling places in many areas, but there were no incidents.[24]

The soldier vote had no sooner been counted than charges of fraud were made. Governor Curtin had appointed some Democratic commissioners to collect the votes at the front. They were arrested under Stanton's orders,as they passed through Washington and sent to Old Capitol Prison.[25] Democratic commissioners from New York suffered similar indignities at the hands of Stanton's minions. One man claimed such actions cost the Democrats 20,000 votes in New York.[26] In October the administration ordered a military commission to investigate charges that the Democrats had substituted McClellan ballots for Lincoln ballots in the original envelopes submitted to soldiers. The democrats were adjudged guilty of fraud, and the government announced its determination to protect the soldiers from further "copperhead machinations."[27]

The Democrats found a chance to counterattack by claiming that the government had carried Indiana by fraud. Marble announced that soldiers from eight other states had voted there. The *Herald* was unmoved by these charges and insisted the Indiana vote was a case of "diamond cut diamond, in which delightful game the administration has been a little ahead of the opposition in getting the first cut. . . . these awful discoveries have made quite a sensation but we guess it is nothing more than the old affair of the mountain in labor, destined to end in the delivery of a ridicu-

[23] Butler to Stanton, November 7, 1864, in Marshall, *op. cit.*, V, 326.

[24] Dix, *op. cit.*, II, 94; Myers, *op. cit.*, 460; C. W. Thompson to Johnson, October 26, 1864, Johnson Papers.

[25] McClure, *Lincoln and Men*, 177–78, 200; Meade to his wife, November 9, 1864, in Meade, *op. cit.*, II, 239–40. S. A. Purviance to Cameron, July 22, 1864; A. B. Hutchinson to Cameron, August 31, 1864; Merrell to Cameron, August 31, 1864, Cameron Papers.

[26] Milton, *The Age of Hate*, 238; Stewart Mitchell, *op. cit.*, 378–81; Alexander, *op. cit.*, III, 124.

[27] Gurowski, *op. cit.*, III, 383.

lous little mouse."[28] A Union journal in Indiana candidly admitted that there had been fraud but added, "It were better that half a dozen Massachusetts regiments should vote, than that the state should fall into the hands of the opponents of the administration. Does anyone think that the administration is going to allow the state of Indiana to fall into the hands of its enemies at a time like this?"[29] There seemed to be no doubt that the administration furloughed home thousands of soldiers to bolster the vote in doubtful areas; if these men voted as decisively for Lincoln as did their comrades in the field, they added greatly to the success of the Union party. Charles Dana noted in his recollections that he was busy in the war office as a constant succession of telegrams arrived asking that leaves be granted to men "whose presence in close districts was deemed of especial importance, and there was a widespread demand that men on detached service and convalescents in hospitals be sent home." In Indiana one Democrat drily noted, "Indiana soldiers seem to be rather sickly. So one would judge by the number who are at home on sick leaves." E. H. Wright, a friend of McClellan's said years later that on October 29 he had met Allan Pinkerton, who told him Lincoln would be elected by any majority that might be desired.[30] This was undoubtedly an overstatement, but in many cases majorities were increased by a judicious use of the soldier vote.

Lincoln would have won the election without the soldier vote, but the electoral vote would have been closer. If one assumes that New York, Connecticut, Maryland, and Indiana would have gone Democratic without the army vote, the final result would have stood at 153 to 80 electoral votes. Since there was some justification for believing that intimidation and fraud had actually been used in employing the soldier vote, the Democrats were probably justified in maintaining that they would not accept the final outcome of the election if it were determined by the soldier vote.

Much effort was directed toward winning the support of urban labor. At the beginning of the conflict many workers had been

---

[28] *New York World*, October 26, 28, 1864; *New York Herald*, October 29, 1864.
[29] *Indianapolis Gazette*, October 17, 1864.
[30] Dana, *Recollections of the Civil War*, 261; Rulkotter, "Civil War Veterans in Politics" (Ph.D. dissertation), 17–23; Eckenrode and Conrad, *op. cit.*, 273–74.

The Month of Decision

reluctant to lend it support, and this attitude was nurtured by some trade union leaders who took the position that the fight against Northern wage slavery was as important as that against chattel slavery. The patriotic spirit of the workingmen ultimately asserted itself over the official attitude of many unions. Some German-Americans, who had organized communist *Arbeitbunds*, gave official support to the war against slavery, and others soon joined them. Official labor papers such as *Fincher's Trades Review* adopted a pro-Lincoln platform, and workingmen's associations in New York, Philadelphia, Boston, and Chicago urged his reelection. Realizing the importance of the labor vote, Lincoln received a deputation from the Workingmen's Association of New York early in March. In a brief address he attempted to show them that the South was waging a war which was basically an attack upon the rights of all workingmen.[31]

The Union party was often tempted to spell out the struggle in terms of a conflict between aristocracy and democracy. The Southern planters appeared in campaign literature characterized invariably as "a proud insurgent aristocracy." Yet the issue was in itself a two-edged sword, for the Union party drew much of its support from powerful financial nabobs of the North who could have been denounced on similar grounds.[32] The issue was introduced only occasionally and then under the most guarded circumstances. Since it was known that the President was a humble, self-fashioned man of the people, party workers could and did remind labor that he understood fully the nature of the workers' problem through personal experience. One example serves to illustrate the point:

Mr. Lincoln is the only President we have ever had who may be said to be from the working class of people. . . . No other President has ever worked with his hands for a livelihood after arriving at the full maturity of manhood. This familiarity with the pursuits and feelings of the great laboring class of his coun-

---

[31] Norton, *op. cit.*, 28–29; Nicolay and Hay, *Abraham Lincoln: A History*, IX, 60–61.

[32] Arthur Cole, *Era of the Civil War*, 325–26.

Lincoln & the Party Divided

trymen, has doubtless given him some advantages in conducting public affairs.[33]

The Democrats also recognized the necessity of winning the
support of urban labor and commissioned McDonough Bucklin
to organize the Workingmen's United Political Association of the
City and County of New York. This was a Copperhead organization and never gained the support of many laborers or their unions.
The Democratic press warned workers in New York that "the
very object of arming the Negroes is based on the constructive idea
of using them to put down the white laboring class," and concluded by asking them to "unite in one grand effort to get the
present administration out of power."[34] The *New York Daily
News* used the aristocracy issue and ascribed the "reign of blood
and debt" to the "New England oligarchy."[35] The *Chicago Times*
commended the workingmen of that city for opposing the draft,
but warned them that they were only delaying the evil day unless
they "at the proper time, also rid themselves and the country of
Mr. Lincoln and his war policies." The *Workingmen's Advocate*
replied to this attack by denouncing Editor Storey as "a traitor to
his countrymen, to his God, and to the workingmen."[36]

War prosperity may have helped the Union party quell much
of the spirit of discontent which could have developed in the
North. Many people benefited from the general condition of
prosperity throughout the nation, but since wages rose about 39
per cent during the war and retail prices advanced about 70 per
cent, the plight of the poor and the unskilled workers must have
been serious.[37] Evidence of this is to be found in the number of
violent strikes which occurred during the election year. During
the same period about two hundred new union locals were
formed.[38] Businessmen predicted that the unions would throw the

[33] Sandburg, *op. cit.*, II, 591.

[34] *New York Daily News*, August 5, 1864.

[35] *Ibid.*, April 14, 1864.

[36] *Chicago Times*, October 1, 1864; *Workingmen's Advocate*, November 5,
1864, in Klement, "Middlewestern Copperheadism: Jeffersonian Democracy in
Revolt" (Ph.D. dissertation), 293.

[37] Wesley C. Mitchell, *Gold Prices and Wages Under the Greenback Standard*,
I, 279.

[38] There were about one hundred strikes during 1864.

The Month of Decision

nation into confusion which would result in "widespread beggary, with all its attending evils—suffering, bread riots, pillage, and taxation."[39] These dire predictions failed to materialize. Although certain classes must have suffered severely, the nation as a whole was prosperous. One report published in August, 1864, in Cincinnati pointed out:

The prosperity of the commercial, agricultural, and manufacturing classes, has been greater and more general, during the past than it was the previous year; and the wealth of all who engage in those departments has increased to an extent almost incredible, because, not only have all been fully employed, but the rapid advances in goods made the merchants, the manufacturers, and the farmers rich while they slept. . . . The whole people in the loyal states are rich beyond their anticipations, and they feel it and are extravagant beyond precedent: and there is not a city, town, village, or hamlet, throughout these states which has not reaped the advantage of this. We could not reasonably expect a different result, when we consider that the government has spent close up to two billion dollars already, in the prosecution of the war.[40]

A reporter for the London *Times* commented that the country was enjoying "a prosperity so enormous as almost to challenge belief." The same observer also puts his finger on the fundamental weakness of the Democrats' position when he wrote, "Nothing is strange, nothing is unusual, nothing is unconstitutional, nothing is wicked to people, who are prospering upon the war."[41] The Democrats seeking to rally the voters upon an issue of war weariness and Lincoln's usurpations of civil liberty failed to realize that while the people were prospering and hoping for a successful termination of the war these other things might appear troublesome but not intolerable. So important was the general economic situation in determining the outcome of the election that some

[39] *Detroit Tribune,* July 25, 1864.
[40] Klement, "Middlewestern Copperheadism: Jeffersonian Democracy in Revolt" (Ph.D. dissertation), 301.
[41] *Ibid.,* 302.

Lincoln & the Party Divided

Democrats deliberately became involved in plots to upset the economy of the country by driving the price of gold beyond all reasonable limits. "Every Union vote is wanted and Copperhead speculators in gold have hit upon a method that will deprive us of thousands of votes," said a worried Unionist to the Secretary of the Treasury.[42]

To assess accurately the role of urban labor in determining the outcome of the election is a difficult task, but some general observations are apparent when one considers the election results in the urban counties of the North. Shortly before the Chicago convention, John Hay wrote to his fellow secretary that "there is throughout the country, I mean the rural districts, a good healthy Union feeling, and an intention to succeed in the military and political contest; but everywhere in the towns the copperheads are exultant, and our own people either growling and despondent or sneaking apologetic."[43] It must be remembered that this letter was written during the depths of despondency which characterized the summer months; it was written two days after Lincoln had drawn up the document pledging to support the next administration. Two questions naturally arise. Was Hay's observation correct? If so, did the situation remain until November, or was there a change during the later months of the canvass?

In appraising the source of Lincoln's strength, the *New York Times* pointed out that it lay primarily among the farming classes, as well as the skilled workers and professional men of the cities. McClellan's strength, on the other hand, came from the unskilled laborers and foreign-born voters.[44] This evaluation would seem to substantiate Hay's earlier appraisal. In evaluating the voting in urban county areas, one finds the percentage of votes cast for Lincoln was in a majority of cases below the percentage cast for him in the other areas of each state.

For purposes of comparison one may take the nineteen major cities (each contained at least 40,000 persons) and the county in which each city was located. In all cases a majority of the popula-

[42] Lawton White to Fessenden, November 2, 1864; William Ropell to Fessenden, November 1, 1864, Fessenden Papers. John Bigelow to Seward, October 15, 1864, in Bigelow, *Retrospections of an Active Life*, II, 229.

[43] Hay, *op. cit.*, I, 219.

[44] *New York Times*, November 12, 1864.

The Month of Decision

tion in the county resided within the city limits. The first problem was to ascertain the percentage of voters in each urban county who voted for Lincoln. This figure was then divided by the percentage cast for Lincoln in the state in which the county was located. Any result greater than 1.00 indicated that the urban county gave Lincoln greater support than the rest of the state, while an answer less than this amount would indicate the converse to be true. The results shown below indicate that a majority of the urban counties studied gave Lincoln less support than the rural or less urbanized areas of the state. This at least indicates that Lincoln was more popular among the rural folk. As was indicated in an earlier chapter, even during the difficult period in July and August Lincoln still continued to hold the support of the rural press, while many of the large city dailies were calling for his removal and a new convention. It was pointed out at that time that since these small-town papers were reflectors of the popular will, it might be assumed Lincoln was still favored among the rural folk.

City	County	Percentage for Lincoln Urban county	State	Result
Baltimore	Baltimore	84.28	55.08	1.53
Chicago	Cook	81.09	54.41	1.49
Pittsburgh	Allegheny	63.41	51.75	1.22
Cleveland	Cuyahoga	60.92	56.31	1.08
Philadelphia	Philadelphia	55.07	51.75	1.06
Newark	Essex	50.43	47.16	1.04
Rochester	Monroe	52.83	50.46	1.04
San Francisco	San Francisco	60.24	58.14	1.03
Cincinnati	Hamilton	55.87	56.31	.99
Providence	Providence	60.29	61.78	.97
Buffalo	Erie	49.41	50.46	.97
Boston	Suffolk	63.71	72.22	.88
St. Louis	St. Louis	61.22	69.38	.88
Brooklyn	Kings	44.75	50.46	.88
Albany	Albany	44.10	50.46	.87
Louisville	Jefferson	24.39	30.19	.80
Detroit	Wayne	43.66	55.88	.78
New York	New York	33.22	50.46	.65
Milwaukee	Milwaukee	31.59	55.88	.56[45]

Lincoln & the Party Divided

Within the cities themselves it is more difficult to arrive at a satisfactory answer concerning how the residents voted, but it is illuminating to note that in the wards which were inhabited by the poor laborers, Germans, and Irish immigrants, McClellan's vote was greater than Lincoln's. If one chooses the seven wards comprising the principal residence of the proletariat in New York City, one gets some highly interesting results. In New York County, Lincoln polled only a scant 33.22 per cent of the vote, while in the state as a whole he polled 50.46 per cent. In four of the seven wards under consideration his vote fell below this first figure.

	McClellan vote	Lincoln vote
Ward 1	2,161	213
Ward 4	2,379	435
Ward 6	3,457	329
Ward 11	5,532	1,990
Ward 14	4,229	859
Ward 17	7,031	3,425
Ward 18	4,424	2,678

It would seem that Lincoln drew his principal support from the rural areas and from the better residential districts of the greater cities, while McClellan's friends were among the poorer classes and among the immigrant groups. No hard and fast rule, however, is possible. The farming classes benefited greatly from the war prosperity which was at its height in 1864. Since the beginning of the war, farm prices had risen 143 per cent. Some of the farmers located in the lands adjacent to the Ohio River had been encouraged by the Southern withdrawal from the Union to cultivate those crops which normally had been raised almost entirely in the Confederacy. Tobacco acreage increased greatly even in Wisconsin, while farmers in other areas turned to cotton, flax, and sugar beets as sources of revenue. In 1862 the farmers in southern Illinois produced only 1,416 pounds of cotton, but by the end of the war they had boosted this to more than half a million pounds.[46] Such

---

[45] It must be kept in mind that the presence of troops in Baltimore, as well as the city's previous experience with McClellan in 1861, probably resulted in such an overwhelming vote for Lincoln in that city.

[46] Arthur Cole, *Era of the Civil War*, 378–79.

The Month of Decision

unprecedented wealth which found its way into the farmers' hands must have done much to influence their vote.

Of the foreign voters the Irish and Germans seemed to have favored McClellan. The Irish were traditionally Democratic, and in 1864 they showed no tendency to depart from their normal pattern. "They voted against us almost to a man," said one Union party leader.[47] In some localities priests stood all day at the polls to see that their flocks voted for McClellan. Edward Everett noted in his diary, "It was truly disgusting to see the vote distributors of the Democratic party in our ward—the very dregs of the Irish population."[48]

Throughout most of the year Lincoln had been noticeably worried over the German vote, and he confessed to Koerner that he feared it would cost him Missouri, Wisconsin, and Illinois, where the Germans held the balance of power. Koerner refused to concur in such a pessimistic view and insisted they would support him even though there was much grumbling about his policies. Their discontent, said Koerner, would die down if Blair were removed from the cabinet.[49]

Both parties directed much of their propaganda toward the German voters. Many documents were issued in German translation, and several were written expressly for them. The Unionists took the stand that the Democratic party was composed of anti-German Know-Nothings and men who hoped to see America broken into a collection of "pumpernickel sovereignities" like Germany.[50] The Democrats retaliated by insisting that the administration was rigging draft quotas so that only Germans would have to go. Lincoln did this, the Democrats claimed, in order to gain revenge for the Germans' growing estrangement from his administration.[51]

One is faced with another difficult task in trying to ascertain whether or not the Germans supported Lincoln in 1864. Joseph Schafer in his study on German voting in Wisconsin during 1860 concluded that "a fairly comprehensive sampling of the Wisconsin

[47] Pierce, *op. cit.*, IV, 201.
[48] Frothingham, *op. cit.*, 464–65.
[49] Koerner, *op. cit.*, II, 423–33.
[50] Francis Lieber, *Lincoln or McClellan*, 1–8.
[51] *Chicago Times*, October 4, 7, 8, 9, 1864.

Lincoln & the Party Divided

election vote of 1860 shows few German communities that were
. . . favorable to Lincoln."[52] Using Schafer's findings as a basis,
we can examine the election returns from Wisconsin in 1864 in an
attempt to determine what the German voters did in that election.
Lincoln polled fewer votes in 1864 than he had four years earlier.
In 1860 he polled 86,110 votes for 56.58 per cent of the total cast,
and in 1864 he garnered only 83,458 for a percentage of 55.88. As
there is no noticeable alteration in the vote in German-inhabited
counties, it may be safely concluded that the Germans in Wisconsin did not support Lincoln in 1864 either. It would be impossible
to conclude that it followed *ipso facto* that their German compatriots in other states such as Illinois, Ohio, and New York followed a similar voting pattern. The lack of a full set of election
poll books for all states makes a comprehensive study impossible,
but one may draw a few conclusions from the material available.

The evidence would seem to indicate that Lincoln lost most
of the counties where at least one-third of the population was
foreign born, or he polled a percentage less than he received for
each state as a whole. Of eighteen Wisconsin counties in which the
foreign born constituted at least one-third of the population, Lincoln lost thirteen, fell below the percentage cast in the state in two,
and carried only three of them by a percentage greater than he received throughout the entire state. The same seems to have been
true in Minnesota. Of sixteen counties of the above type Lincoln
lost seven, and of the remainder carried five by a smaller percentage
than he polled in the state. In five Iowa counties the President
carried only one by a greater percentage than he polled in the
state and lost two others to McClellan. Erie, Kings, and New York
counties in the Empire State voted against him, while he carried
Monroe County by a smaller percentage than he polled in the state.
With only a few exceptions this situation seems to have been true
throughout the North.

The greatest Union party strength lay in the Yankee counties
rather than in those settled by German or Irish immigrants; those
counties in which a larger percentage of the population came from
the older states of the Eastern seaboard, or was native to the state,

[52] Joseph Schafer, "Who elected Lincoln?", *American Historical Review*, Vol.
XLVII (October, 1941), 57.

Lincoln full-face, from Mathew B. Brady's
photograph of February 9, 1864

or where there was an admixture of English and Scots seemed to prefer Lincoln. The counties of northeastern Ohio, for example, the Western Reserve, with its population largely recruited from New England, gave Lincoln much greater support (as they did the Free-Soil movement years earlier) than did those along the Ohio River, including Hamilton County and Cincinnati with its large German population of nearly 50,000.

In examining the election returns from the counties of each state, one cannot escape noticing that McClellan drew much support from areas in which Breckinridge had polled heavily in 1860. The *New York Times* called attention to this fact on November 12 when it appraised the final outcome of the election. In hundreds of counties the vote polled by McClellan was approximately equal to the vote polled by Douglas and Breckinridge four years earlier. Those who voted for the Bell-Everett ticket in 1860 apparently threw their support to Lincoln. Edward Everett was most active throughout the campaign, speaking in New York and New England in an attempt to turn his former supporters into Lincoln's camp. When the ballots were counted, he wrote to Charles Adams expressing personal satisfaction that his former supporters had gone for Lincoln.[53] He felt that these men held the balance of power in states such as New York and Pennsylvania and were responsible for Lincoln's victories there. In many counties it was true that the vote polled by Lincoln was equivalent approximately to the vote polled by Bell and Lincoln in 1860, a fact which lends some support to Everett's contention.

Various churches in the North had been converted to an active support of the war effort since 1861. Catholics, Episcopalians, Presbyterians, Methodists, Baptists, and Congregationalists had taken a conservative stand in relation to the slavery controversy in the period before 1860.[54] It was generally true that once the fighting began Lincoln drew much support from Protestantism. Most ministers regarded the conflict as an issue of human freedom. The Congregational church, for example, proclaimed early in the war that it was a struggle in which "every Christian may rise from his

[53] Everett to Adams, December 18, 1864, in Frothingham, *op. cit.*, 466–67.
[54] William E. Dodd, "Fight for the Northwest—1860," *American Historical Review*, Vol. XVI (July, 1911), 774–88.

Lincoln & the Party Divided

knee to shoulder his rifle."[55] Methodist Bishops Matthew Simpson, Thomas A. Morris, and Edward R. Ames threw their support to the administration. By the election year most of the Protestant faiths were firmly committed to supporting the administration in the war effort. The United Presbyterian church, which had considerable strength in Pennsylvania, Ohio, Indiana, and Illinois, held a general assembly in Philadelphia, on June 2, 1864, and adopted a resolution expressing "deep sympathy and earnest co-operation" with the government. The General Synod of the Reformed Presbyterian church met in the same city on May 18 and declared that it was the church's duty to "encourage and sustain the government . . . in all that they do for the . . . freedom of the enslaved, the mitigation of the inevitable evils of war, and the preservation, at all hazards, of the national life, integrity, and power." About the same time a general assembly of the new school of the Presbyterian church met in Dayton, Ohio, and renewed its allegiance to the government. The Congregational church held general association meetings in June and adopted similar resolutions to attest its loyalty to the government. The annual conference of the Methodist church, which met it Pittsburgh in September, declared "its loyalty to the Government of the United States and its approval of the Administration of Abraham Lincoln." It further advised all its members "to be faithful to the Administration in all its efforts to maintain the Union." Many other denominations hastened to urge their members to support Lincoln's government.[56]

With the principal Protestant churches throwing their influence to the administration and urging their members to support it for the sake of victory, there can be no doubt that Lincoln drew significant support from this source.

By way of recapitulation one may say that Lincoln won the election because of the support given him by the agricultural areas inhabited largely by native-born citizens, former Bell-Everett voters, and the skilled urban workers and professional classes. Mc-

---

[55] *Chicago Tribune,* April 22, 1861.

[56] McPherson, *op. cit.,* 471, 473, 476, 477, 481, 482, 483, 493, 499–500; Chester Dunham, *The Attitude of the Northern Clergy toward the South,* 1860–1865, 115–19; Louis Vander Velde, *The Presbyterian Church and the Federal Union,* 1861–1869, 351, 384–86.

Clellan drew his best support from the immigrant proletariat and from rural areas in which the foreign element predominated. Those who supported Breckinridge in 1860 seem in a large measure to have voted for McClellan in 1864. Most Protestant denominations urged support of the administration, while the Irish element of the Catholic church supported McClellan. There remains only to consider the election itself and to attempt to interpret briefly the significance, if any, of the outcome.

On election day the President's earlier trepidations returned, and he confessed to Noah Brooks that he "was just enough of a politician to know that there was not much doubt about the results of the Baltimore convention, but about this thing [he was] very far from certain."[57] Later that evening he went with Stanton to the War Office to wait for the returns to arrive. Welles and Gustavus Fox ultimately joined the Chief Executive, who as the good news came over the wire, grew more genial, ate some oysters, and disgusted Stanton by reading to them the latest exploits of Petroleum V. Nasby.[58]

With only the Union states voting, it was difficult to beat Lincoln. The final electoral vote stood 213 to 21 (one elector from Nevada died, thereby giving Lincoln only 212), a count that would seemingly indicate a smashing victory. The popular vote, on the other hand, told a different story, and there was some disappointment among the President's managers. "The size of his majority did not come up to the expectation of Lincoln's friends," said Carl Schurz many years later.

The President polled 339,308 more votes in 1864 than he had in his first election. He had 55.08 per cent of the vote cast, and thereby removed from his shoulders the stigma of being a minority president. He carried five more states than in his first election: Missouri, Maryland, West Virginia, Kansas, and Nevada. Delaware and Kentucky voted against him on both occasions, and in the second election they were joined by New Jersey, which had given Lincoln four of its electoral votes in 1860. In 1864, Kansas, West Virginia,

[57] Brooks, *Washington in Lincoln's Time*, 216–17.

[58] Dana, *Recollections of the Civil War*, 261–62; Dennett, *Lincoln and the Civil War*, 233, 235; Richard West, *Gideon Welles—Lincoln's Navy Department*, 299.

and Nevada voted in the presidential race for the first time. In four states—Maine, New Hampshire, Michigan, and Wisconsin—the President polled fewer votes than in 1860, and in nine states (the above four plus Connecticut, Minnesota, New York, Pennsylvania, and Vermont) his percentage of the votes polled was diminished.

All this adds up to indicate that a change of a few thousand votes in certain key states would have thrown the election to McClellan. It also seems to indicate that the country was still normally Democratic. With many in that party committed temporarily to co-operating with the Unionists, with thousands of soldiers brought home to influence the election in some states, and with the party's strongholds in the South not counted, the Democratic candidate was beaten by a rather narrow margin.

In appraising the significance of the election, it might be well first to call attention to what contemporaries believed it indicated. Many insisted that the election meant the end of "Copperheadism" and that it had buried forever the forces of "domestic treason."[59] These persons, of course, were carried away by the fury of their own party's campaigning. The threat of domestic treason had been present at least incipiently in the minds of a few fanatical and overzealous Democrats, who dreamed of the golden opportunity to erect a confederacy in the old Northwest in which they could have reaped the advantages of power and place. These men were the spiritual heirs of the old school that believed the South and the West to be natural allies against the East. This situation had been true before the war, but times had changed. The agricultural West was now riveted indissolubly to the East. Gone were the days when the West looked down the Mississippi to the South for its principal markets and means of egress. This addled minority was at no time a serious threat to the government. Their nebulous, poorly conceived schemes were easily thwarted. In the final analysis the "lunatic fringe" of the Democratic party did great service to their opponents by providing them with the most damning accusations which could be directed against the Democrats in general.

[59] Ware, *op. cit.*, 143; Charles F. Adams to Henry Adams, November 14, 1864, in Worthington Ford (ed.), *A Cycle of Adams' Letters*, 1861–65, II, 223.

The Month of Decision

Greeley reported that the outcome of the election clearly indicated that slavery was no longer to be tolerated in the United States.[60] Lincoln later in his annual message said that the election indicated "the purpose of the people within the loyal states to maintain the integrity of the Union." This purpose, he continued, "was never more firm nor more nearly unanimous than now."[61] Unquestionably both Lincoln and Greeley were correct in their interpretation of what the election indicated. Most Americans would never accept peace without the restoration of the Union. This was the reason they fought. It was a tenacious struggle fought with great vigor by both sides; the cost had been heavy and there had been some disillusionment in 1864. The great victories, however, convinced the majority that the suffering had not been in vain, and they turned to rededicating themselves to see the struggle to its conclusion. Attention has already been called to the fact that the question of emancipation and the Thirteenth Amendment had been introduced by both parties and became one of the most widely discussed issues of the campaign. We must consider the heavy gains made by the Union party in the Congressional elections as proof of a popular mandate to abolish the hated institution in all sections of the nation.

In trying to evaluate the reason for the Democrats' defeat, most persons were agreed that they failed because of the ambiguous expressions in their platform and because of the questionable principles of some of the men who played prominent roles at the convention. They had foolishly taken up the cry of peace, denounced all others as abolitionists, organized secret societies, and written a platform to conciliate a minority group that was running the party. All these factors combined to bring about their downfall. "I am here by the blunders of the Democrats," admitted Lincoln, and many agreed with him.[62]

Even had the party not drawn up the ill-timed platform or permitted a minority faction to jeopardize the position of the

---

[60] *New York Tribune*, November 10, 1864.

[61] Nicolay and Hay, *Abraham Lincoln: A History*, IX, 383–84.

[62] William Weeden, *War Government: Federal and State in Massachusetts, New York, Pennsylvania, and Indiana, 1861–1865*, 261; Barnes, *op. cit.*, 447-48; McCulloch, *op. cit.*, 162; James Randall, *Civil War and Reconstruction*, 622.

majority, there were other weaknesses in its make-up. The party offered nothing which would draw any support away from Lincoln. There was in the North a nucleus of party voters composed of those who had supported the rival nominees Douglas and Breckinridge in 1860. Their combined vote had fallen below Lincoln's vote in the North at that time. The only way the Democrats could have won was to make serious inroads upon Republican strength, and this they failed to do. The Republicans were in a position to weaken their opponents. They created the Union party and thereby offered a basis upon which Democrats, Bell-Everett men, and others could join them in prosecuting the war.

The Democrats deluded themselves on the false premise that the South was anxious to restore the Union and would do so voluntarily if its right to own slaves was recognized and protected. They failed to realize the economic basis of the war, the desire of the South for independence.

McClellan recognized the necessity of making a restoration of the Union an integral part of the peace, and he maneuvered himself into a position where he was standing on the same platform with Lincoln. Since both candidates stood essentially for the same things and Lincoln's administration was, after September 1, proving that it could wage war successfully, there was no reason why the voters should wish to select another leader.

The course of the war was not determined by the outcome of this presidential election. Even had McClellan been elected, the war would have continued much the same. It was true that McClellan was a man who might have been influenced by the peace men of his party, but by March 4, when he would have assumed the reins of power, the work would already have been pushed to the point where the Confederacy had but a short time to live. McClellan, even had he been influenced by the peace men, could not have halted the inevitable march of conquest. Even had he wished to do so, Congress would have presented an insuperable obstacle to such a decision.

The most significant outcome of the election of 1864 was the capture of Congress by the Republican-Union party, as well as the fact that it controlled nearly all the state governmental organizations. With the power of the party completely in the ascendency

The Month of Decision

throughout the North, the President, regardless of his party affiliation, would have been impotent before it. The election of 1864, like the state elections of the preceding year, was merely indicative that the Republican party was fastening itself upon the nation's government and would remain in control for many years. The nation as a whole was still Democratic, but Republican leaders, now in control of the agencies of the federal and state government in the North, had no intention of permitting the Democratic party to unite its strength to oust them from power. Difficult times were ahead for the Democrats and their Southern stronghold.

Republican leaders hailed the election as a triumph for the party and not for the administration. In this belief they were correct. Buchanan remarked shortly after the smoke had cleared, "The Republicans have won the elephant; and they will find difficulty in deciding what to do with him."[63] One can almost imagine that the elephant he had in mind was Abraham Lincoln. Unconditional leaders had supported him reluctantly only when they realized they could find no other man to run. As one of Trumbull's friends wrote, "I have felt and do feel that he lacks much of firmness, decision, and sternness with which God so usefully blessed Andrew Jackson. But I made up my mind, months ago, that we could not risk a change."[64] Bates predicted that the victory of the Unconditionals might be "a melancholy defeat for their country."[65] The fact that Lincoln still stood as the spokesman for the moderate cause made him a white elephant to the Unconditionals because he would oppose their program. On April 11, 1865, Lincoln, apparently realizing the inevitable march of events, announced that he was ready to alter his position, but he did not live to disclose his plans. It will never be known whether he intended to defy the Unconditionals or yield to their pressure.[66] It could almost be said that a kindly Fortune removed him from the scene before he had to fight his greatest battle.

The young Unconditionals such as Conkling, Blaine, Sherman,

[63] Buchanan to John Blake, November 21, 1864, in James Buchanan, *Works,* XI, 377.

[64] G. T. Allen to Trumbull, October 4, 1864, Trumbull Papers.

[65] Beale, *op. cit.,* 412.

[66] Arthur Cole, "Lincoln and the Presidential Election of 1864," *Illinois State Historical Society Transactions* (1917), 137–38.

Garfield, and others were in the saddle after 1864. Their strength had been greatly implemented by the heavy gains from Congressional and state elections that year. The Unconditional clique, which at the outbreak of the war was a minority, had by 1864 become the controlling element of the party. They could keep moderate Republicans in check and, by controlling the reconstruction processes, keep the Democrats powerless to reassert themselves. So strong did they feel that before 1865 was far advanced they could think of abandoning the Union party and the Republican party began to reappear.

For the next few years this militant group, speaking for the industrial capitalistic society of the North, mastered the political agencies in Washington. The opposition party was kept in check in the South by their program of reconstruction and in the North by reviving whenever convenient the myths of conspiracies. The election of 1864 is important in that it marked the passing of power into the hands of the Unconditional spokesmen of Northern industrial capitalism as opposed to the older radicals who thought only in terms of abolition. In all this change Abraham Lincoln, with his great popularity among the common citizens, was useful only in that he could be put up as a symbol of unity around which the people could rally and vote.

Had the Democrats won the national, Congressional, and state elections, things would have been different. Perhaps by 1865 the Southern states would have been readmitted with their great Democratic blocs of voters and that party would have continued to dominate the government. By losing, however, the Democrats were deprived of their chance for a generation. For the Republicans, therefore, 1864 was the year of decision. It had been a year that began in doubt and uncertainty. Lincoln was confronted by a divided country and a dividing party. He faced the twofold task of reuniting the former and preventing the disruption of the latter. There had been at that time a danger that Lincoln's entire moderate program would be lost if the party divided, and an even greater threat that in the event this division occurred the cause of national unity would be lost too. The division of Lincoln's party might have thrown the country into the hands of men dedicated to the cause of appeasement and disunity.

The Month of Decision

At the year's end Lincoln had saved his country. In fact, he did such an effective job of waging war that by November, even had the Democrats won the election, the unity of the country would probably have been assured. During those uncertain months he had also held his party together, fought off his rivals, and secured his re-election. Yet though it was a popular endorsement of Lincoln the man, it was not necessarily an endorsement of the program for which that man stood. It was his personal popularity and hold upon the affection of the American public that gave him victory at the polls. In holding the party together, he did much to assure the ultimate victory of the Unconditional program he had so long opposed.

Bibliography

MANUSCRIPTS

Library of Congress: Blair family Papers; Simon Cameron Papers; William E. Chandler Papers; Zachariah Chandler Papers; Salmon P. Chase Papers; Schuyler Colfax Papers; John A. J. Creswell Papers; Anna Dickinson Papers; James R. Doolittle Papers; William P. Fessenden Papers; Joshua Giddings and George Julian Papers; Horace Greeley Papers; Adam Gurowski Papers; Joseph Holt Papers; Andrew Johnson Papers; Reverdy Johnson Papers; Robert T. Lincoln Papers; John A. Logan Papers; Manton M. Marble Papers; Charles Mason Diary; George B. McClellan Papers; Edward McPherson Papers; Justin S. Morrill Papers; Samuel F. B. Morse Papers; Carl Schurz Papers; John Sherman Papers; Edwin M. Stanton Papers; Thaddeus Stevens Papers; Lyman Trumbull Papers; Benjamin F. Wade Papers; Elihu Washburne Papers; Gideon Welles Papers.
Ohio State Museum: Samuel Medary Papers.
Pennsylvania State Historical Society: Salmon P. Chase Papers.
Western Reserve Historical Society: Thomas Gregg Papers; Albert G. Riddle Papers; Clement L. Vallandigham Papers; A. J. Warner Papers.

Brackney, Clarence C. "Samuel Medary: A Peace Democrat." Unpublished Master's thesis, Department of History, Ohio State University, 1931.
Clark, Charles B. "Politics in Maryland During the Civil War." Un-

published Ph.D. dissertation, Department of History, University of North Carolina, 1941.

Friedel, Frank B. "The Life of Francis Lieber." Ph.D. dissertation, Department of History, University of Wisconsin, 1941.

Hardie, Anna. "The Influence of the Union League of America on the Second Election of Lincoln." Unpublished Master's thesis, Department of History, Louisiana State University, 1937.

Hare, John S. "Allen G. Thurman: A Political Study." Unpublished Ph.D. dissertation, Department of History, Ohio State University, 1933.

Hogen, Mildred E. "The Attitude of the New York Press Toward Lincoln and the Slavery Question." Unpublished Ph.D. dissertation, Department of History, Marquette University, 1944.

Klement, Frank L. "Middlewestern Copperheadism: Jeffersonian Democracy in Revolt." Unpublished Ph.D. dissertation, Department of History, University of Wisconsin, 1946.

McKinney, Effie May. "The Cleveland Convention." Unpublished Master's thesis, Department of History, Western Reserve University, 1928.

McReynolds, Edwin C. "The Influence of the Cabinet During the American Civil War." Unpublished Ph.D. dissertation, Department of History, University of Oklahoma, 1945.

Robinson, Elwyn B. "The Public Press of Philadelphia During the Civil War." Unpublished Ph.D. dissertation, Department of History, Western Reserve University, 1936.

Rulkotter, Marie L. "Civil War Veterans in Politics." Ph.D. dissertation, Department of History, University of Wisconsin, 1938.

Smith, George W. "Generative Forces of Union Propaganda: A Study in Civil War Pressure Groups." Unpublished Ph.D. dissertation, Department of History, University of Wisconsin, 1940.

Stampp, Kenneth M. "Indiana in the Civil War." Ph.D. dissertation, Department of History, University of Wisconsin, 1941.

Stipp, John L. "Economic and Political Aspects of Western Copperheadism." Unpublished Ph.D. dissertation, Department of History, Ohio State University, 1944.

GOVERNMENT PUBLICATIONS

The Congressional Globe
The Congressional Record
United States Statutes at Large

Bibliography

The War of the Rebellion: A Compilation of the Official Records of the Union and Confederate Armies. 70 vols. Washington, 1880–1901.

NEWSPAPERS

Albany Argus
Albany Evening Journal
Baltimore Clipper
Baltimore Gazette
Baltimore Sun
Boston Daily Journal
The (Boston) *Liberator*
Boston Post
Boston Transcript
Canton, Ohio, *Stark County Democrat*
Chicago Times
Chicago Tribune
Cincinnati Commercial
Cincinnati Daily Enquirer
Cincinnati Gazette
Cleveland Herald
Cleveland Daily Leader
Cleveland Plain Dealer
Cleveland *Waechter am Erie*
Columbus, *Ohio State Journal*
The (Columbus) *Crisis*
Detroit Advertiser and Tribune
Detroit Free Press
Frank Leslie's Illustrated Weekly
Harper's Weekly
Hartford Daily Courant

Indianapolis Gazette
Indianapolis Daily Journal
Indianapolis State Sentinel
Madison (Wisconsin) *Patriot*
Milwaukee Sentinel
New York *National Anti-Slavery Standard*
New York Evening Post
New York Herald
New York Independent
New York Journal of Commerce
New York Sun
New York Times
New York Tribune
New York World
Philadelphia Evening Bulletin
Philadelphia Press
Pittsburgh Post
St. Louis *Missouri Democrat*
St. Louis *Missouri Republican*
Washington Daily Chronicle
Washington Daily National Republican
Washington National Intelligencer
Wilkes' Spirit of the Times

ARTICLES

Abrahams, Samuel. "Lincoln's Political Opposition in 1864," *Negro History Bulletin,* Vol. XII (1948–49), 7–9, 18.

Boyer, Margarette. "Morgan's Raid in Indiana," *Indiana Magazine of History,* Vol. VIII (December, 1912), 149–65.

Brillhart, Norman C. "Election of 1864 in Western Pennsylvania,"

Lincoln & the Party Divided

Western Pennsylvania Historical Magazine, Vol. VIII (January, 1925), 26–36.

Brooks, Noah. "Lincoln's Re-election," *The Century Magazine,* Vol. XLIX (April, 1895), 865–72.

———. "Two War-Time Conventions," *The Century Magazine,* Vol. XLIX (March, 1895), 723–36.

Butler, Benjamin F. "Vice-Presidential Politics in '64," *North American Review,* Vol. CXLI (October, 1885), 331–34.

Canup, Charles. "Conscription and Draft in Indiana During the Civil War," *Indiana Magazine of History,* Vol. X (June, 1914), 70–83.

Carr, Clark E. "Why Lincoln Was Not Renominated by Acclamation," *The Century Magazine,* Vol. LXXII (February, 1907), 503–506.

Clark, Charles B. "Politics in Maryland During the Civil War," *Maryland Historical Magazine,* Vol. XXXVI (September, 1941), 239–62; (June, 1942), 171–92; (December, 1942), 378–99; Vol. XXXVIII (September, 1943), 230–60; Vol. XXXIX (June, 1944), 149–61; (December, 1944), 315–31; Vol. XL (September, 1945), 233–41; (December, 1945), 295–309; Vol. XLI (June, 1946), 132–58.

Cochrane, William C. "The Dream of a Northwestern Confederacy," *Proceedings of the Wisconsin State Historical Society* for 1916, 213–53.

Cole, Arthur C. "Lincoln and the Presidential Election of 1864," *Illinois State Historical Society Transactions* for 1917, 130–40.

———. "President Lincoln and the Illinois Radical Republicans," *The Mississippi Valley Historical Review,* Vol. IV (March, 1918), 417–37.

Coleman, Charles H. "The Middlewest Peace Democracy, 1861–1865," *The Mississippi Valley Historical Review,* Vol. XXVIII (September, 1941), 209–10.

———. "The Use of the Term 'Copperhead' During the Civil War," *The Mississippi Valley Historical Review,* Vol. XXV (September, 1938), 263–64.

Cunz, Dieter, "The Maryland Germans in the Civil War," *Maryland Historical Magazine,* Vol. XXXVI (December, 1941), 394–419.

Dennett, Tyler. "Lincoln and the Campaign of 1864," *Abraham Lincoln Association Papers* for 1935, 31–58.

De Witt, David M. "Vice-President Andrew Johnson," *Publications of the Southern Historical Association,* Vol. VIII (November, 1904), 437–42; Vol. IX (January, 1905), 1–24; (March, 1905), 71–87; (May, 1905), 151–60; (July, 1905), 213–26.

Bibliography

Dodd, William E. "The Fight for the Northwest—1860," *American Historical Review*, Vol. XVI (July, 1911), 774–88.

———. "Lincoln's Last Struggle—Victory?" *Abraham Lincoln Association Papers* for 1927, 49–98.

Dorpalen, Andreas. "The German Element and the Issues of the Civil War," *The Mississippi Valley Historical Review*, Vol. XXIX (June, 1942), 55–76.

Dudley, Harold M. "The Election of 1864," *The Mississippi Valley Historical Review*, Vol. XVIII (March, 1932), 500–18.

Dunning, William A. "The Second Birth of the Republican Party," *American Historical Review*, Vol. XVI (October, 1910), 56–63.

Ellis, L. E. "The *Chicago Times* During the Civil War," *Illinois State Historical Society Transactions* for 1932, 135–82.

Ewbank, Louis B. "Morgan's Raid in Indiana," *Publications of the Indiana State Historical Society*, Vol. VII, 131–83.

Fesler, Mayo. "Secret Political Societies in the North During the Civil War," *Indiana Magazine of History*, Vol. XIV (September, 1918), 183–286.

Foraker, Joseph B. "Salmon P. Chase," *Ohio State Archaeological and Historical Publications*, Vol. XV (1906), 312–41.

Friedel, Frank. "The Loyal Publication Society: A Pro-Union Propaganda Agency," *The Mississippi Valley Historical Review*, Vol. XXVI (December, 1939), 359–76.

Glonek, James H. "Lincoln, Johnson, and the Baltimore Ticket," *Abraham Lincoln Quarterly*, Vol. VI (March, 1951), 255–71.

Green, Anna H. "Civil War Opinion of General Grant," *Journal of the Illinois State Historical Society*, Vol. XXII (April, 1929), 1–64.

Greene, Evart B. "Some Aspects of Politics in the Middle West, 1860–1872," *State Historical Society of Wisconsin Proceedings* for 1911, 60–76.

Grover, George S. "Civil War in Missouri," *Missouri Historical Review*, Vol. VIII (October, 1913), 1–28.

Hamilton, E. Bentley. "The Union League: Its Origin and Achievements in the Civil War," *Illinois State Historical Society Transactions* for 1921, 110–15.

Harbison, Winifred A. "Indiana Republicans and the Re-election of President Lincoln," *Indiana Magazine of History*, Vol. XXXIV (March, 1938), 42–64.

———. "Zachariah Chandler's Part in the Re-election of Abraham Lincoln," *The Mississippi Valley Historical Review*, Vol. XXII (September, 1935), 267–76.

Hines, Thomas H. "The Northwest Conspiracy," *The Southern Bivouac: A Monthly Literary and Historical Magazine*, Vol. II (January, 1885), 506–10.

Hofer, J. M. "Development of the Peace Movement in Illinois During the Civil War," *Journal of the Illinois State Historical Society*, Vol. XXIV (April, 1931), 110–24.

Hubbart, Henry C. " 'Pro-Southern' Influences in the West, 1840–1865," *The Mississippi Valley Historical Review*, Vol. XX (June, 1935), 45–62.

Kaplan, Sidney. "The Miscegenation Issue in the Election of 1864," *Journal of Negro History*, Vol. XXXIV (July, 1949), 274–343.

Kimball, E. L. "Richard Yates, His Record as Civil War Governor of Illinois," *Journal of the Illinois State Historical Society* Vol. XXIII (April, 1930), 1–83.

Laughlin, Sceva B. "Missouri Politics During the Civil War," *Missouri Historical Review*, Vol. XXIII (April, 1929), 400–26; (July, 1929), 583–618; Vol. XXIV (October, 1929), 87–113; (January, 1930), 261–84.

Lewis, Lloyd. "The Man the Historians Forget," *Kansas Historical Quarterly*, Vol. VIII (February, 1939), 85–113.

Luthin, Reinhard H. "A Discordant Chapter in Lincoln's Administration," *Maryland Historical Magazine*, Vol. XXXIX (March, 1944), 25–49.

Matthews, Albert. "A Last Word on 'Copperhead,' " *The Nation*, Vol. XVI (June, 1918), 758.

———. "Origin of 'Butternut' and 'Copperhead,' " *Publications of the Colonial Society of Massachusetts*, Vol. XX (April, 1918), 205–37.

McDougal, H. C. "A Decade of Missouri Politics—1860 to 1870—from a Republican Viewpoint," *Missouri Historical Review*, Vol. III (January, 1909), 126–53.

Merrill, Louis T. "General Benjamin F. Butler in the Presidential Campaign of 1864," *The Mississippi Valley Historical Review*, Vol. XXXIII (March, 1947), 537–70.

Moore, Charles. "Zachariah Chandler in Lincoln's Second Campaign," *The Century Magazine*, Vol. XXVIII (July, 1895), 476.

Potter, Marguerite. "Hamilton R. Gamble, Missouri's War Governor," *Missouri Historical Review*, Vol. XXXV (October, 1940), 25–71.

Pritchett, John P. "Michigan Democracy in the Civil War," *Michigan History Magazine*, Vol. XI (January, 1927), 92–109.

Randall, James G. "Has the Lincoln Theme Been Exhausted?" *American Historical Review*, Vol. XLI (January, 1936), 270–95.

Bibliography

Robertson, J. R. "Sectionalism in Kentucky, 1855 to 1865," *The Mississippi Valley Historical Review*, Vol. IV (June, 1917), 49–64.

Ross, Earle D. "Northern Sectionalism in the Civil War Era," *Iowa Journal of History and Politics*, Vol. XXX (October, 1932), 455–512.

Russ, William A. "Disfranchisement in Maryland, 1861–67," *Maryland Historical Magazine*, Vol. XXVIII (December, 1933), 309–28.

Sanger, Donald B. "The *Chicago Times* and the Civil War," *The Mississippi Valley Historical Review*, Vol. XVII (March, 1931), 557–80.

Schafer, Joseph. "Who Elected Lincoln?" *American Historical Review*, Vol. XLVII (October, 1941), 51–63.

Shepard, Frederick J. "The Johnson's Island Plot," *Publications of the Buffalo Historical Society*, Vol. IX (1906), 1–52.

Smith, George W. "A Strong Band Circular," *The Mississippi Valley Historical Review*, Vol. XXIX (March, 1943), 557–64.

Smith, Paul S. "First Use of the Term 'Copperhead,'" *American Historical Review*, Vol. XXXII (July, 1927), 799–800.

Smith, William E. "The Blairs and Frémont," *Missouri Historical Review*, Vol. XXIII (January, 1929), 214–60.

Spring, Leverett W. "The Career of a Kansas Politician," *American Historical Review*, Vol. IV (October, 1898), 80–104.

Stampp, Kenneth M. "The Milligan Case and the Election of 1864 in Indiana," *The Mississippi Valley Historical Review*, Vol. XXXI (June, 1944), 41–58.

Stevens, Walter B. "Lincoln and Missouri," *Missouri Historical Review*, Vol. X (January, 1916), 63–120.

Tasher, Lucy L. "The Missouri Democrats and the Civil War," *Missouri Historical Review*, Vol. XXXI (July, 1937), 402–19.

Townshend, N. S. "Salmon P. Chase," *Ohio State Archaeological and Historical Quarterly*, Vol. I (September, 1887), 111–26.

Vallandigham, Edward N. "Clement L. Vallandigham, 'Copperhead,'" *Putnam's Monthly*, Vol. II (August, 1907), 590–97.

Van Fossan, W. H. "Clement L. Vallandigham," *Ohio State Archaeological and Historical Quarterly*, Vol. XXIII (1914), 256–67.

Williams, T. Harry. "Voters in Blue: The Citizen Soldiers of the Civil War," *The Mississippi Valley Historical Review*, Vol. XXXI (September, 1944), 187–204.

Wilson, Buford. "Southern Illinois During the Civil War," *Illinois State Historical Society Transactions* for 1911, 93–106.

Wilson, Charles R. "McClellan's Changing Views on the Peace Plank of 1864," *American Historical Review,* Vol. XXXVIII (April, 1933), 498–510.

——. "New Lights on the Lincoln-Blair-Frémont 'Bargain' of 1864," *American Historical Review,* Vol. XLII (October, 1936), 71–78.

——. "The Original Chase Organization Meeting and *The Next Presidential Election,*" *The Mississippi Valley Historical Review,* Vol. XXIII (June, 1936), 61–79.

Winchell, J. M. "Three Interviews with President Lincoln," *Galaxy,* Vol. XVI (July, 1873), 33–41.

Woodburn, James A. "Party Politics in Indiana During the Civil War," *American Historical Association Annual Report* for 1902, 223–52.

Yager, Elizabeth F. "The Presidential Campaign of 1864 in Ohio," *Ohio State Archaeological and Historical Quarterly,* Vol. XXXIV (October, 1925), 549–86.

Young, James H. "Anna Elizabeth Dickinson and the Civil War: For and Against Lincoln," *The Mississippi Valley Historical Review,* Vol. XXXI (June, 1944), 59–80.

Zornow, William F. "The Attitude of the Western Reserve Press on the Re-election of Lincoln," *Lincoln Herald,* Vol. L (June, 1948), 35–39.

——. "Campaign Issues and Popular Mandates in 1864," *Mid-America,* Vol. XXXV (October, 1953), 195–216.

——. "The Cleveland Convention, 1864, and Radical Democrats," *Mid-America,* Vol. XXXVI (January, 1954), 39–53.

——. "Confederate Raiders on Lake Erie: Their Propaganda Value in 1864," *Inland Seas,* Vol. V (Spring, 1949), 42–47; (Summer, 1949), 101–105.

——. "Indiana and the Election of 1864," *Indiana Magazine of History,* Vol. XLV (March, 1949), 13–38.

——. "The Kansas Senators and the Re-election of Lincoln," *Kansas Historical Quarterly,* Vol. XIX (May, 1951), 133–44.

——. "Lincoln and Chase: Presidential Rivals," *Lincoln Herald,* Vol. LII (February, 1950), 17–28; (June, 1950), 6–12, 21.

——. "Lincoln, Chase, and the Ohio Radicals in 1864," *Bulletin of the Historical and Philosophical Society of Ohio,* Vol. IX (January, 1951), 3–32.

——. "Lincoln Voters among the Boys in Blue," *Lincoln Herald,* Vol. LIV (Fall, 1952), 22–25.

——. "Lincoln's Influence in the Election of 1864," *Lincoln Herald,* Vol. LI (June, 1949), 22–32.

——. "McClellan and Seymour in the Chicago Convention of 1864,"

Bibliography

Journal of the Illinois State Historical Society, Vol. XLIII (Winter, 1950), 282–95.

————. "Some New Light on Frémont's Nomination at Cleveland in 1864," *Lincoln Herald,* Vol. LI (October, 1949), 21–23, 25.

————. "Treason as a Campaign Issue in the Re-election of Lincoln," *Abraham Lincoln Quarterly,* Vol. V (June, 1949), 348–63.

————. "The Unwanted Mr. Lincoln," *Journal of the Illinois State Historical Society,* Vol. XLV (Summer, 1952), 146–63.

————. "The Union Party Convention at Baltimore in 1864," *Maryland Historical Magazine,* Vol. XLV (September, 1950), 176–200.

————. "Words and Money to Re-elect Lincoln," *Lincoln Herald,* Vol. LIV (Spring, 1952), 22–30.

ELECTION PAMPHLETS

Address by the Union League of Philadelphia to the Citizens of Pennsylvania, in Favor of the Re-election of Abraham Lincoln. Philadelphia, 1864.

Address of the National Democratic Committee. The Perils of the Nation. Usurpations of the Administration in Maryland and Tennessee. Washington, 1864.

Bristed, Charles A. *The Cowards' Convention.* Loyal Publication Society, No. 68. New York, 1864.

Brooks, James. *Remarks of Mr. Brooks in the House of Representatives, March 7th.* Papers of the Society for the Diffusion of Political Knowledge, No. 20. New York, 1864.

————. *Speech of the Honorable James Brooks at 932 Broadway, Tuesday Evening, December 30, 1862.* Papers of the Society for the Diffusion of Political Knowledge, No. 3. New York, 1864.

Brough, John. *The Defenders of the Country and Its Enemies. The Chicago Platform Dissected. A Speech at Circleville, Ohio, September 3, 1864.* Cincinnati, 1864.

Brown, B. Gratz. *Freedom and Franchise, Inseparable.* Washington, 1864.

————. *Let Us Have Genuine Freedom in Missouri.* St. Louis, 1864.

————. *Immediate Abolition of Slavery by Act of Congress—Speech in the Senate, March 8, 1864.* Washington, 1864.

Chandler, William E. *The Soldiers' Right to Vote. Who Opposes It? Who Favors It? Or the Record of the McClellan Copperheads Against Allowing the Soldier Who Fights, the Right to Vote While Fighting.* Washington, 1864.

Chase, Salmon P. *Speeches of Salmon P. Chase, Secretary of the Treasury, During His Visit to Ohio, with His Speeches at Indianapolis and at the Mass Meeting in Baltimore.* Washington, 1863.

The Chicago Copperhead Convention. Washington, 1864.

Church, Sanford E. *Speech by Hon. Sanford E. Church at Batavia, October 13, 1863. Papers* of the Society for the Diffusion of Political Knowledge, No. 16. New York, 1864.

Clinton, Henry L. *Speech of Henry L. Clinton of New York at Patchogue, Long Island, October 1, 1864.* N.p., n.d.

Colfax and the Union League Committee. With the Letters of President Lincoln to A. G. Hodges of Kentucky. Washington, 1864.

Comstock, George F. *Let Us Reason Together. Speech Delivered at the Brooklyn Academy of Music.* Papers of the Society for the Diffusion of Political Knowledge, No. 18. New York, 1864.

Congressional Address. Washington 1864. By Members of the 38th Congress, Politically Opposed to the Present Federal Administration and Representing the Opposition Union Sentiment of the Country. N.p., n.d.

Conkling, Henry. *An Inside View of the Rebellion. An American Citizen's Textbook.* Chicago, 1864.

Cooper, Jacob. *The Loyalty Demanded by the Present Crisis.* Philadelphia, 1864.

Corruptions and Frauds of Lincoln's Administration. N.p. 1864.

Cowan, Edgar. *Speech of Honorable Edgar Cowan of Pennsylvania in the Senate of the United States, June 27, 1864.* New York, 1864.

Crosby, Edward. *The Letter of a Republican, Edward N. Crosby, of Poughkeepsie to Prof. S. F. B. Morse, February 25, 1863, and Prof. Morse's Reply, March 2, 1863.* Papers of the Society for the Diffusion of Political Knowledge, No. 4. New York, 1864.

Curtis, George T. *Address of Hon. George T. Curtis at Philadelphia, September 30, 1864.* New York, 1864.

———. *Honorable George T. Curtis on Constitutional Liberty.* New York, 1864.

———. *The True Conditions of American Loyalty. A Speech Delivered by George Ticknor Curtis Before the Democratic Union Association, March 28, 1863.* Papers of the Society for the Diffusion of Political Knowledge, No. 5. New York, 1864.

Curtis, George W. *The President. Why He Should Be Re-elected.* New York, 1864.

Davis, Henry W. *Speech of Hon. H. Winter Davis of Md. on Confis-*

Bibliography

cation of Rebel Property. Delivered in the House of Representatives, January 14, 1864. Washington, n.d.

————. *Speech of Hon. W. Winter Davis of Md. on the Expulsion of Mr. Long. Delivered in the House of Representatives, April 11, 1864.* Washington, n.d.

————. *Speech of Hon. W. Winter Davis of Md. on the Resolution Offered by Mr. Colfax Proposing the Expulsion of Mr. Long. Delivered in the House of Representatives, April 11, 1864.* Washington, n.d.

Democratic Campaign Songs. New York, 1864.

The Democratic Party the Soldiers' Friend. Legislation That Speaks for Itself. N.p., n.d.

A Democratic Peace Offered for the Acceptance of Pennsylvania Voters. Philadelphia, 1864.

Democratic Platform for Fifty Years. The Immortal Kentucky and Virginia Resolutions of 1798, with Their History and Application to the Present Convention. Chicago, 1864.

Doolittle, James R. *The Rebels and Not the Republican Party Destroyed Slavery. Speech Delivered in the Senate, February 9, 1864.* Washington, n.d.

Drake, Charles D. *Speech of Hon. Charles D. Drake. Delivered Before the National Union Association of Cincinnati, October 1, 1864.* n.p., 1864.

Edge, Frederick M. *Whom Do English Tories Wish Elected to the Presidency?* Loyal Publication Society, No. 69. New York, 1864.

Emancipation and Its Results. Papers of the Society for the Diffusion of Political Knowledge, No. 6. New York, 1864.

Gallatin, James. *Address of Hon. J. Gallatin Before the Democratic Union Association, October 8, 1864.* N.p., 1864.

Grand Lincoln and Johnson Ratification Meeting at Washington, D.C., June 15, 1864. Washington, 1864.

The Great Surrender to the Rebels in Arms. Washington, 1864.

Hamilton, John C. *Coercion Completed or Treason Triumphant.* Loyal Publication Society, No. 66. New York, 1864.

Hamilton, Edward. *A Republican's Views of the Administration Policy.* Boston, 1864.

Harlan, James. *The Constitution Upheld and Maintained. Speech of Hon. James Harlan of U.S. Senate.* Washington, 1864.

Hear Honorable George H. Pendleton. N.p., n.d.

Hopkins, John D. *Bible View of Slavery.* Papers of the Society for the Diffusion of Political Knowledge, No. 8. New York, 1864.

Lincoln & the Party Divided

Howard, Jacob M. *Report of Hon. Mr. Howard in the U.S. Senate on Interference in Elections by Military and Naval Officers.* Philadelphia, 1864.

Hunt, Washington. *Speech of Ex-Governor Hunt at Lockport. Papers* of the Society for the Diffusion of Political Knowledge, No. 14. New York, 1864.

Johnson, Alexander B. *The Approaching Presidential Election.* Utica, 1864.

Johnson, Reverdy. *Reply of Hon. Reverdy Johnson to the Paper Which Judge Advocate Holt Furnished to the President, Urging General Porter's Condemnation.* N.p., n.d.

———. *Speech of Hon. R. Johnson of Md. Delivered Before the Brooklyn McClellan Association, October 21, 1864.* N.p., n.d.

Julian, George W. *Homesteads for Soldiers on the Lands of Rebels. Speech of Hon. Geo. W. Julian of Indiana Delivered in the House of Representatives, March 18, 1864.* Washington, 1864.

Ketchum, Hiram. *General McClellan's Peninsular Campaign.* New York, 1864.

Kettell, Thomas P. *The History of the War Debt of England; The History of the War Debt of the United States, and the Two Compared. Papers* of the Society for the Diffusion of Political Knowledge, No. 17. New York, 1864.

de Laboulaye, Edouard R. L. *Professor Laboulaye. The Great Friend of America, on the Presidential Election.* Washington, 1864.

Letters of Loyal Soldiers. Loyal Publication Society, No. 64. New York, 1864.

Letter to Rev. Nathaniel Hall of Dorchester, Mass. by Nahum Capen on Politics from the Pulpit. New York, 1864.

Lieber, Francis. *Lincoln or McClellan.* Loyal Publication Society, No. 67. New York, 1864.

The Life and Services of Gen. George B. McClellan. New York, 1864.

The Lincoln and Johnson Union Campaign Songster. Philadelphia, 1864.

The Lincoln Catechism Wherein the Eccentricities and Beauties of Despotism Are Fully Set Forth. New York, 1864.

Mr. Lincoln's Arbitrary Arrests: The Acts Which the Baltimore Convention Approves. New York, 1864.

Lincoln's Treatment of Grant. Mr. Lincoln's Treatment of Gen. McClellan—The Taint of Disunion. New York, 1864.

The Loyalty for the Time. A Voice from Kentucky, April, 1864. Philadelphia, 1864.

Bibliography

Marble, Manton. *Freedom of the Press Wantonly Violated. Letter of Mr. Marble to President Lincoln.* Papers of the Society for the Diffusion of Political Knowledge, No. 22. New York, 1864.

Mason, Charles. *The Election in Iowa.* Papers of the Society for the Diffusion of Political Knowledge, No. 11. New York, 1864.

McClellan, George B. *Complete Report of the Organization and Campaigns of the Army of the Potomac.* New York, 1864.

———. *The Harrison's Bar Letter of Gen. McClellan.* New York, 1864.

———. *Letter of Acceptance.* New York, 1864.

———. *West Point Oration.* New York, 1864.

The Military and Naval Situation and the Glorious Achievements of the Soldiers and Sailors. Washington, 1864.

Miscegenation Endorsed by the Republican Party. New York, 1864.

Morse, Samuel F. B. *An Argument on the Ethical Position of Slavery in the Social System, and Its Relation to the Politics of the Day.* Papers of the Society for the Diffusion of Political Knowledge, No. 12. New York, 1864.

———. *The Constitution. Addresses of Prof. Morse, Mr. George T. Curtis, Mr. S. J. Tilden.* Papers of the Society for the Diffusion of Political Knowledge, No. 1. New York, 1864.

Naglee, Henry M. *The Two Letters of General H. M. Naglee about Gen. McClellan.* New York, 1864.

Negro Suffrage and Social Equality. N.p., 1864.

Ovation at the Academy of Music, July 4, 1863. Papers of the Society for the Diffusion of Political Knowledge, No. 7. New York, 1864.

A Page of History from the New York Journal of Commerce. Papers of the Society for the Diffusion of Political Knowledge, No. 19. New York, 1864.

Parker, Amasa. *Speech of the Hon. Amasa J. Parker at the Cooper Institute.* Papers of the Society for the Diffusion of Political Knowledge, No. 15. New York, 1864.

Parker, Joel. *Speech of Governor Parker at Freehold, N.J., August 20, 1864.* New York, 1864.

Peace To Be Enduring Must Be Conquered. New York, 1864.

Pendleton, George H. *Congressional Record of George H. Pendleton.* Philadelphia, 1864.

———. *George H. Pendleton: The Copperhead Candidate for Vice-President.* Washington, 1864.

Philadelphia Union League. *Abraham Lincoln.* Philadelphia, 1864.

Lincoln & the Party Divided

The Policy of Congress in Reference to the Restoration of the Union. Washington, 1864.

The Presidential Election Appeal of the National Union Committee of the People of the United States. N.p., n.d.

Pugh, John. *Speech of Mr. Pugh to 50,000 Voters Who Nominated Vallandigham and Resolved to Elect Him Governor of Ohio.* Papers of the Society for the Diffusion of Political Knowledge, No. 9. New York, 1864.

Rebel Terms of Peace. Washington, 1864.

Reply to President Lincoln's Letter of June 12, 1863. Papers of the Society for the Diffusion of Political Knowledge, No. 10. New York, 1864.

Report of the Judge Advocate General on "The Order of American Knights," Alias "The Sons of Liberty." A Western Conspiracy in Aid of the Southern Rebellion. Washington, 1864.

Republican Opinions about Lincoln. N.p., 1864.

Seymour, Horatio. *Speech of Governor Seymour at Philadelphia.* New York, 1864.

Sights and Notes by a Looker-on in Vienna. Washington, 1864.

Smith, Gerrit. *Gerrit Smith on McClellan's Nomination and Acceptance.* Loyal Publication Society, No. 63. New York, 1864.

Smith, John. *Speech of John Smith, Esq. Not Delivered at Smithville, September 15, 1864.* New York, 1864.

Stevens, John A. *Sherman vs. Hood. "A Low Tart Inclined To Be Very Sweet"—Something for Douglas Democrats To Remember—An Appeal to History—Where Governor Seymour Got His Lesson—On the Chicago Surrender.* Loyal Publication Society, No. 61. New York, 1864.

The Submissionists and Their Record. Loyal Publication Society, No. 65. New York, 1864.

Swinton, William. *The War for the Union from Fort Sumter to Atlanta.* N.p., n.d.

Treasonable Designs of the Democracy. The Issue Before the People—Another Civil War—The Proof from Their Own Record. Washington, 1864.

Turpie, David. *Speech of Mr. David Turpie, Delivered in the Senate of the United States, February 7, 1863.* Papers of the Society for the Diffusion of Political Knowledge, No. 2. New York, 1864.

Voorhees, Daniel W. *Speech of Hon. D. W. Voorhees of Indiana, Delivered in the House of Representatives, March 9, 1864.* Washington, 1864.

Bibliography

The Votes of the Copperheads in the Congress of the United States. Washington, 1864.

Wade, Benjamin F. *Facts for the People. Ben Wade on McClellan. And Generals Hooker and Heintzelman's Testimony. A Crushing Review of Little Napoleon's Career.* Cincinnati, 1864.

Walker, Robert J. *Letter of Hon. R. J. Walker in Favor of the Reelection of Abraham Lincoln.* New York, 1864.

Wilkes, George. *"McClellan" Who He Is and "What He Has Done" and Little Mac: "From Ball's Bluff to Antietam."* New York, 1864.

The Will of the People. Philadelphia, 1864.

Winthrop, Robert C. *Great Speech of Hon. R. C. Winthrop at New London, Conn., October 18, 1864.* New York, 1864.

———. *Speech of Hon. R. C. Winthrop at the Great Ratification Meeting in Union Square, New York, September 17, 1864.* New York, 1864.

PUBLISHED LETTERS AND SPEECHES

Agassiz, George R. (ed.). *Meade's Headquarters, 1863–1865. Letters of Col. Theodore Lyman.* Boston, 1922.

Angle, Paul M. (ed.). *New Letters and Papers of Lincoln.* Boston, 1930.

Belmont, August. *Letters, Speeches, and Addresses of August Belmont.* N.p., 1890.

Boutwell, George S. *Speeches and Papers Relating to the Rebellion and the Overthrow of Slavery.* Boston, 1867.

Buchanan, James. *Works.* 12 vols. Philadelphia, 1910.

Cook, Thomas M., and Thomas W. Knox (eds.). *Public Record Inducing Speeches, Messages, Proclamations, Official Correspondence, and Other Public Utterances of Horatio Seymour.* New York, 1868.

Curtis, G. W. (ed.). *The Correspondence of John Lothrop Motley.* 3 vols. New York, 1889.

Dickinson, John R. *Speeches, Correspondence, etc. of the Late Daniel S. Dickinson.* 2 vols. New York, 1867.

Ford, Worthington C. (ed.) *A Cycle of Adams' Letters, 1861–65.* 2 vols. Boston, 1920.

Garrison, Wendell P. and Francis J. *The Words of Garrison.* Boston, 1905.

Gray, Jane (ed.). *Letters of Asa Gray.* 2 vols. Boston, 1893.

Julian, George W. *Speeches on Political Questions, 1850–1868.* New York, 1872.

Lincoln & the Party Divided

Lincoln Letters Hitherto Unpublished in the Library of Brown University and Other Providence Libraries. Providence, 1927.

Marshall, Jessie A. (ed.). *Private and Official Correspondence of General Benjamin F. Butler.* 5 vols. Norwood, Mass., 1917.

Nicolay, John, and John Hay (eds.). *Complete Works of Abraham Lincoln.* 12 vols. Harrogate, Tenn., n.d.

Nunns, Annie A. (ed.). "Some Letters of Salmon P. Chase, 1848–1865," *American Historical Review,* Vol. XXXIV (April, 1929), 536–56.

Phillips, Wendell. *Speeches, Lectures, and Letters.* 2 vols. Boston, 1891.

Schafer, Joseph (ed.). *Intimate Letters of Carl Schurz, 1841–1869. Publications* of the State Historical Society of Wisconsin, Vol. XXX. Madison, 1928.

Sumner, Charles. *Works.* 15 vols. Boston, 1870–1883.

Thorndike, Rachel S. (ed.). *The Sherman Letters.* New York, 1894.

Tracy, Gilbert A. (ed.). *Uncollected Letters of Abraham Lincoln.* Boston, 1917.

Vallandigham, Clement L. *Speeches, Arguments, Addresses and Letters.* New York, 1864.

Voorhees, Daniel W. *Forty Years of Oratory.* 2 vols. Indianapolis, 1898.

AUTOBIOGRAPHIES, MEMOIRS, AND REMINISCENCES

Adams, Charles F. *Autobiography,* Boston, 1916.

Bancroft, Frederic, and William A. Dunning (eds.). *The Reminiscences of Carl Schurz.* 3 vols. New York, 1909.

Beale, Howard K. (ed.). *The Diary of Edward Bates, 1859–1866.* Annual Report of the American Historical Association for 1930, Vol. IV. Washington, 1933.

Bigelow, John. *Retrospections of an Active Life.* 5 vols. New York, 1909.

Blaine, James G. *Twenty Years of Congress.* 2 vols. Norwich, Conn., 1884.

Boutwell, George S. *Reminiscences of Sixty Years in Public Affairs.* 2 vols. New York, 1902.

Butler, Benjamin F. *Autobiography and Personal Reminiscences.* Boston, 1892.

Chase, Salmon P. *Diary and Correspondence. Annual Report* of the American Historical Association for 1902, Vol. II. Washington, 1903.

Chittenden, L. E. *Personal Reminiscences, 1840–1890.* New York, 1893.

Bibliography

Cole, Cornelius. *Memoirs.* New York, 1908.

Conway, Moncure D. *Autobiography, Memoirs, and Experiences.* 2 vols. Boston, 1904.

Cox, Samuel S. *Three Decades of Federal Legislation.* Providence, 1885.

Cullom, Shelby M. *Fifty Years of Public Service.* New York, 1911.

Dana, Charles A. *Recollections of the Civil War.* New York, 1913.

Dennett, Tyler (ed.). *Lincoln and the Civil War in the Diaries and Letters of John Hay.* New York, 1939.

Depew, Chauncey M. *My Memories of Eighty Years.* New York, 1922.

Field, Maunsell B. *Memories of Many Men and Some Women.* New York, 1874.

Gerry, Margarita S. (ed.). *Through Five Administrations, Reminiscences of Colonel William H. Crook.* New York, 1910.

Gilmore, James R. *Personal Recollections of Abraham Lincoln and the Civil War.* Boston, 1898.

Greeley, Horace. *Recollections of a Busy Life.* New York, 1872.

Gurowski, Adam. *Diary.* 3 vols. Washington, 1866.

Hay, John. *Letters of John Hay and Extracts from His Diary.* 3 vols. Washington, 1908.

Hughes, Sarah F. (ed.). *Letters and Recollections of John Murray Forbes.* 2 vols. Boston, 1899.

Julian, George W. *Political Recollections, 1840–1872.* Chicago, 1884.

Koerner, Gustave. *Memoirs of Gustave Koerner, 1809–1896.* 2 vols. Cedar Rapids, 1909.

Lusk, D. W. *Eighty Years of Illinois Politics and Politicians. Anecdotes and Incidents, 1809–1889.* Springfield, Ill. 1889.

McClure, Alexander. *Recollections of Half a Century.* Salem, Mass., 1902.

McCulloch, Hugh. *Men and Measures of Half a Century.* New York, 1888.

Morse, Edward L. *Samuel F. B. Morse: His Letters and Journals.* 2 vols. Boston, 1914.

Pease, Theodore C., and James G. Randall (eds.). *The Diary of Orville Hickman Browning, 1850–1864.* 2 vols. Collections of the Illinois State Historical Library, Vols. XX and XXII. Lincoln Series, Vols. II and III. Springfield, Ill., 1925.

Poore, Ben: Perley. *Perley's Reminiscences of Sixty Years in the National Metropolis.* 2 vols. New York, 1886.

Riddle, Albert G. *Recollections of War Times.* New York, 1895.

Schofield, John. *Forty-six Years in the Army.* New York, 1897.

Lincoln & the Party Divided

Sherman, John. *Recollections of Forty Years in the House, Senate, and Cabinet.* 2 vols. Chicago, 1895.

Stanton, Theodore, and Harriet Blatch (eds.). *Elizabeth Cady Stanton as Revealed in Her Letters, Diary, and Reminiscences.* 2 vols. New York, 1922.

Stephenson, Nathaniel W. *An Autobiography of Abraham Lincoln. Consisting of the Personal Portions of His Letters, Speeches, and Conversations.* Indianapolis, 1926.

Stoddard, William O. *Inside the White House in War Time.* New York, 1890.

Villard, Oswald. *Fighting Years: Memoirs of a Liberal Editor.* New York, 1939.

Weed, Harriet A. (ed.). *Autobiography of Thurlow Weed.* Boston, 1884.

Welles, Gideon. *Diary.* 3 vols. Boston, 1911.

White, Andrew D. *Autobiography.* 2 vols. New York, 1905.

BIOGRAPHIES

Bacon, G. W. *Life and Speeches of President Andrew Johnson.* London, n.d.

Bancroft, Frederic. *The Life of William H. Seward.* 2 vols. New York, 1900.

Barnes, Thurlow W. *Memoir of Thurlow Weed.* Boston, 1884.

Barton, William E. *The Life of Abraham Lincoln.* 2 vols. Indianapolis, 1925.

Bates, David H. *Lincoln in the Telegraph Office.* New York, 1907.

Bigelow, John. *The Life of Samuel J. Tilden.* 2 vols. New York, 1895.

Biographical Sketch of Andrew Johnson. Washington, 1864.

Bloss, G. M. D. *Life and Speeches of George H. Pendleton.* Cincinnati, 1868.

Brigham, Johnson. *James Harlan.* Iowa City, 1913.

Brooks, Noah. *Abraham Lincoln and the Downfall of American Slavery.* New York, 1896.

Brown, Francis. *Raymond of the "Times."* New York, 1951.

Buckingham, Samuel G. *The Life of William A. Buckingham: The War Governor of Connecticut.* Springfield, Mass., 1894.

Carpenter, F. B. *Six Months at the White House with Abraham Lincoln.* New York, 1866.

Chapman, John J. *William Lloyd Garrison.* Boston, 1913.

Bibliography

Zachariah Chandler. An Outline Sketch of His Life and Public Services. Detroit, 1880.

Charnwood, Lord. *Abraham Lincoln.* Garden City, N. Y., 1938.

Chittenden, L. E. *Recollections of President Lincoln and His Administration.* New York, 1891.

Clarke, Grace. *George Julian.* Indianapolis, 1932.

Conkling, Alfred R. *The Life and Letters of Roscoe Conkling.* New York, 1889.

Cornell, William M. *The Life and Public Career of Hon. Horace Greeley.* Boston, n.d.

Cortissoz, Royal. *The Life of Whitelaw Reid.* 2 vols. New York, 1921.

Current, Richard N. *Old Thad Stevens. A Story of Ambition.* Madison, 1942.

Dana, Charles A. *Lincoln and His Cabinet.* Cleveland, 1896.

Dennett, Tyler. *John Hay From Poetry to Politics.* New York, 1934.

Dittenhoefer, Abram J. *How We Elected Lincoln.* New York, 1916.

Dix, Morgan. *Memoirs of John Adams Dix.* 2 vols. New York, 1883.

Dodd, William E. *Lincoln or Lee.* New York, 1928.

Eckenrode, H. J., and Bryan Conrad. *George B. McClellan the Man Who Saved the Union.* Chapel Hill, N. C., 1941.

Fessenden, Francis. *Life and Public Services of William Pitt Fessenden.* 2 vols. Boston, 1907.

Field, Henry M. *The Life of David Dudley Field.* New York, 1898.

Flower, Frank A. *Edwin McMaster Stanton.* New York, 1905.

Foster, Lilian. *Andrew Johnson. President of the United States: His Life and Speeches.* New York, 1866.

Foulke, William D. *Life of Oliver P. Morton.* 2 vols. Indianapolis, 1899.

Frothingham, Paul R. *Edward Everett: Orator and Statesman.* Boston, 1925.

Fuess, Claude M. *Carl Schurz: Reformer, 1829–1906.* New York, 1932.

Garrison, Wendell P. and Francis J. *William Lloyd Garrison, 1805–1879.* 4 vols. New York, 1885–1889.

Gorham, George C. *Life and Public Services of Edwin M. Stanton.* 2 vols. Boston, 1899.

Gresham, Matilda. *Life of Walter Quintin Gresham, 1832–1895.* 2 vols. Chicago, 1919.

Hall, Clifton R. *Andrew Johnson Military Governor of Tennessee.* Princeton, 1916.

Hamlin, Charles E. *The Life and Times of Hannibal Hamlin.* Cambridge, Mass., 1899.

Harris, Wilmer C. *Public Life of Zachariah Chandler, 1851–1875.*

University of Michigan Series II, Michigan Historical Studies. Lansing, 1917.

Hart, Albert B. *Salmon Portland Chase.* Boston, 1899.

Herndon, William, and Jesse W. Weik. *Abraham Lincoln: The True Story of a Great Life.* 2 vols. New York, 1920.

Holcombe, John W., and Hubert M. Skinner. *Life and Public Services of Thomas A. Hendricks with Selected Speeches and Writings.* Indianapolis, 1886.

Hollister, O. J. *Life of Schuyler Colfax.* New York, 1886.

Jones, James S. *Life of Andrew Johnson.* Greeneville, Tenn., 1901.

Julian, George W. *The Life of Joshua R. Giddings.* Chicago, 1892.

Lamon, Ward H. *Recollections of Abraham Lincoln, 1847–1865.* Chicago, 1895.

Lothrop, Thornton K. *William Henry Seward.* Boston, 1896.

Maverick, Augustus. *Henry J. Raymond and the New York Press.* Hartford, 1870.

Macartney, Clarence E. *Lincoln and His Cabinet.* New York, 1931.

McCall, Samuel W. *Thaddeus Stevens.* Boston, 1899.

McClure, Alexander. *Abraham Lincoln and Men of War-Times.* Philadelphia, 1892.

———. *Lincoln as a Politician.* Putnam, Conn., 1916.

———. *Our Presidents and How We Make Them.* New York, 1900.

McGrane, Reginald. *William Allen. A Study in Western Democracy.* Columbus, 1925.

Meade, George (ed.). *The Life and Letters of George Gordon Meade.* 2 vols. New York, 1913.

Merriam, George S. *The Life and Times of Samuel Bowles.* 2 vols. New York, 1885.

Miller, Alphonse B. *Thaddeus Stevens.* New York, 1939.

Milton, George F. *The Age of Hate. Andrew Johnson and the Radicals.* New York, 1930.

Mitchell, Stewart. *Horatio Seymour of New York.* Cambridge, Mass., 1938.

Morse, John T. *Abraham Lincoln.* 2 vols. Boston, 1898.

Myers, William S. *General George Brinton McClellan. A Study in Personality.* New York, 1934.

Nevins, Allan. *Frémont, Pathmarker of the West.* New York, 1939.

———. *Frémont the West's Greatest Adventurer.* 2 vols. New York, 1928.

Nicolay, Helen, *Lincoln's Secretary.* New York, 1949.

Bibliography

Nicolay, John, and John Hay. *Abraham Lincoln: A History.* 10 vols. New York, 1890.

Oberholtzer, Ellis P. *Jay Cooke, Financier of the Civil War.* 2 vols. Philadelphia, 1907.

Ogden, Rollo. *Life and Letters of Edwin Lawrence Godkin.* 2 vols. New York, 1907.

Orcutt, William D. *Burrows of Michigan and the Republican Party.* 2 vols. New York, 1917.

Pearson, Henry G. *The Life of John A. Andrew, Governor of Massachusetts, 1861–1865.* 2 vols. Boston, 1904.

Pierce, Edward L. *Memoir and Letters of Charles Sumner.* 4 vols. Boston, 1877–1893.

Radcliffe, George L. *Governor Thomas Hicks of Maryland and the Civil War.* Johns Hopkins University *Studies in Historical and Political Science,* Series XIX, No. 11. Baltimore, 1901.

Randall, James G. *Lincoln the Liberal Statesman.* New York, 1947.

Rankin, Henry B. *Personal Recollections of Abraham Lincoln.* New York, 1916.

Raymond, Henry J. *Lincoln, His Life and Times. Being the Life and Public Services of Abraham Lincoln.* New York, 1865.

Riddle, Albert G. *The Life of Benjamin F. Wade.* Cleveland, 1888.

Rothschild, Alonzo. *Lincoln Master of Men: A Study in Character.* Boston, 1906.

Salter, William. *The Life of James W. Grimes.* New York, 1876.

Sandburg, Carl. *Abraham Lincoln: The War Years.* 4 vols. New York, 1939.

Schuckers, James W. *The Life and Public Services of Salmon Portland Chase.* New York, 1874.

Seitz, Don C. *Horace Greeley.* Indianapolis, 1926.

———. *The James Gordon Bennetts: Father and Son.* Indianapolis, 1928.

———. *Lincoln the Politician.* New York, 1931.

Seward, Frederick W. *Seward at Washington as Senator and Secretary of State.* 3 vols. New York, 1891.

Smith, Donnal V. *Chase and Civil War Politics.* Ohio Historical Collections, Vol. II. Columbus, 1931.

Smith, Theodore C. *The Life and Letters of James Abram Garfield.* 2 vols. New Haven, 1925.

Smith, Willard H. *Schuyler Colfax: The Changing Fortunes of a Political Idol.* Indianapolis, 1952.

Smith, William E. *The Francis Preston Blair Family in Politics.* 2 vols. New York, 1933.

Speer, John. *Life of General James H. Lane.* Garden City, Kansas, 1896.

Stearns, Frank P. *The Life and Public Services of George Luther Stearns.* Philadelphia, 1907.

Steiner, Bernard C. *Life of Reverdy Johnson.* Baltimore, 1914.

Stephenson, Wendell H. *The Political Career of General James H. Lane. Publications* of the Kansas Historical Society, Vol. III. Topeka, 1930.

Stoddard, Henry L. *Horace Greeley, Printer, Editor, Crusader.* New York, 1946.

Storey, Moorfield. *Charles Sumner.* Boston, 1900.

Stryker, Lloyd P. *Andrew Johnson: A Study in Courage.* New York, 1929.

Swift, Lindsay. *William Lloyd Garrison.* Philadelphia, 1911.

Tarbell, Ida M. *The Life of Abraham Lincoln.* 2 vols. New York, 1900.

Thayer, William R. *The Life and Letters of John Hay.* 2 vols. Boston, 1915.

Thornton, Willis. *The Nine Lives of Citizen Train.* New York, 1948.

Vallandigham, James. *Life of Clement L. Vallandigham.* Baltimore, 1872.

Van Deusen, Glyndon G. *Thurlow Weed, Wizard of the Lobby.* Boston, 1947.

Warden, Robert B. *An Account of the Private Life and Public Services of Salmon Portland Chase.* Cincinnati, 1874.

West, Richard S. *Gideon Welles—Lincoln's Navy Department.* Indianapolis, 1943.

Williams, T. Harry. *Lincoln and the Radicals.* Madison, 1941.

Wilson, James H. *The Life of Charles A. Dana.* New York, 1907.

Winston, Robert W. *Andrew Johnson: Plebeian and Patriot.* New York, 1928.

Winthrop, Robert C. *A Memoir of Robert C. Winthrop.* Boston, 1897.

Wittke, Carl. *Against the Current: The Life of Karl Heinzen, 1809–80.* Chicago, 1945.

Woodburn, James A. *The Life of Thaddeus Stevens.* Indianapolis 1913.

Woodley, Thomas F. *Thaddeus Stevens.* Harrisburg, Pa., 1934.

SECONDARY ACCOUNTS AND MONOGRAPHS

Alexander, DeAlva S. *A Political History of the State of New York.* 3 vols. New York, 1909.

Bibliography

Ayers, S. H. M. *Iowa in War Times.* Des Moines, 1888.

Bartlett, Ruhl J. *John C. Frémont and the Republican Party.* Ohio State University Studies: *Contributions in History and Political Science,* No. 13. Columbus, 1930.

Benton, Elbert J. *The Movement for Peace Without Victory During the Civil War.* The Western Reserve Historical Society Collections, No. 99. Cleveland, 1918.

Brooks, Noah. *Washington in Lincoln's Time.* New York, 1896.

Brummer, Sidney. *Political History of New York State During the Period of the Civil War.* New York, 1911.

Carman, Harry J., and Reinhard H. Luthin. *Lincoln and the Patronage.* New York, 1943.

Cole, Arthur C. *The Era of the Civil War, 1848–1870* Vol. III of *The Centennial History of Illinois,* by T. C. Alvord. 5 vols. Springfield, 1919.

Coulter, E. Merton. *The Civil War and Readjustment in Kentucky.* Chapel Hill, 1926.

Doyle, Henry G. *Catholicism in the Civil War and Reconstruction.* Boston, 1923.

Dunham, Chester F. *The Attitude of the Northern Clergy Toward the South, 1860–1865.* Toledo, Ohio, 1942.

Ellison, Joseph. *California and the Nation, 1850–1869.* University of California *Publications in History,* Vol. XVI. Berkeley, 1927.

Fahrney, Ralph R. *Horace Greeley and the Tribune in the Civil War.* Cedar Rapids, 1936.

Faust, Albert B. *The German Element in the United States.* 2 vols. Boston, 1909.

Fertig, James W. *The Secession and Reconstruction of Tennessee.* Chicago, 1898.

Gray, Wood. *The Hidden Civil War. The Story of the Copperheads.* New York, 1942.

Greeley, Horace. *The American Conflict, 1861–1865.* 2 vols. Hartford, 1866.

———. *Proceedings of the First Three Republican National Conventions of 1856, 1860, and 1864.* Minneapolis, 1893.

Gue, Benjamin F. *History of Iowa.* 4 vols. New York, 1903.

Harper, Robert S. *Lincoln and the Press.* New York, 1951.

Heathcote, Charles W. *The Lutheran Church and the Civil War.* Chicago, 1919.

Hesseltine, William B. *Lincoln and the War Governors.* New York, 1948.

Hosmer, James K. *Outcome of the Civil War, 1863–1865.* Vol. XXI of *The American Nation: A History,* ed. by A. B. Hart. 28 vols. New York, 1904–1918.

Kent, Frank. *The Democratic Party.* New York, 1928.

Kirkland, Edward C. *The Peacemakers of 1864.* New York, 1927.

Knapp, Charles M. *New Jersey Politics During the Period of the Civil War and Reconstruction.* Geneva, N. Y., 1924.

McClure, Alexander. *Old Time Notes on Pennsylvania.* Philadelphia, 1905.

McMaster, John B. *History of the United States During Lincoln's Administration.* New York, 1927.

McPherson, Edward. *A Political History of the United States of America During the Great Rebellion.* Washington, 1866.

Milton, George F. *Abraham Lincoln and the Fifth Column.* New York, 1942.

Minor, Henry. *The Story of the Democratic Party.* New York, 1928.

Mitchell, Wesley C. *Gold Prices and Wages under the Greenback Standard.* Berkeley, 1908.

Norton, Lee. *War Elections, 1862–1864.* New York, n.d.

Patton, James W. *Unionism and Reconstruction in Tennessee, 1860–1869.* Chapel Hill, N. C., 1934.

Pollard, E. A. *The Lost Cause.* New York, 1866.

Porter, George H. *Ohio Politics During the Civil War Period.* Columbia University *Studies in History, Economics, and Public Law,* Vol. XL. New York, 1911.

Randall, James G. *The Civil War and Reconstruction.* Boston, 1937.
———. *Constitutional Problems under Lincoln.* New York, 1926.

Rhodes, James F. *History of the United States from the Compromise of 1850 to the Final Restoration of Home Rule at the South in 1877.* 7 vols. New York, 1893–1922.

Roseboom, Eugene C. *The Civil War Era, 1850–1873.* Vol. IV of *The History of the State of Ohio,* ed. by Carl Wittke. 6 vols. Columbus, 1944.

Schouler, William. *A History of Massachusetts in the Civil War.* 2 vols. Boston, 1868–1871.

Scott, Eben G. *Reconstruction During the Civil War in the United States of America.* Boston, 1895.

Shutes, Milton. *Lincoln and California.* Stanford, 1943.

Stanwood, Edward. *A History of the Presidency.* Boston, 1903.

Stidger, Felix. *Treason History of the Order of the Sons of Liberty.* Chicago, 1903.

Bibliography

Sweet, William W. *The Methodist Church and the Civil War.* Cincinnati, 1912.

Vander Velde, Louis G. *The Presbyterian Church and the Federal Union, 1861–1869.* Cambridge, Mass., 1932.

Ware, Edith E. *Political Opinion in Massachusetts During the Civil War and Reconstruction.* Columbia University *Studies in History, Economics, and Public Law,* Vol. XXIV. New York, 1916.

Warren, Louis A. *Lincoln's Second Term Preliminaries.* Harrogate, Tenn., 1940.

Weeden, William B. *War Government: Federal and State in Massachusetts, New York, Pennsylvania, and Indiana, 1861–1865.* Boston, 1906.

MISCELLANEOUS PUBLICATIONS

Appleton's Annual Cyclopedia for 1863, 1864, and 1865. New York, 1864–1866.

Ayer, I. W. *The Northwest Conspiracy in All Its Startling Details.* Chicago, 1865.

Cincinnati Convention, October 18, 1864, for the Organization of a Peace Party Upon States Rights, Jeffersonian Democratic Principles and for the Promotion of Peace and Independent Nominations for President and Vice-President. N.p., n.d.

Edmunds, James M. *A Circular Letter of James M. Edmunds to the Councils of the Union League of All the States To Be Read in Open Council, October 19, 1864.* N.p., n.d.

Meeting of the Grand National Council, Union League of America, Baltimore, Md., June 6, 1864. N.p., n.d.

Murphy, D. F. *Presidential Election, 1864, Proceedings of the National Union Convention Held in Baltimore, Md., June 7 and 8, 1864.* New York, 1864.

Official Proceedings of the Democratic National Convention Held in 1864 at Chicago. Chicago, 1864.

Pitman, Benn (ed.). *The Trials for Treason at Indianapolis.* Cincinnati, 1865.

Tribune Almanac for 1863, 1864, and 1865. New York, 1864–1866.

The Union Campaign Committee Herewith Respectfully Presents to the Contributors a Statement of Receipts and Expenditures of the Fund Raised by Them for the Union Campaign of November, 1864. N.p., n.d.

Index

Index

Index

Cooley, D. N.: 188
Cooper, Peter: 186
Copperheads: 105, 120–21, 124, 128, 138, 154–55, 160, 163, 198, 199;
  opposition to McClellan, 123, 130–38
Copperheadism repudiated in 1864: 216
Corning, Erastus: 122
Corry, William: 138
Covode, John: 30
Cox, Samuel: 111n., 123n., 125, 127, 193, 196
Creswell, John: 188
Crisis, The: 127, 137, 170
Cullom, Shelby: 19, 21
Curtin, Andrew: 30, 60n., 61, 193, 203

Dana, Charles: 12, 204
Dana, Richard Henry: 61
Davis, David: 56
Davis, Henry Winter: 91, 104, 108, 112, 115, 145–47, 201
Davis, Jefferson: 109, 110, 141, 142, 163
Defrees, John: 51
Delano, Columbus: 52
Delaware: 93, 194, 195, 197, 201, 215
Democratic party: 76, 88, 119, 120–21, 125, 127, 129, 144–45, 170, 171,
  211; cause of defeat, 8, 161; accused of treason, 8, 148, 150, 158,
  183; factionalism, 119–22, 125, 127–28, 137–39; supports war
  policies of Lincoln, 120–21; uncertainty of position in campaign,
  139–40; asserts not disloyal, 153–54; attacked by War-Democrats,
  159–60; favors reunion, 162–63; view on reconstruction, 165–67;
  view on emancipation, 168–69; view on civil liberty, 171–73; attacks on Lincoln, 173–75, 177; attitude on Union party, 175–76;
  campaign literature, 180–83; methods of conducting campaign,
  181–82; campaign expenses, 184; October elections, 191–95; losses
  in Congress, 198; weakness, 217–18; position as result of election,
  218–20
Democrats: 6, 13, 17, 22, 45, 78, 86, 118, 119, 124, 162, 187; protest
  against doctrine of military necessity, 7; denounce military failures,
  106; denounce conscription, 109; reconciling differences, 121–22;
  denounce Chicago platform, 141; association with treason, 149,
  150–51, 153–54, 157–61, 163–64; war weariness, 169–71
Dennison, George: 27
Dennison, William: 41, 92

253

Index

Index

Index

Index

Index

ature, 179–83; fate after war, 175–76; victories in October, 192–93; predictions of victory after October results, 194–95; gains in Congress and the states, 198; views on what election outcome meant, 217

Unionists: 142; factionalism, 13, 22, 119; attitude on Wickliffe resolution, 135; similarity of views with those of Democrats, 120–21; use of treason issue, 149–53, 157; attack on McClellan and Pendleton, 158–61

Urban voting: 208–209

Vallandigham, Clement: 29, 123 n., 124, 126 n., 127, 132–35, 137–38, 163, 172, 193, 194

Vermont: 190, 216

Veteran Union Club: 199

Vindictives: *see* Unconditionals

Virginia: 93, 106, 169

Wade, Benjamin: 15, 27, 28, 39, 108, 112, 115, 145–47

Wade-Davis Bill: 108–109, 167

Wade-Davis Manifesto: 111–12, 174

Walbridge, Hiram: 159

Wales, William: 34

Walker, John: 157

Wallace, Lew: 202

War-Democrats: 65, 67, 81–82, 88, 99, 102, 111, 114, 120–21, 129, 136, 159–60, 163, 183, 186

"War-Failure" plank: 132–33, 141–42, 159–60, 171, 177

War prosperity: 206–208

Washburne, Elihu: 63, 113, 188, 202

Washington Constitutional Union: 52

Weed, Thurlow: 9, 32, 37–38, 41–45, 48, 55–56, 101, 110, 114, 123 n., 143, 161

Welles, Gideon: 11, 18, 25, 27, 29, 37, 41, 47, 48, 61, 84, 97, 103, 104, 129, 215

West Point oration: 128

West Virginia: 93, 215

Whig party: 13, 45, 129

White, Andrew: 91

Wickliffe, Charles: 134

Wilkes, George: 34, 45, 114–16, 143, 146

Wilkes' Spirit of the Times: 34, 114